The Reflective Cycle of the Teaching Practicum

Reflective Practice in Language Education
Series Editor: Thomas S. C. Farrell, Brock University

This series covers different issues related to reflective practice in language education and includes an introductory book which introduces these areas. The other books in the series clarify the different approaches that have been taken within reflective practice and outline current themes that have emerged in the research on various topics and methods of reflection that have occurred.

Published:

Reflective Practice in ELT
Thomas S. C. Farrell

Cooperative Learning through a Reflective Lens
George M. Jacobs, Anita Lie, and Siti Mina Tamah

Exploring the Principles of Reflective Practice in ELT: Research and Perspectives from Turkey
Edited by Bahar Gün and Evrim Üstünlüoğlu

Micro-Reflection on Classroom Communication: A FAB Framework
Hansun Zhang Waring and Sarah Chepkirui Creider

Reflecting on Leadership in Language Education
Edited by Andy Curtis

Reflective Practice in TESOL Service-Learning
Cynthia J. Macknish

Using Video to Support Teacher Reflection and Development in ELT
Laura Baecher, Steve Mann, and Cecilia Nobre

Forthcoming:

English Language Teacher Beliefs
Farahnaz Faez and Michael Karas

Language Teacher Identity and Reflective Practice
Zia Tajeddin

Surviving the Induction Years of Language Teaching: The Importance of Reflective Practice
Thomas S. C. Farrell

Teachers Reflecting on Boredom in the Language Classroom
Mirosław Pawlak, Mariusz Kruk, and Joanna Zawodniak

The Reflective Cycle of the Teaching Practicum

Fiona Farr and Angela Farrell

SHEFFIELD UK BRISTOL CT

Published by Equinox Publishing Ltd.
UK: Office 415, The Workstation, 15 Paternoster Row, Sheffield, South Yorkshire S1 2BX
USA: ISD, 70 Enterprise Drive, Bristol, CT 06010

www.equinoxpub.com

First published 2023

British Library Cataloguing-in-Publication Data
A catalogue record for this book is available from the British Library.

ISBN-13 978 1 78179 848 5 (hardback)
978 1 78179 849 2 (paperback)
978 1 78179 850 8 (ePDF)
978 1 80050 401 1 (ePub)

Library of Congress Cataloging-in-Publication Data

Names: Farr, Fiona, 1971- author. | Farrell, Angela, author.
Title: The reflective cycle of the teaching practicum / Fiona Farr and Angela Farrell.
Description: Sheffield, South Yorkshire ; Bristol, CT : Equinox Publishing, 2023. | Series: Reflective practice in language education | Includes bibliographical references and index. | Summary: "This book focuses on the practice cycle, or practicum, of ELT education programmes"-- Provided by publisher.
Identifiers: LCCN 2023002809 (print) | LCCN 2023002810 (ebook) | ISBN 9781781798485 (hardback) | ISBN 9781781798492 (paperback) | ISBN 9781781798508 (pdf) | ISBN 9781800504011 (epub)
Subjects: LCSH: English teachers--Training of. | Student teaching. | Reflective teaching. | English language--Study and teaching--Foreign speakers. | Second language acquisition.
Classification: LCC PE1128.A2 F2843 2023 (print) | LCC PE1128.A2 (ebook) | DDC 428.0071--dc23/eng/20230607
LC record available at https://lccn.loc.gov/2023002809
LC ebook record available at https://lccn.loc.gov/2023002810

Typeset by S.J.I. Services, New Delhi, India

Contents

Series Editor's Preface

The Reflective Cycle of the Teaching Practicum by Fiona Farr and Angela Farrell is an excellent text for learner language teachers and their supervisors to reflect on when engaging in teaching practice in any certificate or graduate program on language teacher education. The book attempts to balance the theory learner language teachers receive in their teacher education with the practice they will engage in during their practicum experiences. Fiona and Angela have managed such a wonderful balancing act by drawing on the practices and research from the context of their own pre-service MA in TESOL program featuring novices with little or no prior teaching experience.

The contents of the book are primarily based on their implementation of a reflective practice framework they call PENSER, which they point out is from the French verb 'penser' that means to think or reflect. This five-step reflection model for student teachers consists of **P**uzzle identification, **E**mbracing, **N**oticing, **S**olving, and **E**xperimentation and **R**esearch. The cycle of these five steps is repeated three times over the course of an academic year. Farr and Farrell specify that the starting point of the PENSER approach is to ask each of the student teachers to identify *one* aspect of their teaching practice where they felt particularly challenged, which would provide the focus of their reflections over the following five-week cycle.

The first chapter provides a theoretical introduction to the notion of reflective practice, its origin, how it has been defined in the literature, various evidence-based perspectives on how effective it is, as well as some of its associated pros and cons. The introduction necessarily takes us outside of the realm of language teaching and teacher education, back to some philosophical accounts as well as to the field of general education. This discussion, like those included in later chapters, is embedded in the context of the practicum component of TESOL education programs with a focus on novice teachers. After introducing the concept of reflective practice in Chapter 1, the authors give details of their PENSER approach in Chapter 2. The remaining chapters outline and discuss the results of how they implemented the PENSER model in an Irish context during teaching practice with learner teachers. Chapter 3 outlines holistic transitioning support for teachers as they near their time to engage in real professional classroom practice. Throughout the chapter, Farr and Farrell note, the potential of complementary dialogic reflection with other participants such as mentors, cooperating teachers, and peers, is explored to uncover the ways in which novice teachers can co-construct knowledge in collaboration with others. Chapters 4–7 draw on the PENSER reflective data to trace the reflective thinking and professional development of a group of ten student teachers of EFL in Ireland over the course of their teaching practice (TP) journey. In Chapter 4, the focus is on their reflections on the various challenges associated with the preparation and planning of lessons in the early days of their TP. Chapter 5 deals with their reflections on specific issues in the area of classroom management and teacher/learner relationships. Chapter 6 is focused on issues related to teaching language skills such as grammar, vocabulary, and pronunciation. In Chapter 7, the authors discuss awareness of teacher talk and interactional skills, showing how teachers play a central role in the processes of language acquisition through their talk and interactions with learners. Chapter 8 is designed to help prepare for and engage in the post-observation discussions that take place between student teachers and mentors or supervisors. This focus, the authors point out, is a very important part of the reflective process as it provides the opportunity for support, direction, and insight from those more experienced as a way to guide and deepen student teachers' own reflective endeavours. Chapter 9 concludes the book and points out that the contents can heighten theoretical understanding of the complexities involved in becoming an EFL teacher today in terms of the knowledge base, skills, and critical insights this now requires. This book also presents practical tasks in the form of pauses for reflection, as well as strategies and techniques that can be applied by teacher educators, teachers, and researchers to their own context.

Farr and Farrell note that the research presented in this book can serve as a springboard for further RP-based research in the ELTE field, to help bring a more bottom-up empirical perspective to the academic literature in this field. Thus pre-service (and in-service) language teachers, language teacher educators, and teacher educators beyond language education will find the rich extracts of real interactions between learner teachers and teacher supervisors and educators a useful, engaging, and enlightening window into the real world of learning to teach on the practicum. *The Reflective Cycle of the Teaching Practicum* by Fiona Farr and Angela Farrell is truly a welcome addition to the series *Reflective Practice in Language Education* and I thank them for all their hard work to produce such a wonderful book.

Thomas S. C. Farrell
Series Editor, *Reflective Practice in Language Education*

To our MA in TESOL students, past and present,
in this significant 30th anniversary year
since the program began

Acknowledgments

This book is about our many and varied educational engagements, how we do the things we do, and how we say the things we say in our everyday professional lives. It is about helping ourselves and others to understand reflective interactions and the development of teaching practices. All of this requires communicating with and collaborating with many people, to whom we are extremely grateful. Much appreciation goes to all of our wonderful TESOL colleagues at the University of Limerick, especially to those who never say 'no' when we come wanting to collect yet more data. Elaine Riordan deserves a very special mention in the context of the data included in this book, and for previous joint research using the Teacher Education Corpus, much of which provided foundations for the present volume.

We are continuously thankful to our wonderful MA students for their contributions, without which there would be no book. Not only do they allow us to gather their artifacts to scrutinize, but they do so at times when they are often struggling with the demands of becoming a teacher and are feeling particularly vulnerable, stressed, or anxious. Their selflessness will perhaps help other student teachers to have smoother journeys.

Equinox Publishers had the foresight to become invested in this reflective practice book series and we are very grateful that they did. It has already produced a number of valuable volumes and we feel privileged to be part of it. Many thanks to the editorial board, the commissioning editors, and all of those involved in the copy-editing and production process at Equinox.

We owe a mountain of gratitude to our friend and colleague Tom Farrell for inviting us into his world of reflective practice. He always says that he is standing on the shoulders of giants, but he has well and truly become one of those giants, for us and for other scholars of reflective practice long into the future. From the initial invitation to get involved in this wonderful series, to the final editorial comment, his insights, positivity, and good humour have provided a much-appreciated buoyancy to the entire journey. Go raibh míle maith agat, a Thomás!

List of Acronyms

CALL:	Computer-Assisted Language Learning
CL:	Corpus Linguistics
CLT:	Communicative Language Teaching
CM:	Classroom Management
CoP:	Community of Practice
CPD:	Continuing Professional Development
DDL:	Data-Driven Learning
EFL:	English as a Foreign Language, used to refer to English language learning for typical short-term stay students in private language centres, or school or university exchange programs in Ireland
ELT:	English Language Teaching
ELTE:	English Language Teacher Education
ESL/EAL:	English as a Second/Additional Language, used to refer to English language learning for those who have immigrated to Ireland for various political or economic reasons
INSET:	In-Service Education and Training
L1:	First Language
L2:	Second Language
NEST/NNEST:	Native/Non-Native English Speaker Teacher
PENSER:	Puzzle identification, Embracing, Noticing, Solving, and Experimentation (or Exploring) and Research, a framework of reflective practice proposed by the authors
PRESET:	Pre-Service Education and Training
RP:	Reflective Practice
SBE/SAE:	Standard British English/Standard American English
SLA:	Second Language Acquisition
ST:	Student Teacher
TBTL:	Task-Based Teaching and Learning
TE:	Teacher Educator
TEC:	Teacher Education Corpus

TEFL: Teaching English as a Foreign Language, a rather dated term in the Irish context often now used to refer to short English language teaching courses on offer in the private sector; it has typically now been replaced with ELT or TESOL

TESOL: Teaching English to Speakers of Other Languages

TP: Teaching Practice, usually taking place in universities or private language schools teaching English to international students

ZPD: Zone of Proximal Development

Chapter 1

An Introduction to Reflective Practice and the Practicum

INTRODUCTION

Many good, and some not-so-good, writings have been published on what has come to be commonly known as 'Reflective Practice.' In teaching circles, this is a broad and general notion that refers to an ability to think purposefully and critically about our professional actions so that we might continue doing what we do well, make changes to any practices that need to be improved, and remove or replace any that need to be discontinued. A personal professional judgment is required to conduct such evaluations and reach decisions. Of course, a big challenge is having the appropriate skills to successfully engage in such an endeavor, particularly in a self-assessment context where the practices we are reviewing are those which we have carefully planned and prepared because we deemed them to be appropriate and predicted that they would be successful. An added challenge comes for those whose natural disposition is more action-focused and therefore may not be naturally reflective or pensive. The result of this can be that such individuals may not place a high value on reflective endeavors and may find it difficult to perceive how they might be operationalized in a way that is practically useful. We have encountered teachers at both ends of the spectrum over the course of our professional lives as teacher educators, and many who fall somewhere in between. We have heard say that reflective practice is a waste of time and conversely that it has been transformative for some of our student teachers. However, the one thing that they all have in common is the need to understand and learn the practical tools of reflective practice, so that such efforts move beyond the realm of mere musing or navel gazing.

This understanding, we argue, must begin in the teacher education context in a very structured and applied way, preferably within the teaching practicum component of the program. If the appropriate skills and tools are honed at this stage of a professional life, they are likely to become embedded in future in-service contexts to facilitate continuous professional development. This ability to reflect and modify may be what saves many new teachers when they are confronted with the reality of the classroom and feel ill-prepared by their teacher education program for these realities (Baguley, 2019; Farrell, 2021: Chapter 2). In fact, as we write this volume during the global Covid pandemic with its associated lockdowns and forced mass move to online education, never has the ability to critically reflect on, evaluate, and adapt our practices been so crucial. And ironically, equally within this context, there has never been so much, and yet so little, time for reflection. Hence, the initial development of reflective abilities in teacher education contexts is crucial to their normalized integration into later practices. Based on this fundamental belief, this volume aims to examine in some detail appropriate ways in which reflective practice skills can be developed as part of the teaching practice component of initial teacher education programs in a TESOL context.

We are also firm believers in the notion of a theory-practice balance in the sense that student teachers should have a conceptual understanding of what they are doing and why they are doing it before moving to the practical application. This relationship can then become more iterative as the practice develops and the theoretical understanding expands over time. This book aims to achieve a theory-practice balance, and in all instances is based on evidence from our own practically-oriented research into reflective practice in the teacher education context in which we work together. This first chapter provides a theoretical introduction to the notion of reflective practice, its origin, how it has been defined in the literature, various evidence-based perspectives on how effective it is, as well as some of its associated pros and cons. The introduction necessarily takes us outside of the realm of language teaching and teacher education, back to some philosophical accounts as well as to the field of general education. This discussion, like those included in later chapters, is embedded in the context of the practicum component of TESOL education programs with a focus on novice teachers.

Pause for Reflection

1. Do you think you are a naturally reflective person or not? What evidence from your past behaviors do you have for this?
2. Do you feel you are well-prepared to engage in reflective practice as part of your education program or ongoing professional development? Say why or why not.
3. Which is more important to you – reflection or action? Why?

REFLECTIVE PRACTICE, DEWEY AND SCHÖN

Musing, thinking, reflecting, whatever we might prefer to call it, has probably existed since close to the origins of human existence. In terms of pinpointable historical timeframes, accounts of the great philosophers of the Classical period, such as Socrates and his student Plato, suggest its formal origins are approximately 400–300 years BC. In the Socratic Method, a teacher asks many questions to prompt student thinking and guide them to learning. 'It was a dialectical method that employs critical inquiry to undermine the plausibility of widely-held doctrine' (Brickhouse & Smith, 2000: 53). This period also saw the importance of lifelong education for all as an imperative for a civilized and lawful society. The links to the formation of the State, morals, ethics, and the law were much more explicit at a time when the norms of modern society were at the relatively early stages of development. In accounts of Socrates and Plato we see strong echoes of what we now understand to be the fundamental principles of reflective practice.

More contemporary recognition of the importance and integration of reflective practice in various fields of education has most often been credited to John Dewey, and later Donald Schön (for a summary account see Farrell, 2012, 2022). Dewey (1859–1952) was an American educational reformer, a philosopher and a psychologist. After having tried teaching at both primary and secondary levels but finding these contexts did not suit him, he became an academic and wrote many influential texts about education, democracy, and ethics, among other subjects. He was a strong believer in testing philosophy and theory in authentic educational contexts to determine their validity in practice. He published numerous works and the two we have always found most influential and relevant to language teacher education and particularly reflective practice in this context are *Democracy in Education* (Dewey, 1916) and *How We Think: A Restatement of the Relation of Reflective Thinking to the Educative Process* (Dewey, 1933). In many of his works written about education, primarily in relation to the education of children, he stresses the importance of active and interactive (social) engagement by pupils in their education. His ideas articulate the fundamental principles on which many more recent methods in general education and language education are based. These include the many approaches associated with task-based learning, problem-based learning, and the flipped classroom. And although he does not write directly about it, many of his ideas, principles, and espoused practices have been transposed to the teacher education context over the last 50–60 years in particular. In the following annotated list, we summarize Dewey's most important contributions to reflective practice in language teacher education.

1. *Education for the present with a focus on the process*
   Dewey rejected a focus on education to achieve some future goal, which in the life of most children is irrelevant because of its temporal distance and will not serve as a motivator. People in general, and especially children, find it difficult to appreciate and connect with eventualities which will occur at some distant point in the future (one of the reasons for the general ineffectiveness of anti-smoking campaigns which focus on future ill-health, or for the tardiness of governments and individuals to react more robustly to climate change issues). Student teachers may have the same challenges if theory is divorced from the implementation into practices which will not occur until sometime down the road. Hence the need for inclusion of a practicum early on in teacher education programs, to create an urgency and connection with the present. This, combined with critical reflective practice, maintains a focus on the developmental processes of what is happening, when it is happening.

2. *Education as the reconstruction of experience*
   Experiencing an issue, a problem, or a dilemma in a social context is the starting point for deconstructing it, understanding it, and reconstructing it so that one is prepared for similar future realities. 'Such a view of education connects ends and means, unifies thought and action, and links past, present, and future. It is a continuous interplay of actions and ideas that lead to increased understanding and personal agency over time' (Feiman-Nemser, 2006: 133). In terms of teacher education, one of these experiences is the social environment of the classroom that student teachers encounter in the practicum. Through this interactive experience both the teacher and the environment are changed and through critical reflective practice the teacher can begin to reconstruct the experience in order to learn from it and prepare for the future.

3. *The place of practice*
   Closely related to the previous point on the reconstruction of experience is the centrality that Dewey placed on practical experimentation in the classroom. This 'doing,' according to Schwab (1959: 158) is 'to go hand in hand with reading, reflecting and remembering.' As a pragmatist, Dewey was committed to the student encountering a genuine situation to provoke thinking when faced with an issue or incident. This encounter would then trigger a cognitive process dedicated to understanding and learning, supported by sufficient previous theoretical and practical understandings to allow for an effective response. This very much relates to his idea that

one educates indirectly and not directly, and that experience is the basis for development. It allows one to form appropriate habits, but habits which are not routine and are kept flexible through constant reasoning and suitable judgment (Farrell, 2012: 9). It is clear that Dewey favors an experimental approach to teaching rather than the apprenticeship of the craft, both of which we will return to in the next section. He advocates for teachers who know how to learn from all of their experiences.

4. *Reflection as emancipator from routine activity*
   Directly associated with his thoughts on experience and practice, Dewey outlined the five main phases of reflective thought, which he considered could take place in any particular order (Dewey, 1933: 18). This is an early framework, from which many others have derived fundamental concepts, and it includes the following:
   a. ***Suggestions*** about a questionable situation in which the mind jumps forward to a potential solution.
   b. An ***intellectualization*** of the difficulty or perplexity that has been felt (directly experienced) into a problem to be solved.
   c. The use of one suggestion after another as a ***leading idea***, or hypothesis, to initiate and guide observation and the collection of factual material.
   d. ***Reasoning*** as the mental elaboration of the leading idea that reflective thought has generated.
   e. ***Hypothesis testing*** by overt or imaginative action.

Donald Schön (1930–1997), another American thinker who originally studied philosophy and music before going on to complete his doctoral research, focused on Dewey's theory of inquiry. He elaborated on Dewey's ideas, which he sought to 'rethink and reconnect' (Schön, 1983: 357) and is best remembered for his more explicit attention to reflective practices and learning systems within both organizations (Schön, 1983) and other communities, including educational (Schön, 1987). 'He was, by his own account, a displaced philosopher working in (among other places) a management consulting firm, a governmental agency, a non-profit center for social development, and finally a university department of urban planning. He used his marginal position in the design professions to reframe professional practice generally' (Waks, 2001: 37). His work addressed the same questions as that of Dewey, but it differed in the answers it provided to some. A key point of departure is their relative perspectives on the relationship between reflection and practice. In simple terms, Dewey believes that knowledge is constructed during time-out periods from practice, during which reflection can take place. He suggests a separation between knowledge construction and live practice. Schön, on the other hand, believes that practitioners also have knowledge codes built into and integrated into their practices. In other words, they construct meaning and knowledge during critical moments in their practice, and practice is also knowledge.

It is worth noting that much of Schön's original empirical work was conducted with music and design professionals, which surely influenced this perspective. He was keenly interested in and provides many examples of how professionals engaged in 'reflection-in-action,' during the course of authentic professional activities. In the case of teaching, this might mean, for example, how a teacher responds to an unanticipated problem (something which Schön calls 'backtalk') that arises during the course of one of their classes. For example, a student might display an unanticipated (by the teacher) difficulty pronouncing a certain sound in English because of a mild hearing impediment. In this context, an experienced teacher will draw on her/his resources and experiences to create a way (in other words, build knowledge) to guide the student through this issue as it happens in the classroom in real time. This is often referred to as 'tacit' or 'practical' knowledge (Golombek, 1998), which is learned in use rather than in abstract theoretical terms. In teacher education settings, the site for learning how to reflect-in-action is in a practicum setting, which is designed to approximate the real-world teaching setting in which teachers will find themselves in their future careers. Although there are constraints, or gaps (Baguley, 2019) between the two contexts, the practicum provides a useful starting point. Schön also recognizes the importance of what he refers to as 'reflection-on-action,' which is more akin to Dewey's ideas. This involves deliberate review and reasoning as part of the reflective process (Munby, 1989: 34). This usually happens retrospectively and once removed from the actual context, often with the support of a peer, a mentor, or an expert.

The important influence of both Dewey and Schön's thinking on the field of language teacher education, and more specifically on reflective practice in this arena, cannot be underestimated, although some constraints have been identified (Farrell, 2022: 14). In a general sense, it has been credited with causing a major shift away from more traditional transmission-based models to a philosophical and practical stance that teacher education must be constructivist and social in nature and, as such, is inevitably a life-long endeavor. In a recent volume, Mann & Walsh (2017: 7) suggest that 'partly because of the value put on autonomy and reflection by Dewey and his followers, there has been a general trend away from the notion of teacher training towards one of teacher education. This is often characterised as a movement from transmission to constructivism.'

Pause for Reflection

1. Which of Dewey's concepts outlined in bullets 1–4 above resonate most with you and why?
2. Do you align more with notions of refection-on-action or reflection-in-action and why?

TEACHER KNOWLEDGE AND APPROXIMATIONS OF PRACTICE

Although somewhat delayed, the practical effects of the teachings of the educational thinkers and reformers discussed in the previous section have now found their way into most, if not all, teacher education contexts around the world, although admittedly to various degrees. ELT education has moved 'away from top-down prescriptions for practice to an appreciation of the importance of teachers' own contextually based reflections and understandings for their professional development' (Hall, 2019: 285–286). Understandings *of* and *for* teachers are core to this paradigm. The former, the understanding of teachers, has manifested itself in terms of research and practice agendas around, for example, teacher cognition/thinking (Borg, 2006; Li, 2019) and teacher beliefs and identity (Barkhuizen, 2017; Morton & Gray, 2018). Focused research in these areas help us to gain better insights into the cognitive and related psychological dimensions of teachers and their teaching. It is assumed that one of the functions of this enhanced understanding is to help inform the professional development of prospective and practicing teachers. This brings us to understanding *for* teachers on the other hand, which can begin its life in the classroom or during teacher education programs (see also Farrell, 2016c: 352, for his thoughts on research written *for* teachers and *by* teachers). In terms of deciding the appropriate content and approach in teacher education contexts, it is generally the community of teacher educator professionals which decides. The teacher educator profession 'functions as a sort of gate-keeper and sustainer of what counts as worth knowing in ELT' (Freeman et al., 2019: 13). This is influenced by a number of factors: history and tradition, new insights, research (as mentioned above), trial and error, and prevailing models in other similar contexts, to name but some. What constitutes the appropriate content, or knowledge, for prospective teachers is not static. It changes over time as our experiences and understandings as a community of professionals advance, in terms of what we know about both English language teaching and English language teacher education.

Looking at the macro-context of ELTE knowledge, there have been some influential representations of what this should, or does, look like (for a fuller account see Farr & O'Keeffe, 2019: 268–269). Shulman (1986) articulated the concept of content, pedagogy, and pedagogic content knowledge as being core for teachers. In other words, knowing what we are teaching, knowing how to teach, and knowing how to best go about teaching it in the relevant context. This was expanded to include technological knowledge and use as this became more pervasive in all social settings, including the classroom (Mishra & Koehler, 2006). Later, Shulman elaborated on the notion of 'wisdom of practice' (Shulman, 2004) to include the type of experiential knowledge that is gleaned from being engaged in real practice, much akin to Dewey and Schön's ideas explored above. Freeman (2016: 115) presents a knowledge-generation framework, which consists of the following:

- First generation: disciplinary knowledge. The focus here was on the ***what*** of teaching with much content centered around linguistics and psychology (at the time, behaviorism).
- Second generation: teaching-knowledge as pedagogy. Attention shifted away from a relatively exclusive focus on what was taught to ***how*** it was taught. The fields of applied linguistics and second language acquisition were born and strongly influenced this generation, with its resultant variety of methods and approaches.
- Third generation: teaching knowledge as in-person, in-place. This is the generation in which Shulman's framework was born. The focus here is on teachers taking the *what* and *how* of the previous two generations and combining them with the ***who*** and ***where*** of the contexts in which they are teaching.
- Fourth generation: knowledge-for-teaching. The key concept in this generation is a focus on the student in relation to the subject matter, and the commonalities that identify English language teachers as distinct from other teachers. So, the question becomes ***why*** do we teach English the way we do? In other words, what makes it different from teaching maths or science or history, for example.

It was during the second generation of knowledge in ELTE that grounded practice (Jenset et al., 2018) began to gain traction, a traction which has become stuck fast within the fabric of teacher education programs. A priority was placed on the application of theory to practice, and also on providing opportunities for student teachers to learn from the experiences of engaging in various practice-oriented activities in a scaffolded environment, or in Vygotskian terms, within the Zone of Proximal Development (Vygotsky, 1978). This zone is the conceptual plane where learning can take place with the aid and support of a more experienced other (a teacher, a mentor, a peer, etc.), in order to reach a point of understanding which could not have been reached alone.

Pause for Reflection

1. Have you ever engaged in any kind of teaching or teaching practice? If so, reflect on your experiences and what you learned from them. If not, what do you expect it to be like?
2. Reflect on and create lists for what you anticipate might be included in a/your teacher education program in terms of the following:
   - Disciplinary knowledge (what you will be teaching)
   - Teaching/pedagogic knowledge (how you will be teaching)
   - People and places (the who and where of teaching contexts)
   - The subject matter (why we teach English the way we do as distinct from teaching other subjects).

Following an audit of English language teacher education programs at MA level in UK universities, it was reported that, 'students consider practical teaching experience an important part of their programs and report that they would like more course time to be spent on it' (Papageorgiou et al., 2019: 154), in a context where only 34 of the 141 programs under scrutiny offered a practicum as part of the curriculum. There are practical, financial, and ethical constraints which have caused and maintained such a low level of practicum offerings. We encounter them periodically in our own context, but through tenacity, commitment, and hard work on the part of the teacher education team we have managed over the 30 years of our MA in TESOL program to keep a strong practical stream as a central offering for our student teachers. In contexts where this is not possible, or as in our case, as transitionary supports in the move towards real classroom practice, alternatives may be on offer. These can come in the form of 'representations of practice' (Grossman, 2011: 2837), which 'include all the different ways in which the work of practitioners is made visible to novices during professional education. Such representations include everything from the stories told by practitioners about practice, to written narratives and cases of practice, to videos of actual practice. Representations also include artifacts from practice, including case records of clients, lesson plans, student work, and live observations of practitioners, be they in field experience or observation of live therapy from behind a one-way mirror.' Such approaches are also known as grounded practice, and Jenset et al. (2018: 187) examine a range of these (planning and practicing for teacher roles; analyzing pupils' leaning; engaging with teaching materials and resources; taking pupils' perspectives, seeing models of teaching; engaging with national or state curricula) and how they are implemented across a number of international contexts. By their very nature, no representations provide a complete and holistic experience of practice for student teachers, but they are helpful.

There may also be opportunities on teacher education programs to engage in one or more of a number of 'approximations of practice' (Grossman, Compton, et al., 2009), all of which align with Dewey's notion of 'laboratory' approaches mentioned in the introduction to this chapter – to allow teachers to try things out, to experiment, and to reflect on and evaluate the consequences. According to Grossman, Compton, et al. (2009: 2840), 'virtually all professional education includes opportunities for students to engage in approximations of practice. In activities ranging from roleplays to moot court and student teaching, approximations require students to engage in practice that is related, but not identical, to the work of practicing professionals.' Typically, in a teacher education context these come in two related forms: micro-teaching and team teaching. Representations and approximations of practice can play a crucial role in teacher education programs as they can provide a much-needed bridge between theory and practice in a low-risk environment for student teachers.

The practicum, also known as teaching practice, teaching placement, teaching internship, etc., can take various forms depending on context and sometimes tradition. A relatively typical, and, in our experience, prevalent practicum model operating on ELTE programs would look something like a variant of the following:

Observation of Teaching

- Observation of more experienced teachers (either live or pre-recorded)
- Structured and supported reflection of the observation

Peer Teaching

- Supported preparation for peer teaching (teaching other student teachers in a simulated setting, sometimes known as micro-teaching, although micro-teaching can also have different meanings)
- Structured peer teaching
- Structured and supported reflection of peer teaching

Team Teaching

- Supported preparation for team teaching (teaching together with a more experienced teacher in a shared and supportive environment)
- Structured team teaching
- Structured and supported reflection of team teaching, usually with the team teacher

Individual Teaching

- Supported preparation for individual teaching (often observed by a mentor)
- Individual teaching
- Structured and supported reflection of teaching, usually with the mentor who has observed.

We have purposely refrained from assigning this list numbers as we do not necessarily see this as a linear or sequential process, but rather one of repeat cycles and overlaps as appropriate for the context and/or the individual. Represented visually, it might look something like the examples presented in Figures 1.1 and 1.2, although we could also envision other possibilities.

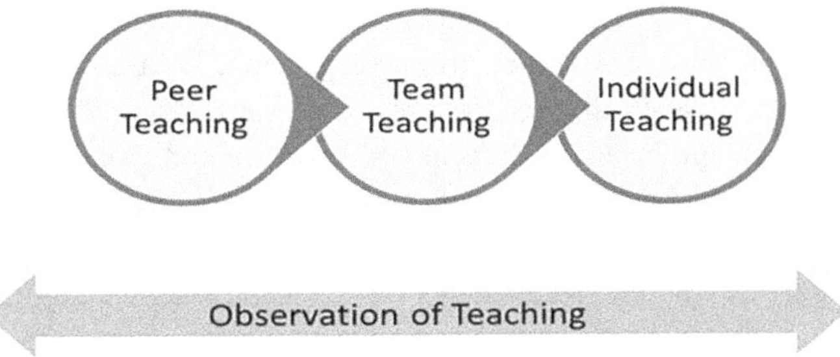

Figure 1.1. Overlapping cycles of the practicum on an ELTE program: Example 1.

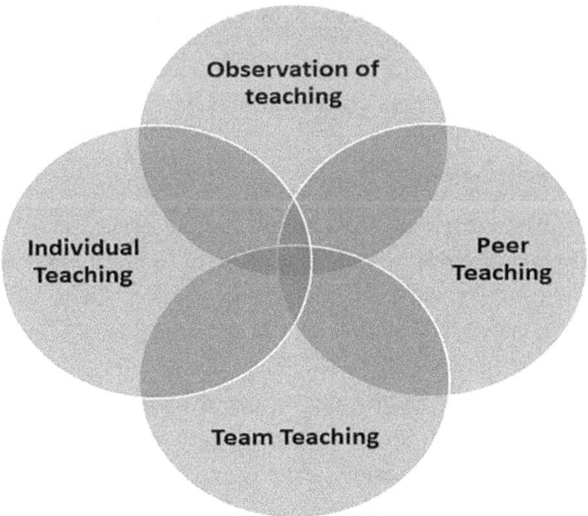

Figure 1.2. Overlapping cycles of the practicum on an ELTE program: Example 2.

Contextual factors such as duration of the program, access to English language classes and teachers, as well as resources (human and other) will determine the most appropriate components and model used on a specific ELTE program. On a short two-day introductory or in-service program, you might expect to see teachers perhaps engaging in just two components briefly. On the other hand, a year-long MA program might afford a much more elaborate offering of several cycles of each of the components. The latter reflects the context of our experiences discussed in this book, but we suggest that much of this is also relevant to other contexts and can be appropriated with due consideration and adaptation. And, of course, the thread stringing each of the four components together is structured and supported critical reflection, which is the main focus of the remainder of the chapters of this book.

Figures 1.1 and 1.2 perhaps suggest that the practicum is a fairly linear, albeit overlapping, and smooth journey. In our experience, both as teachers and as teacher educators, this is absolutely not the case for most student teachers. There are many bumps and bends on the route, with u-turns and roundabouts aplenty. In fact, an early challenge comes with the recognition that teachers' developmental paths and concerns do not always match the type of practicum model and associated reflective activities presented as part of their teacher education program. In fact, one widely cited example of an empirically constructed theory of teacher development can be found in the work of Fuller and her colleagues (Fuller, 1969; Fuller & Brown, 1975). Their model suggests that teachers go through stages of concern when learning to teach. The three-stage framework suggests that teachers move through the stages, progressing to the next only when the current concerns are resolved:

- concerns about self and their own adequacy
- concerns about tasks and teaching
- concerns about student learning.

Researchers have empirically mapped such development with novice teachers, and some have even extended the framework to include a progressive movement towards concern with personal and professional development to grow as teachers in a state of heightened reflexivity (Conway & Clark, 2003). Others still recommend that teacher educators align their efforts to relevant teacher concerns at the appropriate times rather than 'teaching against the tide' (Feiman-Nemser, 2006: 132). This is something of which we are acutely aware and embed within the framework and activities we include in later chapters of this book.

Pause for Reflection

1. What do you think the practicum will consist of on your teacher education program? Is this in line with your expectations? Why/why not?
2. How do you feel about taking part in the practicum? Do you have any concerns about yourself, what you will be teaching, or your students?

APPROACH OF THE BOOK

In terms of the approach taken in the remaining chapters, we draw on the practices and research from the context of our pre-service MA in TESOL program featuring novices with little or no prior teaching experience. Over the course of a number of years, we have gathered a range of different datasets to help us understand our teacher education practices and also to investigate the social interactions of our student teachers. We are of the strong view that exploring practices and interactions from this context is not just in our interest but is also our responsibility as teacher educators committed to the principles of research-informed reflective practice and professional development. In Johnson's words, exploring interactions in teacher education 'as they unfold and within the socio-cultural contexts in which they occur, not only opens up the practices of L2 teacher education for closer scrutiny, but it also holds teacher educators accountable to the L2 teachers with whom they work and, of course, the L2 students their teachers teach' (Johnson, 2015: 515). Having said that, this is not a research-oriented account only, but one which aims to bridge the gap between that research (for example, Farr, 2011; Farr et al., 2019; A. Farrell, 2019) and the practices that novice teachers will engage in during their teacher education program.

Various tools and sources of evidence to support the RP process during the practicum are investigated, using the many data-rich examples mentioned above and below. These illustrations do not suppose to be models of best practice, or even good practice in some cases, but examples of real practice, all of which have the potential to provide insights into the teacher development process. They will shed light on the challenges experienced by the novices, as revealed in their spoken and written reflections, and how they endeavor to understand these challenges. In so doing, the reflections will also illuminate the ways in which student teachers addressed these challenges, with the over-arching aim of informing future directions in their teaching. Much of the data is discourse data presented in qualitative ways to encourage a nuanced understanding of the social processes being engaged in and how these are supported by peers and experts. However, we also occasionally use corpus-based techniques (see below), which allow us to quantify some of the linguistic phenomena under investigation in order to draw conclusions about frequency and saliency in the interactions (for a more strongly oriented corpus-based account of such interactions see Farr et al., 2019) .

As already seen, this book also presents practical tasks in the form of pauses for reflection, as well as strategies and techniques that can be applied by teacher educators, teachers, and researchers to their own context. As such, it will demonstrate the ways in which reflective practice can form an integral part of ELTE programs, across a range of modes and tasks, and how this approach can be enhanced by the complementary use of evidence from real reflections in order to gain a deeper understanding of real classroom practices. We aim to demonstrate how this evidence-based approach can enable teacher educators to provide more critically informed and targeted pedagogic guidance to novice teachers, including in teaching practice feedback. The principles underpinning the approach in this volume can be summarized as followed:

- it is evidence-based, drawing on data from a context where we, the teacher educators, have researched our own practice in what is often known as 'ecological research' (Mann & Walsh, 2017: 32), and share this evidence in the form of illustrative examples
- it draws on illustrations from a range of written and spoken discourse contexts
- it values both individual and dialogic/collaborative reflective activities
- it supports, even if not directly addressed, the use of different tools and approaches for practical purposes: narrative enquiry, stimulated recall, dialogic encounters, and appropriate pro-formas (all taking account of the context).

Having generally discussed our approach and our positionality, we outline in some detail in the next section the discourse data that we use to support our discussions in later chapters, and the context from which it emanates. Also included there is a discussion of the issues encountered and identified by novice teachers as they move through their practicum cycles. These issues, challenges, or puzzles, as we call them interchangeably, form the basis for the substantive Chapters 4–7 in this volume.

DATA FOR THE BOOK

The Context

As strong proponents for evidence-based reflective practice, we have been collecting such evidence in the form of data for a considerable number of years. This data, which will be used to exemplify and explore reflective practice in the remainder of this book, comes from student teachers and those who mentor them over the course of the practicum component of an MA TESOL program at the institution where both authors work. In the following sections, we provide a very general demographic profile of the participants and details of the academic program that served as the backdrop for the data-collection and research. This should help to contextualize the subsequent chapters.

The data, or evidence, presented in this book was collected at a higher education institution in Ireland from discourse produced as part of a one-year full time MA TESOL program that runs over three academic semesters (including a summer, research-oriented, semester). The program has the overall aim of providing students with an understanding of the theoretical perspectives which underpin effective English language teaching. Each semester is of 15 weeks and features core modules in conjunction with a range of electives of which teaching practice (TP) is one. This module is, in reality, compulsory for all student teachers with fewer than three years of prior teaching experience. The TP module involves theoretical input, lesson planning, and practice teaching of multicultural English language classes at advanced, upper-intermediate, and intermediate levels within the same higher education institution where the TESOL program is offered. The students taught on the TP module by the student teachers are ERASMUS (European University Exchange) and other third-level international students studying for a university degree on a full-time basis, all of whom speak English as a second or other language. The classroom teaching practice begins halfway through the first semester after an initial period of observation of experienced teachers (informal mentors) and team teaching. The qualified class teacher assumes a mentoring role, engaging in discussion with the student teacher and providing informal feedback on the initial team-teaching stages. Student teachers are typically required to plan for and teach a one-hour lesson every week. TP lessons are routinely recorded and observed by teacher educators (for approximately 60% of an individual's teaching), and they are followed by an individual feedback session with the teacher educator, usually a day or so after the lesson. Supervised lessons are formally graded. The TP module also involves the ongoing observation of qualified and experienced teachers and the writing of a reflective diary, which is formally evaluated and graded.

The practicum is also supported by other modules on the program which explore classroom theory and practice, as well as language systems and phonetics, among others. Figure 1.3 summarizes the participatory framework.

In reality, the mentors are the full-time class teachers and the supervisors can also be lecturers on the program (henceforth we will generally call them teacher educators). So, although performing different roles, the individuals involved cross the participation boundaries, with the exception of the student teachers. The student teachers, usually about 20 per annum, come from a variety of demographic, educational, experiential, cultural, and linguistic backgrounds. In general, in the data described below, about 60% of the student teachers speak English as a first language and 40% as a second or other language, although in more recent years this balance has tilted slightly in favor of the latter group.

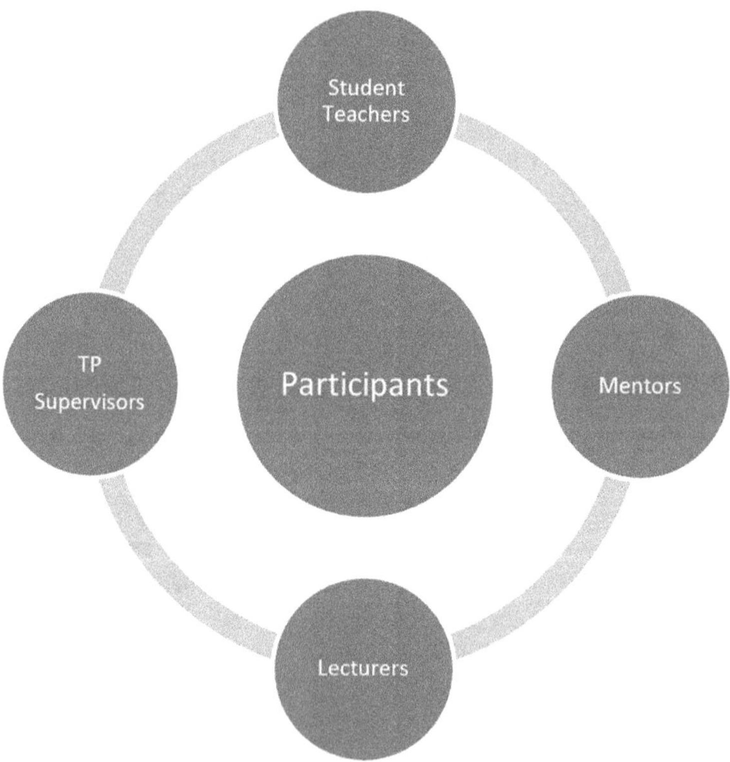

Figure 1.3. The participatory framework.

The Teacher Education Corpus (TEC)

As part of the TP and related modules, the MA students are asked to engage in several reflective practice activities throughout their academic studies. Some of these are individual, some collaborative, some are written while others are spoken, some are formally graded and others not, and some are online while many are face-to-face. For approximately the past 20 years, following the prerequisite ethical approvals, we have been engaged in collecting some of the various artifacts of these reflective practices and storing them as data in the form of what we call the Teacher Education Corpus (TEC), which grows from year to year and now contains approximately half a million words. Elsewhere we have analyzed this corpus from various discourse perspectives (for example, Farr et al., 2019; A. Farrell, 2019; Riordan, 2018). In this volume we use this discourse data in a more qualitative way to exemplify and evidence the reflective practices of those involved. Figure 1.4 presents an overview of the TEC corpus data as it currently stands.

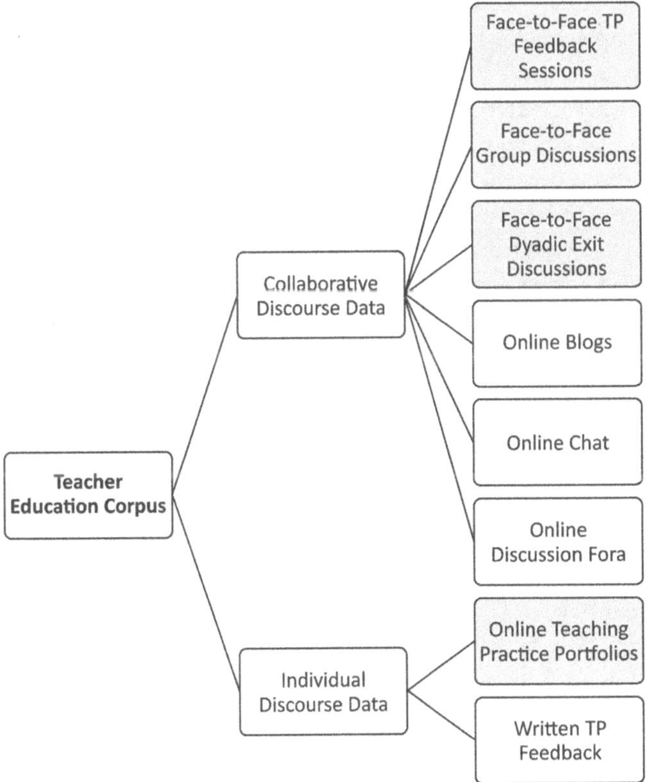

Figure 1.4. The Teacher Education Corpus (TEC).

The highlighted cells in Figure 1.4 represent the categories from which we draw some data for the current volume. We collate this into what we call the PENSER sub-corpus of TEC. All of our corpus data uses pseudonyms for any student teachers involved, of whom there are many, and we use the acronym TE to refer to the teacher educator. In the following subsection, we explain in detail the PENSER process and the data that was collected as part of its implementation over a number of years.

The PENSER Approach and Sub-Corpus

Over a period of about 5 years we have been implementing what we term the PENSER (the French verb 'penser' means to think or reflect) approach in our TP modules (Farr & Farrell, 2017) to provide a five-step structure for students to reflect on their practices (see also Chapter 2). The cycle of these five steps is repeated three times over the course of the academic year. In this section we detail its implementation over the course of one academic year by way of exemplification. The starting point of the PENSER approach is to ask each of the student teachers to identify *one* aspect of their teaching practice where they felt particularly challenged (similar to what some term a 'critical incident,' but we felt this terminology sounded a bit serious and potentially overwhelming), which would provide the focus of their reflections over the following five-week cycle. This marked a reflection-*on*-action stage of the reflective process (Farrell, 1998: 12) and it was repeated for the following two cycles (three cycles in total over the two semesters). From this, the student teachers were encouraged to articulate the specific nature of the challenge, or puzzle, which then formed the focus for their reflections for that particular cycle, and to begin the process of addressing the challenge over the subsequent weeks of the cycle, which we refer to as embracing, noticing, solving, and experimentation (or exploring) and research. Table 1.1 outlines the stages of the PENSER cycle and a typical timeframe for its implementation.

Table 1.1. The PENSER cycle.

Stage of Cycle	Timeframe/Task	Data Type
1. Puzzle identification	(Week 1): Group discussion 1	Oral
2. Embracing	(Week 2): Group discussion 2	Oral
3. Noticing	(Weeks 2–5): Observation and Online TP portfolio	Written
4. Solving	(Week 4): Group discussion 3	Oral
5. Experimentation and Research	(Week 5): Dyadic exit discussion	Oral

Table 1.1 illustrates, in the last column, the kind of data that is generated and collected as part of the PENSER cycle when students engaged in individual and collective reflections across a range of spoken and written modes of communication, as follows:

1. *Group discussions*
   A total of three group discussions were held in each reflective cycle (Week 1, Week 2, and Week 4), creating opportunities for novices to identify and articulate the challenges they had encountered in their teaching practice, propose and explore hypotheses for these challenges, and share the insights gained from the reflective process with peers. The choice of group discussions was influenced by their successful use in studies by O'Brien & Beaumont (2000) and Farrell (2016b) in the context of reflective practice research amongst novice TESOL teachers. It also addressed three key criteria of reflection proposed originally by Dewey (1933: 7), and others since (Farrell, 2004: 44), which are that it involves naming the puzzle or question(s) that arise out of the experience; that it needs to happen in community in interaction with others; and that it takes place in a low-anxiety context. These discussions were guided by a teacher educator who was also one of the TP supervisors.
2. *Online TP portfolios*
   Online TP portfolios were utilized as a complementary tool with each participant asked to write at least one entry per week between Week 2 and Week 5 of each reflective cycle in relation to the challenge they had selected as the focus of their reflection. The choice of this approach was influenced by Riordan (2018) and Farr et al. (2019), both of which demonstrated the benefits of using online TP portfolios to map the development of student teacher reflective thinking.
3. *Dyadic exit discussions*
   Dyadic discussions lasting 30 minutes in duration and featuring individual student teachers and a teacher educator were held at the end of each of the three five-week cycles in order to informally evaluate the development of their conceptual, practical, and critical knowledge of the specified challenge. This approach was selected following its successful use by Tsui (2003) and Farrell (2016b) for similar purposes.

Accordingly, the PENSER approach featured multiple and varied modes to help facilitate and trace the reflective thinking of student teachers. The choice of this combined approach can be further rationalized following the conclusion reached by Spalding et al. (2002) that while many individual methods have proved effective tools for facilitating the reflective thinking of novices, no single pedagogical strategy is best or sufficient to teach reflective thinking skills or to record its development in terms of the depth and outcomes achieved. The whole process (and the associated data collection) is ongoing, recursive, and dynamic throughout the three reflective cycles. To create what we now call the PENSER sub-corpus of TEC, the data from the guided group discussions and the dyadic exit discussions were audio-recorded, transcribed, and coded thematically alongside the online TP portfolio data. The PENSER corpus is detailed in Figure 1.5.

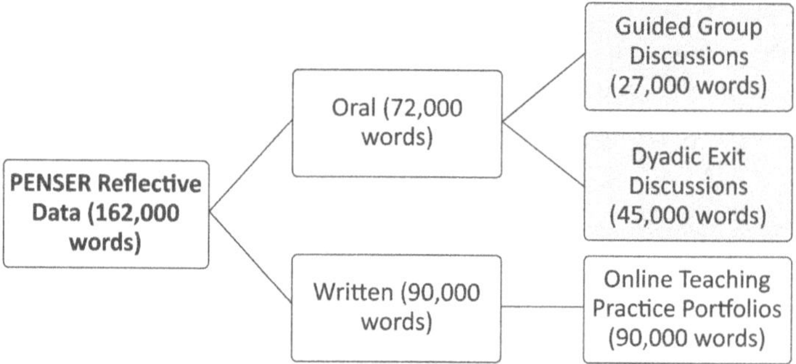

Figure 1.5. The PENSER corpus.

Ultimately, the data used in later chapters of this book comprises the TP feedback sub-corpus and the PENSER sub-corpus of TEC. The PENSER data has been analysed both quantitatively and qualitatively, beginning with an up-close examination of the transcripts of the first group discussion in each of the three reflective cycles. These were coded for references to challenges, issues, or puzzles in the student teachers' verbalizations, whether explicitly or implicitly expressed, tabulated for the number of occurrences, and categorized into broad areas of pedagogical challenge, which are detailed in the next section.

PUZZLES IDENTIFIED BY STUDENT TEACHERS

The initial thematic analysis of the PENSER group discussions revealed a range of 26 issues of concern over the course of the three reflective cycles which were categorized into four, broad pedagogical themes: (i) Planning and Preparation; (ii) The L2 Classroom Environment; (iii) Teaching Grammar, Vocabulary, and Pronunciation; (iv) Teacher Talk and Interactional Skills. From this, the most problematic areas in each of the three reflective cycles were identified, with comparisons made across cycles. Figure 1.6 presents the findings relating to this thematic analysis, with the percentages representing the number of students who mention each challenge.

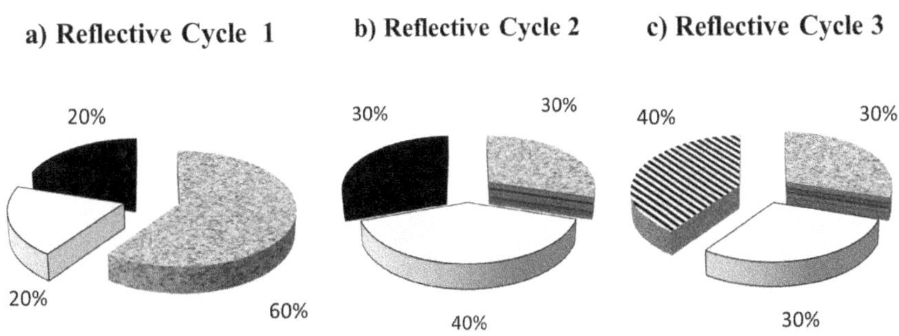

Figure 1.6. Pedagogic puzzles identified in PENSER cycles.

As indicated, there was variability in the prominence of the various types of challenge as the novices moved from one reflective cycle to the next. In PENSER Cycle 1, for instance, problems relating to planning and preparation featured most predominantly in the reflective data followed by issues relating to managing the L2 classroom and the teaching of specific areas of language such as grammar, vocabulary, and pronunciation, while concerns relating to teacher talk and interactional skills were largely absent. By comparison, in PENSER Cycle 2, problems relating to teaching aspects of the English language featured most saliently, followed to a slightly lesser degree by challenges relating to managing the L2 classroom and planning and preparation; but as in PENSER Cycle 1, concerns in relation to teacher talk and interactional skills did not feature. By contrast, in PENSER Cycle 3, the novices were most concerned with challenges relating to their teacher talk and classroom interactional skills; although issues relating to planning and preparation and teaching the language were still salient in the data, classroom management now no longer featured as a challenge. These findings corroborate the conclusions reached by Katz (1972: 52) that in the early days of teaching when novices are in the 'survival' stage, they are more likely to be concerned with their classroom management role, but over time, their focus moves to their classroom teacher role and skills, as would be expected. Table 1.2 summarizes the four broad pedagogical areas identified as puzzles by the student teachers over the course of the three PENSER cycles. It also sets out the specific challenges they pinpointed in each case in the order in which they were most frequently mentioned in the PENSER reflective data.

Table 1.2. Puzzles identified during the PENSER cycles.

Main Areas of Challenge	Specific Issues
(i) Lesson Design and Planning	• Workload • Identifying lesson aims • Writing the lesson plan • Understanding learner abilities • Constraints of the course book • Selecting suitable materials and resources
(ii) The L2 Classroom Environment	• Teacher anxiety • Poor teacher presence • Difficulties building rapport with learners • Low learner engagement • Uneven participation • Managing resources
(iii) Teaching Grammar, Vocabulary, and Pronunciation	• Lack of language awareness and knowledge • Unsuitable level of input • Poor explanations of language points • Overly didactic teaching approach • Lack of confidence teaching grammar • Fear of teaching pronunciation
(iv) Teacher Talk and Interactional Skills	• Quantity of teacher talk • Quality of teacher talk • Suitability of teacher talk • Quantity of student talk • Quality of student talk • Questioning strategies • Poor instructions • Corrective feedback

These puzzles, or challenges, identified by the student teachers, have helped us to organize Chapters 4–7 under these broad themes.

OVERVIEW AND STRUCTURE OF THE BOOK

This introductory chapter has outlined the foundational concepts on which this book sits, including a discussion of educational philosophy and how reflective practice was born therein. An explication of what a typical practicum might look like as part of an ELTE program provides some pragmatic context for student teachers and teacher educators in advance of later chapters. The practicum simply represents one component of how and where teacher knowledge is constructed during education programs and serves to complement others such as content knowledge and pedagogical knowledge, as discussed. In this chapter we also introduced the data which we draw on in later chapters of this volume by way of the TEC and the context in which it is born. More specifically, the PENSER reflective model and data (Farr & Farrell, 2017) is detailed. This data-informed approach towards reflection has been developed and implemented by the present authors to facilitate the processes of reflective thinking of novice teachers during the teaching practicum. The associated data emanating from the implementation of this approach with student teachers is subsequently articulated and now forms the PENSER sub-corpus of TEC. This will be referenced throughout later chapters in order to illustrate the professional growth of the novices over the course of their TP journey.

In summary, this chapter has explored some of the ways in which practice teaching is a key component of all good ELTE programs, and it provides a forum for novice teachers to begin to cross the theory-practice divide in a way which allows them to try out ideas in a classroom setting. This typically happens after a period of theoretical induction and the observation of more experienced teachers, and it can often begin in a highly scaffolded way through micro-teaching or team teaching, before moving to more independence, as detailed in the previous section and further elaborated in Chapter 3. At all stages of this practice-oriented process, reflection is a fundamental and obligatory underlying principle, the integration of which leads to informed decisions on change implementation to improve teaching. In Chapter 2 we address the theory-practice divide that is often quoted in relation to teacher education programs. We do this by presenting a number of practice-oriented reflective practice frameworks found in the literature from the last 40–50 years. Many of these are oriented towards practice in general and not specifically towards the practicum component of ELTE programs, but provide much foundational orientation and content for this volume. This chapter also explores some of the practical challenges associated with the successful implementation of reflective practice and some possible solutions. The focus for Chapters 3–8 is on the practical or practicum component of ELTE programs. Each of these chapters explores reflective practices at various stages and around different topics related to the practicum (observation, lesson planning and preparation, the L2 classroom environment, teaching the language, teacher talk and interactional skills, learner engagement, and the post-practice feedback session). The process of RP as a life-long developmental practice will be explored as the volume concludes. In the exploratory and reflective spirit of this book, we also provide tasks for readers based on the themes explored in each chapter, which offers an opportunity for further reflection.

This book aims to provide a useful practical guide for teachers who are interested in exploring the role and impact of evidence-based reflective practice that is grounded in classroom-oriented reflection and research. Accordingly, it is envisaged that it can serve as a core text for language pedagogy and practicum modules on ELTE programs. It can also be used as a reference book and practical guide for novice teachers engaged on MA TESOL/ELTE programs, or in their early career years, with a view to enabling them to become more confident, better-informed, and more expert teachers in terms of their linguistic knowledge, lesson design, classroom management, and target English skills. It aims to help them to develop a critical understanding of the complex and varied needs of learners in different teaching contexts and the ways in which the changing English language and pedagogic landscapes are impacting on their pedagogical choices and practices. This volume is also likely to be of interest to researchers and postgraduate students (MA and PhD) working in the fields of reflective practice, corpus linguistics, and language teacher education. It will be of particular interest to those engaged in researching corpus-based approaches to reflective practice and the relationship between reflective practice and pedagogical knowledge and skills.

Chapter 2

Frameworks and Approaches for Reflecting on Practice

INTRODUCTION

On several occasions while writing this book we have questioned whether the term reflective practice (RP) is actually an appropriate or accurate term to capture what is intended by this ubiquitous expression in teacher education contexts. 'Practice,' we don't have an issue with, but 'reflective,' as attested to by its many listed synonyms, is suggestive of museful, pensive, and thoughtful processes, and in our experience, RP in teacher education is necessarily a much more serious, structured, and focused intellectual endeavor. It is thinking with purpose, it has aims and intended outcomes which will result in judicious change for improvement, where prudent. In the practicum context, RP relies on systematic exploration of practice, an examination of underlying beliefs and principles, an awareness of practices, an understanding of the shared wisdom of the profession, an insight into the perspectives of all of the participants in the institutional and cultural context under reflection, and finally, an ability for teachers to articulate and abstract this in a coherent way to themselves and to others. This can seem like a daunting and complex task for student and novice teachers, and indeed it is. For this reason, the present volume aims to provide a support and structure to help them to achieve useful reflection and improvements in their practice.

From the outset, it is important to mention that RP has been with us for some time, in lots of professions, and in many micro-contexts within those professions. It has been widely espoused as a professional development framework and for this reason '...there has been a hodgepodge of definitions, activities, strategies, and approaches to reflection presented both in the fields of education and second language education, and there has been no consistency within any of these approaches or models that teachers, regardless of their experience, can apply to their everyday professional practice' (Farrell, 2015: 3). It is not our intention in this book to resolve these issues, as we believe such an attempt would be futile. Instead, in this chapter we begin by presenting a set of practical principles intended to function as suggested predispositions for engaging in RP. This will be followed by a presentation and discussion of some previously published frameworks for doing reflective practice, many of which we have found most useful in our own experiences. Some of the challenges identified in relation to RP are then explored before we propose some possible solutions.

REFLECTIVE PRACTICE: REQUISITE ATTITUDES

Dewey (1933) distinguished between what he called 'routine actions,' which have become habitual, impulsive, and often subconscious for the experienced teacher, and actions that are 'reflective.' Zeichner & Liston (2014: 10) define a reflective action as 'that which involves active, persistent and careful consideration of any belief or practice in light of the reasons that support it and the further consequences to which it leads.' For many, being in a state of reflective action is a way of existing as a teacher in a holistic sense, holistic because it involves both rational problem-solving (a cognitive dimension) as well as emotion and passion (an affective dimension). Bolton (2014: 1) considers RP 'a state of mind, an on-going attitude to life and work, the pearl grit in the oyster of practice and education.' In our experience, being in this reflective state does not come naturally to most people, as many modern-day cultures in the contemporary world foster a more cognitive approach to education and living in general, often to the detriment of the development of emotional intelligence. However, with support, time, and effort to bridge any gaps, we have seen the teachers with whom we work become very adept at thinking and acting reflectively, and this stays with them throughout their teaching lifetimes (see Farrell, 2021 for a full discussion on bridging the gaps in teacher preparation and initial professional practice). The current volume provides some of the support needed on reflective journeys, but the time, effort, and attitude needed must come from the teachers themselves. For Dewey, three attitudes are essential for reflective action. Each of these will now be discussed.

1. *Open-mindedness*

   Open-mindedness means a willingness to consider all possibilities and entails an acceptance that your own beliefs and opinions may not be the only or indeed the correct ones. In other words, you may be wrong! In the 1960s, Wright Mills distinguished between three types of believers (cited in Zeichner & Liston, 2014: 11), and it would be worth considering where you currently sit on this spectrum and where you might ideally prefer to be in terms of open-mindedness:

- Vulgar believers, have no interest in listening to alternative arguments or question their own beliefs
- Sophisticated believers, are interested in what others have to say but only so that they can contradict them through articulating their own beliefs
- Critical believers, are willing to try to see things from other perspectives because they accept that all belief systems have strengths and weaknesses.

The last of these, 'critical believers,' is akin to Dewey's notion of open-mindedness. To be an effective reflective practitioner means being able to genuinely consider a range of other perspectives as being appropriate and having the possibility to help understand or resolve the issue under consideration.

2. *Responsibility*
The second necessary attribute for effective reflective action is to possess and demonstrate the ability to thoughtfully consider the consequences of any of your actions, unintended as well as intended. The consequences of your actions for the students you teach may take different forms. Your actions may affect their personal self-concept, how they think about themselves. They may be more academic in nature, and you may primarily affect their intellectual development. It is also important to think about your students' futures and whether your actions could have any impact on these in terms of social, cultural, and political consequences relating to their opportunities in life. To give a positive example, your considerable efforts at motivating your students to learn English, or indeed other languages, could have a strong impact on their achievement level and therefore their chances of accessing a university program or working for a multinational company and travelling the world in the future.

3. *Wholeheartedness*
The principle behind wholeheartedness is that both open-mindedness and responsibility are genuinely core and central parts of a teacher's life. They should be in no way peripheral or added on. Reflecting in open-minded and responsible ways must be a regular and integrated part of your routine as you strive to understand and improve practice.

With such an unreserved commitment to RP, as advocated by Dewey, comes the inevitable realization that teachers are imperfect in some ways. However, good reflective teachers are not overly harsh or critical towards themselves but look for solutions and move forward with their practice. The major advantage is that reflection 'emancipates us from merely impulsive and routine activity and enables us to direct our actions with foresight and to plan according to ends in view of purposes of which we are aware. It enables us to know what we are about when we act' (Dewey, 1933: 17). Having considered the core requisite attitudes or dispositions to RP, we now explore some of the frameworks previously proposed in the literature, which may help you to put the theory into practice.

Pause for Reflection

1. How open-minded, responsible, and wholehearted are you, in Dewey's terms? Use real examples from your past to evidence your self-assessments.
2. Which of these three attributes do you need to develop most and what specific steps can you take to do this?

REFLECTIVE PRACTICE FRAMEWORKS

As facilitators of reflective practice for our student teachers on pedagogic, practice, and professional development courses over several years, we have become accustomed to citing the core staples of RP frameworks from the literature. Some of these emanate from general education literature and others are more specifically set in and directed towards the TESOL profession, with inevitable overlaps and commonalities. Criticisms of the proliferation of models and frameworks of RP can also easily be found. Mann & Walsh (2017: 15), for example, suggest that practitioners spend too much time and space going through the models rather than showing students/teachers how to do reflective practice. This may be the case, but we think good practitioners can avoid this pitfall: for example, we spend very little instructional time going through the frameworks and get quickly to how they might be adapted and used to facilitate RP. Secondly, they voice an objection to the fact that frameworks suggest a linear order and progression, and this is indeed an issue that we have experienced with our own student teachers and one which must be guarded against. Another major criticism of RP and its related frameworks is that they are not data-led (Akbari, 2007; Walsh & Mann, 2015). Again, this is a criticism with which we strongly align ourselves and have been endeavoring in our various dissemination efforts and publications to counter-balance by ensuring that all of our writings and practices are corpus- or evidence-based (for example, Farr,

2011; Farr et al., 2019; A. Farrell, 2019), as discussed in Chapter 1. In the remainder of this section we present, in summary format, some of the more influential frameworks from past and more recent literature (for a more detailed account see A. Farrell, 2019: Chapter 1).

Kolb's Experiential Learning Cycle

Kolb (1984) introduced a much-used cyclical model to illustrate the process of learning from experience. It draws obviously on earlier work by Dewey as discussed in Chapter 1. It involves four stages, as illustrated in Figure 2.1, combining practical and reflective phases.

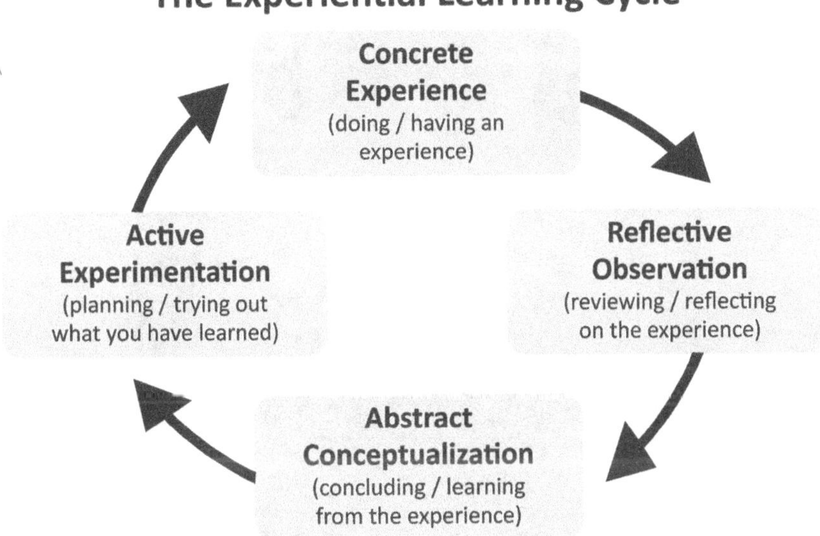

Figure 2.1. Kolb's Experiential Learning Cycle (1984).

In theory, the cycle can begin at any point, although many use the 'concrete experience' as a starting point and the stimulus for reviewing one's practice. Following such review, conclusions are drawn, and a plan formulated, which is in turn applied in practice. This cycle can then continue or be reactivated at any stage in one's professional practice. The model has been applied in various disciplines from nursing to teaching and, in our experience, is one which student teachers generally find conceptually accessible and practically enforceable in its simplest form, although at times they may not feel ready or able to engage with all of the stages during each reflective cycle. This is perfectly fine as student teachers typically move from being legitimate peripheral members to fuller members of the community of teachers (Lave & Wenger, 1991) where they plan to spend their professional lives.

Gibbs' Reflective Practice Cycle

Very soon after the publication of Kolb's work, Gibbs (1988) presented a more nuanced cyclical account of RP. His model suggests a more overtly holistic approach, with an explicit discriminatory focus on cognitive descriptions and the articulation of emotions, as well as an evaluative step which, for most, includes a combination of cognition and emotion (see Figure 2.2).

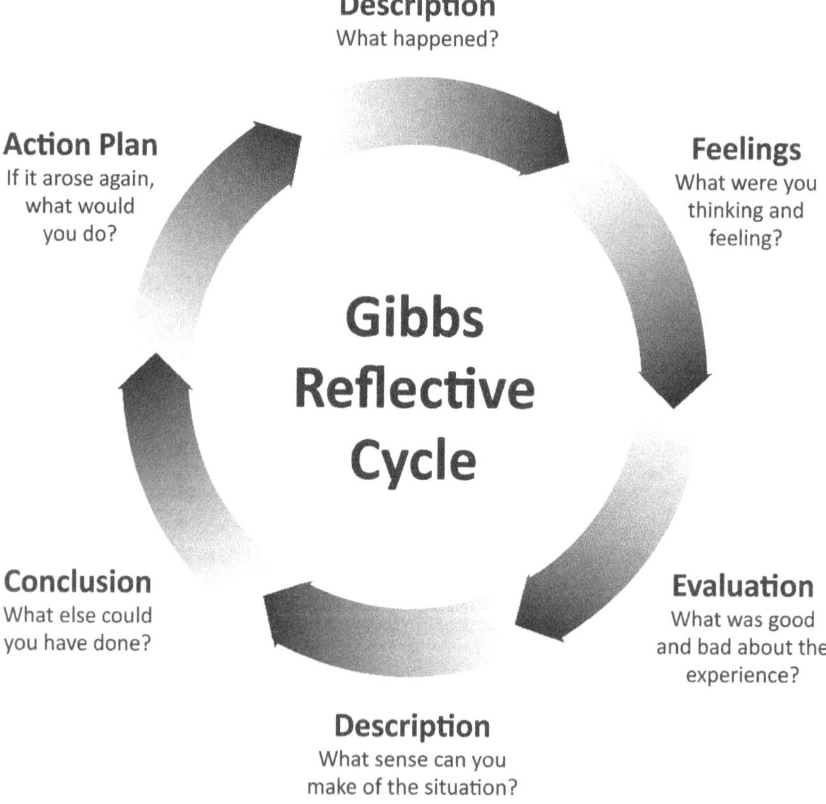

Figure 2.2. Gibbs' Reflective Practice Cycle (1988).

As with previous frameworks, this six-stage model suggests that reflection takes place after an experience, in our case practice teaching. Gibbs worked and researched in higher education teaching, and although many of his publications are contextualized in this setting, they can also be applied to other disciplines and teaching environments. One of the attractive aspects of this approach is that it includes a number of cue questions and provides a checklist to work through. In our experience, student teachers like questions and checklists as a way of focusing attention and eliciting key concepts. Gibbs was adamant that learners should move beyond simple narration and posited that 'learners often lurch from superficial descriptions of what happened to premature conclusions about what to do next, without adequate reflection or analysis' (Gibbs, 1988: 25). Questions and checklists are one of his efforts to promote a more multidimensional and deeper level of reflection, although in themselves they can be restrictive if applied too rigidly. The more explicit focus on emotional as well as cognitive and evaluative dimensions seems to have impacted on the articulation of later models concerned with the higher education teaching context in particular (for example, Brookfield, 1995).

Farrell's Contributions

Since the 1990s, one of the strongest advocates and contributors to the RP discussions (and debates) in the literature and elsewhere, specifically in the English language teaching arena, has been Tom Farrell (for full details see: http://www.reflectiveinquiry.ca/). As a profession we are indebted to him for moderating the prolific work of others in volumes such as his digest of research in the field (Farrell, 2018), but also for his applied work. Some of this practice-facing effort has focused on the development of frameworks for teachers wishing to engage in RP. We present one of them here, as being highly relevant to the practicum context.

Farrell (2015, 2022) presented a comprehensive five-stage framework, peppered with lots of reflective tasks and questions for each of the stages. It is intended to be flexible and suitable for teachers at any stage in their professional careers, from pre-service to highly experienced individuals (see Figure 2.3).

In Farrell's words (2015: 23), 'the framework not only addresses each level from a theoretical perspective but also asks probing questions and outlines strategies to stimulate reflection. Throughout the reflective process, teachers are encouraged not only to describe but also to examine and challenge embedded assumptions at each level so that they can use the framework as a lens through which they can view their professional (and even personal) worlds.' The intention is that teachers can explore the various dimensions of the framework individually or in combination, and in any sequence. This is what gives it flexibility and makes it potentially suitable for teachers at different starting points. We will now briefly explore each of the five stages.

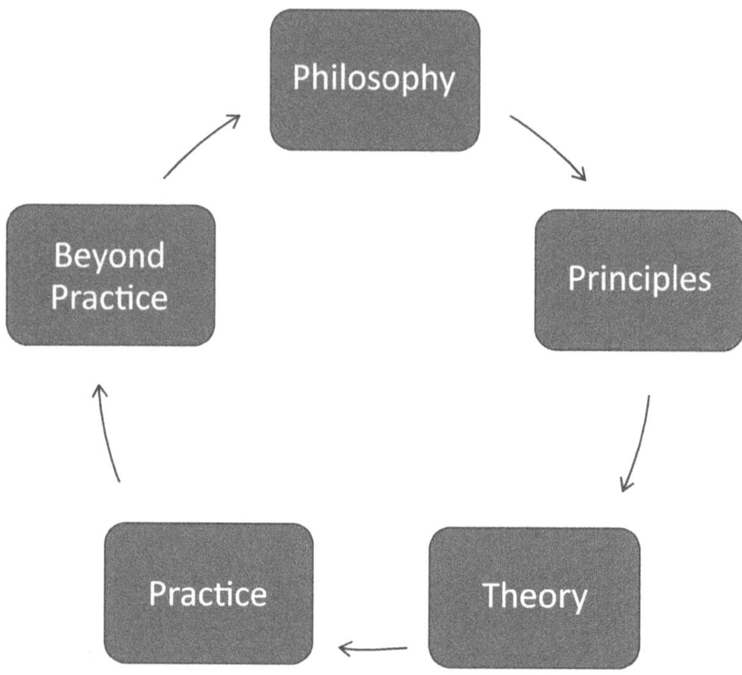

Figure 2.3. Farrell's framework for TESOL professionals (2015: 23).

1. *Philosophy*

   This relates to the underlying philosophy that guides a teacher's actions. Such a philosophy has been developing since birth and, according to Farrell (2015: 24), is strongly influenced by such factors as heritage, ethnicity, religion, family, and personal values, among others. This is where teachers reflect on the self, or 'the self-as-teacher' and, from our reading of it, is strongly related to notions of teacher identity (Barkhuizen, 2017; Farr et al., 2019; Farr & Riordan, 2015; Morton & Gray, 2018). Philosophy often develops and exists in a subconscious way, therefore accessing our thoughts, emotions, and evaluations best happens through a metacognitive process by engaging in specific reflective activities. In reality, the suggestion is that teachers engage in a process of making what is implicit explicit. In Chapter 4 of his book, Farrell outlines ways in which this can be facilitated through contemplation. Taking a rather holistic approach, the chapter explores techniques associated with mindfulness and meditation. Given that the focus is on the reconstruction of previous experiences in order to understand them, a narrative approach is advocated (see also Johnson & Golombek, 2002). This narrative might be constructed chronologically, using Farrell's 'Tree of Life' reflective activity where teachers recount their life stories through a visualization of them as roots (pre-school years), trunk (formative school years), and limbs (beyond high-school). It could also be constructed around critical events to help bring meaning to past and present teaching experiences.

2. *Principles*
At this stage, assumptions, beliefs, and conceptions of teaching and learning are considered. Many may see these three notions as very similar, and indeed there are overlaps. However, Farrell makes subtle but important distinctions between them as a gateway to deeper and more meaningful reflection. *Assumptions*, drawing on Brookfield (1995), he defines within his framework, as 'taken-for-granted beliefs about anything that seems so obvious to us that we do not usually articulate them to ourselves or others' (Farrell, 2015: 50). *Beliefs*, on the other hand, can be conscious or unconscious, and are usually idiosyncratic. Woods (1996: 72) identifies some characteristics of beliefs, as follows:

- they are non-consensual (not everyone agrees)
- they often include a notion of existence (something exists)
- they are highly evaluative
- they are often highly anecdotal
- they can be strong or weak
- they often overlap with beliefs in other areas.

Farrell asserts that beliefs can be complex and difficult to understand, and so, after articulating beliefs, teachers should try to identify their sources so that they can make better sense of them. He draws on Richards & Lockhart (1994) to suggest a variety of possible sources for teachers' beliefs, including: teachers' past experience as students, experience of what works well in their classrooms, established practice within a school, personality factors of teachers, educational or research principles, method-based sources. Finally, *conceptions* are defined as 'an organizing framework through which a teacher understands, interprets, responds to, and interacts with his or her particular teaching environment' (Farrell, 2015: 62).

Pause for Reflection

1. Articulate your philosophy, principles, and beliefs in relation to teaching and say how and why they have developed to be what they are today.
2. Do you anticipate that any of these will change during your teacher education experiences and if so why and how?

3. *Theory*

   In this part of the framework, there is a move away from more introvertly-focused reflections and understandings to what others might have to say about teaching and learning from a theoretical perspective. A lens on theory helps teachers to name their practices and to explain why something is as it is in relation to what others have to say about it. So, for example, a novice teacher might say that they like using pair and group work in their classroom, but by reading appropriate theories in the literature they might understand why this is the case and they will be able to label it a socio-constructivist approach (Vygotsky, 1978). A useful distinction is often made in teaching circles between the more official theories, as found in the educational literature and known by most in the professions, and 'theories-in-use', which are the ideas and concepts that practitioners draw on all the time as they go about their job (Argyris & Schön, 1974). The challenge in reflective practice is how to make these tacit belief systems, or personal theories, more explicit (Freeman, 1991). From a practical perspective, the literature on methods and approaches in English language teaching can often provide a useful starting point for activities such as lesson planning, and Farrell (2015: 68–71) suggests how this might work as a reflective endeavor. Of course, all discussions about theory are caveated with the cautionary note that in educational disciplines, they are only useful if they can be applied in practice, or be useful in explaining practice (Widdowson, 1984). Thornbury (2019: 519–520) advocates that the writers of methodology texts in education should 'have a sense of how to leverage the inexpert teacher into the target discourse community – not necessarily by simply re-packaging the findings of SLA research and applied linguistics, but by inviting the teacher to map those findings on to their own experience, and by "renaming them", gain ownership of them.' Unfortunately, this is not always the case, and it seems to be one of the reasons why Farrell includes the next two practice-oriented levels in his framework, to account for the importance of learning from classroom experience, as well as from theory.

Pause for Reflection

1. How much do you know about educational theories? Which have you heard of in the past (list the theories or their proponents)?
2. In lay terms, can you think of any aspects of your teaching practices in which you think further knowledge of such theories might help you to understand and articulate?

4. *Theory of practice*
   Level 4 of the framework moves from theoretical notions firmly to individual practice, although the link between them is vital. At this stage, 'teachers are encouraged to systematically reflect in their practice to see what they actually do in lessons (rather than what they believe they do)' (Farrell, 2015: 81). This endeavor consists of reflection-in- and on-action (as explored in Chapter 1), and also an added dimension of reflection-for-action, which is very much future-oriented. Two practical avenues for the exploration of practice are detailed. The first is classroom observation, which consists of both self-observation and peer-observation, both seen as particularly useful and insightful. The use of data in the form of audio and/or video recordings is advocated for later perusal and reflection. The use of relatively accessible observation instruments such as the SCORE seating chart (Acheson & Gall, 1987) is discussed as a possible way to access meaningful data for post-observation discussions (see also Farr, 2015: Chapter 4 for other approaches including Walsh's SETT framework (Walsh, 2011)). The second avenue presented is action research, which involves the stages of plan (problem identification), research (literature review), observe (data collection), reflect (analysis), and act (redefining the problem) (Farrell, 2015: 92). This is a localized, practice-oriented research methodology that a teacher can engage in to systematically reflect on practice (see also Burns, 2010; Farr, 2015: Chapter 9).

5. *Beyond practice*
   The final stage of this framework is where Farrell (2015: 95) challenges the teacher to move beyond a consideration of the technical aspects of teaching in order to include the societal context. This, in other educational contexts, has been labelled critical reflection, and can include contemplation of the impact teaching has on moral, social, cultural, and political issues such as equality, gender, and race. The inclusion of this stage aims to uncover whether any teacher practices are 'socially restrictive,' in Farrell's words (2015: 96). There is a specific focus on power relations and dynamics and their impact on learners, or particular groups of learners. More recently, he has placed a renewed focus on emotional reflection through appraisal analysis (Farrell, 2022: 20), which involves exploring language for expressing attitude, including: affect, judgment, and appreciation (White, 2000; see also Farr, 2005, 2006). This level of reflection is more important now than it has ever been, certainly in our lifetimes. The impact of the Covid restrictions of 2020–2022 (to-date), up to and including moving education

exclusively online in many countries, has brought issues of inequality and vulnerability into sharp focus. We have seen teachers' and students' unions strongly influencing and sometimes overturning government decisions: for example, in Ireland, in early 2021, the government announced that all Leaving Certificate (final second-level state examination) students would return to school on January 11. This was despite a national lockdown, with strict instruction for everyone to stay at home, during a period when the country briefly had the highest rate of the disease in the world. Strong objection and outcry from many organized groups culminated in one of the teachers' unions instructing its members not to attend work on the specified date. This in turn led to the Minister for Education announcing a reversal of her decision within a few hours. This is an example of formally organized groups engaging in action to challenge leadership at a national level in consideration of teacher and student welfare issues in the midst of a global pandemic. However, as Farrell outlines, local critical reflection can happen best through dialog with others in what he calls 'Teacher Reflection Groups.' He details how many issues need to be considered when forming such groups, such as, 'the type of group they want, the number of participants to include at formation, the different roles of each participant, what to discuss, how to sustain the group, and how to evaluate the group when the reflection period has ended' (2015: 100).

Pause for Reflection

1. What are the possible ways in which your own planned future teaching career in a specific context might have a social impact on other people, including your learners and fellow professionals?
2. To what extent do you see this as an important aspect of your current and future responsibility as a teacher? Why?

PENSER

In Chapter 1, we briefly introduced the PENSER approach, which represents a staged and cyclical approach to RP that we have designed and finetuned over a number of years to facilitate the process of developing student teachers' reflective thinking around core challenges experienced specifically in teaching practice as part of a teacher education program (Farr & Farrell, 2017). In the absence of a suitable framework in the literature designed specifically for the teaching practice stage, we developed this relatively tightly controlled and scaffolded process suitable for novice teachers, which is designed to work in a linear way and cyclically, and includes five steps, or stages (see Chapter 1 also). These five steps constitute one cycle, which can then be repeated as required for individually identified issues or challenges faced by the practicing teacher. The process involves reflective cycles during which novices engage in teacher educator-guided group discussions, the development of an online TP journal, and individual exit interviews in order to reflect on their experiences of teaching English. This is with the overall aim of facilitating their professional growth and supporting their teacher identity formation over the course of their TP experience. The five stages of the PENSER cycle are encapsulated in Figure 2.4, each of which is elaborated in the following sections.

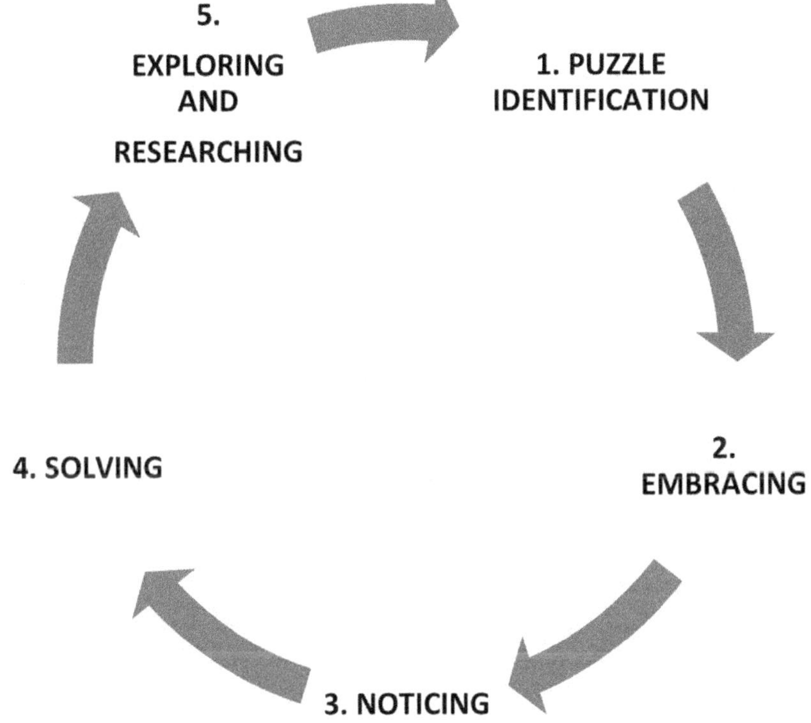

Figure 2.4. The PENSER cycle.

1. *Puzzle identification:* an individual issue, puzzle, problem, or challenge is identified and articulated through observing and reflecting on personal practice. We originally called this step 'problem' identification, aligning it with terminology familiar to our students from action research literature, but have now changed this to 'puzzle' in order to avoid any negative connotations.

2. *Embracing:* the challenge is accepted as an issue in need of further investigation, understanding, and improvement, and there is a commitment to these actions. We purposely included this as a separate step to allow for a more holistic and emotional engagement with the puzzle in a positive way. This and the previous step are facilitated through supported group discussions.
3. *Noticing:* experienced teachers are observed to facilitate a better understanding of the challenge and to provide examples of practice to be considered for assimilation. These observations and their meanings for the novice teachers' own practice are processed and articulated in the form of a TP reflective diary.
4. *Solving:* a solution for personal change to practice is proposed, planned, and implemented. This is again facilitated through supported group discussions.
5. *Exploring and Researching:* the solution is investigated and critically evaluated to determine if the challenge has been appropriately overcome or if further engagement is needed. This final step is facilitated through a dyadic exit interview with an experienced teacher educator, and next steps are determined.

The PENSER process was designed to unfold over a five-week period, which is repeated three times over the course of one academic year. During the various stages of the cycle, novice teachers engage in a variety of written and spoken reflective discussions and tasks using both online and face-to-face modes in the form of individual e-portfolios, teacher educator-guided group discussions in traditional classroom settings, and dyadic exit interviews between TP supervisors and student teachers.

In this section we have reviewed three of the most prominent frameworks for RP in educational and TESOL circles, as well as the approach we use with our own novice teachers. Such frameworks can be useful for guiding and structuring reflection in a way that may prove to be broader and deeper for many practicing and prospective teachers, particularly novice teachers with little experience of formal reflection. They can also provide a useful starting point for discussion and critique among more experienced groups as part of a portfolio of professional development. There are however other useful ways in which to approach reflective practice, which don't necessarily involve a staged or linear approach. We explore some of these in the next section.

OTHER APPROACHES TO RP: DIMENSIONS, CONTEXTS, AND METAPHORS

Dimensions

In *The Teacher's Reflective Practice Handbook*, Zwozdiak-Myers formally presented her account of reflective practice (Zwozdiak-Myers, 2012). It was developed in 2010 as part of her PhD, from teacher responses to a survey, and, as such, is claimed to be closely related to actual habits and practices. It contains nine dimensions of RP which, she suggests, can transpire in non-linear ways. Each dimension is based on the application of various theories from within the relevant literature, many of which are cited in each case. These nine dimensions are presented and explored briefly in this subsection. It is useful to consider them as tools, or techniques, which can be employed at any of the various stages of the frameworks presented in the previous section and have often been used in this way by the teachers we have worked with.

Dimension 1: Teachers study their own teaching for personal improvement. This relates to the teacher's ability to change roles, from being one of the main participants to being the critical observer in the sense of Kolb's 'experiential learning', as discussed in the previous section (Kolb, 1984). It is the ability to psychologically remove yourself from the context in order to objectively critique, yet to retain the insider's (or emic) understanding gained from being a primary participant in that context.

Dimension 2: Teachers systematically evaluate their own teaching through classroom research procedures. This aspect of RP incorporates models of action research (see also Farr, 2015: Chapter 9). These models typically include the following stages: a practice-based problem is identified, defined, and assessed; an action plan to improve practice is then devised, implemented, and evaluated, to decide if the results are satisfactory of if further action and evaluation are needed. Each phase is systematically recorded in the way any formal research study is.

Dimension 3: Teachers link theory with their own practice. Dimension 3 explores how teachers can relate various relevant theories to their classroom practices. This includes formal learning theories as presented in Chapters 1 and 3 of this volume, as well as the type of personal or tacit understandings that teachers gain from their practical experiences. Core to this dimension of RP is the ability to implement this theoretical knowledge appropriately during teaching. According to Shulman (1987), this application involves the stages of *teacher comprehension* (a full understanding of what is to be taught), *transformation* of this understanding into appropriate content for the learners, providing good *instruction* in class, *evaluating* student understanding, *reflecting* on the experience, and achieving *new comprehension* through analysis, discussion, and documentation of the process. In our experience, this can often be a daunting and complex task for novice teachers, and one with which they need support if this is not to become a process of trial and error and anecdotal interpretation.

Dimension 4: Teachers question their personal theories and beliefs. Dimension 4 explores a teacher's individual beliefs, opinions, and values, all of which combine to shape personal professional cognition. These are highly personal and may even be subconscious. This is often more easily done with the help of others, a trusted professional friend or teacher reflection groups, as described in Farrell's framework in the previous section.

Dimension 5: Teachers consider alternative perspectives and possibilities. Dimension 5 is closely related to Dimension 4 and advocates considering different perspectives on how things might be done, different from teachers' existing preferences. It is about exploring available alternatives in line with the development and growth that comes from experience. Alternatives can also emerge through conversations and activities with other teachers, who may have different experiences to share. Mentorship and peer observation processes can aid in this context. Student feedback is also likely to provide suggestions that may not be obvious to the teacher (see Zwozdiak-Meyers, 2012: 100–107 for suggestions of structured activities to assist with this dimension).

Dimension 6: Teachers try out new strategies and ideas. Dimension 6 is about the engagement of all teachers to try new activities that they may have explored during the Dimension 5 thought process. New strategies need to be carefully considered and adapted to the context of your learners, taking account of a range of learner variables and preferences to decide what will work well and reach the widest audience. This can be daunting, especially for novice teachers, but without risk there will be no gain. And while not everything new works well, or works well the first time, some new strategies will improve the teaching and learning experiences and avoid the dangers of monotony inherent in consistently doing the same things in the classroom.

Dimension 7: Teachers maximize the learning potential of all their students. Dimension 7 relates to ensuring an environment of inclusion in educational systems, and is closely related to critical reflection, or Farrell's 'beyond practice' final stage of reflection presented in the previous section. This can be challenging for teachers as they have a range of factors to consider: cultural backgrounds, social, emotional, intellectual, and special needs, a range of learning styles, motivations, and aspirational influences and levels. As mentioned earlier, this is not an easy task and can be daunting for many teachers. Therefore, it needs specific thought and planning and teachers may need to draw on a range of strategies and consult with others from a range of professional backgrounds in particularly demanding circumstances. This might include school leaders, medical professionals, and psychologists, among others.

Dimension 8: Teachers enhance the quality of their own teaching. Dimension 8 addresses the thorny issue of teaching quality. Much research has been done into what constitutes good quality teaching and teachers, and also into learners' perceptions of quality. For a number of years, the language teaching profession spoke of best practice and in many cases still does, although good practice now seems to be the preferred term (Edge & Richards, 1998). Most qualified teachers will have a strong sense of what constitutes good practice from the various criteria articulated during their teacher education programs. In addition, many national and international education-oriented quality assurance agencies and professional bodies publish their criteria in the form of standards, or what have become known as teacher competency frameworks (TCFs) or teacher development frameworks (TDFs). Some of those we often cite and use for the TESOL context include:

- The Equals Framework for Language Teacher Training and Development: https://www.eaquals.org/our-expertise/teacher-development/the-eaquals-framework-for-teacher-training-and-development/The European Profiling Grid: https://egrid.epg-project.eu/
- The Cambridge English Teaching Framework: https://www.cambridgeenglish.org/teaching-english/professional-development/cambridge-english-teaching-framework/
- The ECML Guide to Teacher Competences for Languages in Education: https://www.ecml.at/ECML-Programme/Programme2016-2019/TowardsaCommonEuropeanFrameworkofReferenceforLanguageTeachers/tabid/1850/Default.aspx
- Identifying Teacher Quality Toolbox: http://www.teacherqualitytoolbox.eu/home

In addition, for student teachers who may wish to teach in a state primary, secondary, or tertiary education in the Irish context, we often review:

- The Teaching Council's Cosán (meaning pathway in the Irish language) Framework for Teachers' Learning: https://www.teachingcouncil.ie/en/publications/teacher-education/cosan-framework-for-teachers-learning.pdf
- The National Forum for the Enhancement for Teaching and Learning in Higher Education has also published a Professional Development Framework, which is another useful lens through which to reflect on teaching: https://www.teachingandlearning.ie/our-priorities/professional-development/the-national-professional-development-framework-pdf-for-all-staff-who-teach-in-higher-education/

Although we have serious reservations about the use of such frameworks for formally assessing teaching in summative ways, a discussion of which is beyond the scope of this book, we have found them extremely useful as tools for reflective practice taking formative professional development as the starting point.

Dimension 9: Teachers continue to improve their own teaching. Dimension 9 highlights Continuing Professional Development (CPD) as key. It acknowledges that learning to be a teacher is a lifelong process, one which only begins with initial teacher education. Zwozdiak-Myers (2012: 174), discusses three main sources for CPD: within the school (induction, mentoring, observation, etc.), school networks (cross-school, virtual, etc.), and other external expertise (further study, professional associations, etc.). A number of key questions need to be asked before and after any such activity and all CPD should be recorded in a Professional Development Portfolio as a professional artifact for future use. Never have we been so aware of the need for CPD than during the obligatory move to online teaching during the global Covid pandemic, which saw all professionals upskilling in numerous ways in order to engage with this new mode of engagement with our students and peers.

Contexts

Mann & Walsh's book *Reflective Practice in English Language Teaching: Research-Based Principles and Practices* bears testament to their own strong stance that evidence- and data-based approaches are crucial in the future of RP (Mann & Walsh, 2017). This book exemplifies a principled approach to reflection. It uses a range of vignettes and other types of authentic data, such as classroom discourse and teachers' voices, to illustrate reflection in practice, all the while integrating theoretical and research findings into the discussion. What we particularly like in their approach is the sensitivity to context. There are discrete but related discussions and chapters about pre-service and in-service contexts, about written and spoken modes of reflecting, and individual and dialogic reflection, with an accompanying focus on the important social context of learning. The two latter distinctions we engage with in some detail in the later chapters of this volume, but we do not address the pre- and in-service context in any great detail and so will include a discussion of this here from the context of Mann & Walsh's work. The explicit distinction between PRESET (pre-service education and training of English language teachers) and INSET (in-service education and training of English language teachers) contexts is a concerted effort to avoid a one-size-fits-all approach (Mann & Walsh, 2017: 48). However, they do acknowledge that this distinction in itself is not without its complexities as there is often a mixture of teacher backgrounds and qualifications represented in any one teacher education program. The PRESET contexts explored include CELTA, and BA and MA university programs, while Masters level INSET is covered in their Chapter 4.

Starting with the PRESET CELTA or certificate context, there is an initial acknowledgment that there are obvious time constraints related to not just RP aspects of the program but to all areas of the content to be included. There is also often a contradiction between the espoused aims of such programs in relation to RP and the amount of actual time and attention devoted to it during the reality of what is typically a four-week part-time program. The second issue is the implementation of a strong criterion-based model of assessment, with many and varied standards that need to be evidenced as having been met by the student teachers before they are awarded a certificate (in the Irish context the Quality and Qualifications Ireland [QQI] TESOL standards apply and amount to almost six pages of standards for such a part-time certificate at Level 6 on the National Framework of Qualifications [NFQ]). Both of these factors often stifle opportunities for more independent reflection. Mann & Walsh 'recognize the challenge but do not take the position that reflection is impossible. We would argue for a middle ground' (2017: 48). They go on to discuss the post-observation feedback conference (POC) as the context which offers most affordances and they illustrate through the use of discourse data from this context how reflective talk is and can be promoted more effectively (for more elaborate discussions of post-observation talk in CELTA settings see Copland, 2008, 2010, 2012; Copland & Mann, 2010). On the other hand, by merit of the more extensive nature of BA and MA programs, more opportunities for varied and sustained reflective practice activities are typically included (for example, see Farr & Riordan, 2012; Riordan, 2018). In the selected extracts analyzed, they illustrate how deeper levels of reflection can be achieved in such contexts (Mann & Walsh, 2017: 67), although they do question whether this is necessarily a 'higher' level of reflection as they attribute value to all the different types of reflection with which a teacher engages. Even after having the benefit of more extensive RP experiences in PRESET programs, teachers often do not feel fully prepared for the reality of the classroom after graduation due to what is commonly referred to as the theory-practice gap. Farrell (2021: Chapter 2), suggests that a transitionary period of reflective activities, supported by teacher educators from the PRESET program, is one way to address this issue. He calls this a novice service approach, which expands the PRESET teacher education program support into the first five years of teaching to support novice teachers in their transition. The main tools he advocates for this period are those based around collaborative reflective practice, and it obviously blurs the boundaries between PRESET and INSET contexts. Mann & Walsh (2017: 100) address similar issues under their discussion of 'reflections in the wild,' which examines how reflective practices can be sustained after the completion of a teacher education course (see also Baguley, 2019 for a discussion of the difficulties encountered in the first year of teaching).

Any discussion of reflection in INSET contexts is typically more complex, due to the potential for variety among participants, and also duration and therefore content. Indeed, Mann & Walsh (2017: 74), at the outset of Chapter 4, acknowledge that within the literature there are two very different accounts, one which is 'positively rosy and optimistic' and one which is 'much bleaker.' They discuss MA INSET programs in this chapter and advocate for a systematic integration of RP activities. They present a list of some of the choices available in order to do this (2017: 75–76):

- having a *discrete module* called 'Reflective Practice' within the program
- providing opportunities for *reflective writing across different modules*, perhaps in the form of a reflective portfolio
- incorporating *reflective tasks and discussion* across different modules (modules might involve tasks which encourage the sharing and articulation of learning and teaching experiences; they might also include reflection grids to bring out the significance of tasks)
- enabling teachers and tutors to interact online through wikis, VLEs (virtual learning environments), and other online tools
- evaluating reflection as part of an assignment, either as one of the marking criteria or by requiring a section of the assignment to perhaps reflect on the learning in the module as a whole
- giving feedback in a form which encourages reflection (i.e., formative and dialogic).

These are all good suggestions, many of which we follow in our own practices and will be illustrated in later chapters. We do have some reservations in relation to the summative assessment of RP artifacts and activities. We present these below. The remainder of the discussion on INSET RP by Mann &Walsh includes some detailed vignettes featuring very experienced teacher educators and their insights into how RP can be systematically integrated, and finally many examples of how this might happen in practice. The options for an MA program are varied due to the time available for systematic integration and full advantage should be taken of this.

Metaphors

So far in this section we have examined a dimensions approach to RP, looked at a context-based consideration, and finally we would like to turn to a staple of language teacher education, the use of metaphor. Farrell (2015) chooses a tree as an appropriate metaphor and presents a useful self-reflective tool called the 'Tree of Life,' which contains three parts:

- roots are the early influences, usually in home contexts, which provide the foundations shaping a teacher's early years (family values, heritage, religion, socio-economic status, etc.)
- the trunk represents early school experiences up to the end of second-level education
- limbs signify any beyond-school experiences which happen at any stage of adulthood.

We have found the use of this metaphor to be beneficial to student teachers during their early framing and articulation of reflection, and one which they typically enjoy. From the frameworks and approaches presented in this section and the previous one, there is no shortage of appropriate scaffolding to support reflective endeavors in teacher education. The next section addresses some of the issues we have identified and experienced in relation to RP. While we are strong advocates of RP, we are also critical advocates, and we now share some of these criticisms, or reservations, along with some of our proposed solutions.

Pause for Reflection

1. Do any of the frameworks or conceptualizations of RP presented above appeal to you and how so?
2. Are there any ideas which you don't fully understand, and if so, can you do some simple online searching and reading to help your comprehension?
3. Which of the ideas in this chapter so far do you think will be easiest to apply to the teaching practice context and why?

CHALLENGES AND SOLUTIONS

The implementation of RP in teacher education is challenging in all sorts of ways. Indeed, in much of the related literature it is rather easy to find a range of criticisms leveled against at least one aspect of RP, either at a theoretical or practical dimension. This is probably inevitable and, we believe, healthy, for a practice which has been embedded in teaching and teacher education for such a long period of time. In fact, its ubiquity, in itself, has been cited as an issue: 'It seems to me that reflection represents one of the subtlest threats to successful teacher education and development. This is part of the price it has had to pay for its success, a consequence to some extent of its widespread adoption [...] what once represented an exciting and liberating opportunity has become for many a necessary and almost routine element in the teacher education curriculum, in some cases serving more as an evaluation tool than a key to deeper understanding and professional growth.' (Keith Richards in Mann & Walsh, 2017: 101). In this section, we address some of the challenges we have encountered in our own practices, many of which have also been identified by others, and we propose a range of solutions available to teacher educators and their student teachers.

Challenge 1: Assessment

Evaluating reflective practice is problematic for a number of reasons, and we consider it a double-edged sword. In many contexts, including our own, there are institutional imperatives to assess artifacts presented by students in order to ensure that they have met the learning outcomes of the particular module and program. Often these imperatives are driven by quality agencies, professional bodies, and indeed employers who want to have some way of distinguishing between candidates during teacher recruitment processes. On a more micro-level, assessment can be a motivating factor for student teachers to engage fully and put their best effort into such activities among a competing range of others. As such, formal evaluation bestows a value and a respect for RP activities that it might not otherwise get. However, there are also two major issues. Firstly, there is an issue in relation to the criteria used to assess RP artifacts, such as teaching portfolios or blogs, and how they are applied. The second issue revolves around the complex, and often conflicting, relationships between the various parties involved. We discuss both and propose possible solutions here.

Over many years, we have defined, refined, and re-refined grading criteria and are still not quite satisfied that these criteria can easily be assessed. Why not? Because any assessor is necessarily an outsider who is attempting to access the cognitive processes of another, represented within the many limits of a written or spoken artifact. This leaves a number of questions unanswered: Am I interpreting the account the way that it was intended to be interpreted? Do I understand the issues raised (having not been present for the events described)? Am I confident that the student teacher has engaged in deep reflection and changed action, as opposed to being just good at writing about them – and vice versa – does a poor written account signal poor reflection or practice? Am I assessing the reflections rather than the teaching event, or can these even be separated? Has language been a constraining factor in the reflective account, especially for L2 speakers? These and other such questions have always left us feeling more than slightly uncomfortable about the reliability of evaluative judgments set against detailed marking schemes and grading bands. And while we trust our professional judgments to distinguish between very good and very poor reflective accounts, it is not so easy to distinguish, with confidence, between a B1 grade and a B2 grade, or a 60% and a 65%, or a merit and a distinction. Yet these evaluations may have strong repercussions for an individual student teacher in terms of their award classification, and even their job prospects. We have tried to guard against this danger in a number of ways in our own practices. The following are some of the approaches we have taken:

- ensuring that written artifacts are accompanied by some sort of verbal account in the form of a discussion between the student teacher and the assessor, which allows for clarifications and further interpretations
- allowing for the submission of materials in other modes, such as a recorded oral account, or through a visual representation (this might be more suitable for certain types of student teachers and may also address any issues associated with access to the assignment)
- ensuring that written artifacts are assessed by more than one professional involved in the delivery of the program and that marks are allocated following a discussion and agreement between the assessors
- ensuring that assessment criteria and associated rubrics are explicit, detailed, and gradable, and have been explained in full to the student teachers with the provision of a range of examples (although beware of encouraging them to work to the criteria rather than engaging in reflection which is meaningful to them, and possibly more original and innovative than can be captured in the criteria)
- ensuring that not all artifacts are graded and that student teachers have plenty opportunity for formative feedback in advance of a summative assessment

- exploring the possibility of not applying a detailed marking scheme to such artifacts: for example, at our institution we can apply a Pass/Fail grading type to a module, without further nuance in terms of letter or percentage grades. This is especially suitable for initial RP assignments and has the added bonus of removing some of the risk for students.

The second assessment-related issue revolves around the relationship between the student teacher and the person assessing the RP. Farr (2011: 26), with specific reference to teaching practice feedback as a reflective activity, talks about the 'paradox of facilitator roles.' This refers to contexts where the same teacher educator finds themself in a position of mentoring and advising a student and also having to assess the student on the activities for which this advice has been offered. This can create a paradox, or a dilemma for the tutor because the first relationship requires a level of support and nurturing, and mutually shared trust. The assessor role can then feel like a betrayal of that relationship as the tutor moves to play the part of an objective and detached evaluator. This can cause a lot of discomfort for both student teachers and mentors and may damage the mentorship relation for future encounters due to feelings of betrayal, particularly if the assessment outcome has not been favorable or as anticipated by the student. There is another possible interfering factor, which is the degree to which a student teacher has heeded the advice offered by the mentor at earlier stages. A student may legitimately have decided not to heed some of that advice, for reasons which often remain hidden to the tutor. This may impact the tutor's assessment of the activity or final artifact describing the activity and associated reflections. Some of the actions mentioned in the previous list can guard against some of these issues, such as having more than one person involved in assessment, or even having a different person entirely doing the evaluation. Another course of action is to clearly separate discussions intended for formative purposes from those of a summative nature: for example, in our post-observation feedback sessions with student teachers we generally do not discuss grades or how these were awarded. The focus is sharply on the teaching, how it was good, and also how it could be improved. Grades are allocated after the feedback, taking the student engagement in the reflective activities into account. Should a student teacher wish to then discuss the evaluation, or indeed challenge the grade awarded, a further discussion and process is followed. This also prevents student teachers from conflating teaching development with teaching evaluation and becoming 'grade obsessed' during formative discussions.

Challenge 2: Scaffolding Reflective Practice

The second issue that we have witnessed in our own contexts during our professional lives is not facilitating student teachers to develop the dispositions and skills to support their reflective endeavors. Student teachers do not always find it natural to engage in reflection, and indeed neither do some tutors. A structured induction into reflective practice, what it means, its various frameworks and tools, is needed, particularly at the early stages of a teacher education program. It is not sufficient for students to be told to critically reflect on their teaching. They need to know where to start, what to do, how to structure and how to present those reflections, as well as how to consult and integrate the appropriate literature. A common pitfall which we have seen, often among relatively experienced teachers, is that the excitement of finding their own reflective voices can lead to the exclusion of other voices. Those other voices may come from the literature, from critical friends, or even from students, and will help teachers to consider a range of options for future teaching development, as discussed in the previous sections. Theoretical and applied perspectives on RP should be a core component on a teacher education program and should be completed by all student teachers before they are asked to engage in more independent reflective activities. This echoes some of what we discussed in the previous section in relation to what Mann & Walsh advocate for RP on PRESET programs (2017: 75–76).

Challenge 3: Information vs Reflection

The world has changed unrecognizably over the last 20 years due to advancements in technology. This is especially true since Tim Berners-Lee invented the world wide web in 1989. This is the year in which one of the present authors began as a first-year undergraduate student at university, and happily spent four years hearing only whisperings of what this was and never seeing or experiencing it first-hand. While no-one would dispute the vast affordances and advantages it has brought, we wonder if it has to some extent stifled reflective thinking as a natural human trait. Our minds now tend to focus on information that can easily be accessed online, instead of drawing on our own memories or reflections to find the answers or draw conclusions. By way of anecdote, recently, while watching an animated movie with my (Fiona's) children, we couldn't pinpoint the actor's voice playing the principal character. Within seconds my teenage daughter was reaching for her phone to check. I set a challenge for who could first correctly identify him without searching online, and that same daughter did so within about four seconds, probably far faster than it would have taken her to search online. There seems to have been a shift to the prioritization of information (often inaccurate information) over thought and reflection. And for good reflective engagement, this imbalance needs to be redressed and students often need to relearn how to reflect introspectively and to become comfortable in the presence of their own voices, rather than just the information they get from screens. This often requires creating some quiet spaces and activities for reflective thought as part of the teacher education program, perhaps even through engaging in some meditative activities to reignite our own independent thought processes. Our inner voices have such an important role to play in reflective practice that we need to learn to use them and to listen to them as a starting point. In other words, this needs to be central, and can then be supported, or challenged by some of the other voices we have spoken about in the two previous challenges.

In this section, we have explored what we see as the major challenges to the successful implementation of RP in teacher education programs, but also a range of suggestions and solutions to ensure that they are adequately addressed and resolved. There is also a question about the extent to which teacher educators themselves systematically reflect, which is something to be considered for those involved in this way in the RP of student teachers.

Pause for Reflection

1. Which of the three challenges mentioned above is most concerning for you and why?
2. How do you propose to overcome these concerns so that the RP experience becomes and remains a positive one?

SUMMARY

This chapter has explored the literature related to RP theories, frameworks, and approaches. It begins with a discussion of Dewey's requisite attitudes for effect RP: open-mindedness, responsibility, and wholeheartedness, and what they mean in this context. Next it has outlined some of the dominant frameworks for RP present in the literature and practices integrated in many teacher education programs. The three frameworks presented are Kolb's Experiential Learning Cycle, followed by Gibbs' closely related Reflective Practice Cycle, and finally Farrell's five stage framework for professional development. In the next section other perspectives on RP are outlined, including Zwozdiac-Meyers' dimensions (2012), the PRESET and INSET contexts discussed in Mann & Walsh (2017), and Farrell's tree metaphor (2015). However, if experience has taught us anything, it is that the uncritical adaptation of one framework, model, or approach is not appropriate for teacher education programs which prepare students for as yet an undetermined array of future teaching contexts. Coupled with this is the need to consider the challenges and criticisms associated with RP, its models and frameworks. We have articulated the three which we have considered to be the most significant in our own practices: assessing RP, scaffolding RP, and distinguishing between information and reflection. This discussion provides a backdrop to the first of six substantive chapters dedicated to the various aspects and processes of reflection which can occur as part of the practicum on ELTE programs. Chapter 3 is the first of these and focuses on how novice teachers can engage with those more experienced in a range of ways as a way to learn and improve their own practice.

Chapter 3

Preparing for Teaching: Social Learning, Mentors, and Observations

INTRODUCTION

In all professional and skilled contexts, learning from those more expert and experienced has had a very long tradition. This is true of all fields, from sports to medicine, and is very much embedded in teacher education as a discipline. The apprenticeship model of learning new trades and crafts is 'bound by neither history or culture' (Coy, 1989: xi). It has been socially applied to allow the master to slowly and appropriately reveal the secrets of her/his domain, and also as a way to protect the integrity of that domain from any potential damage that might be caused by novices. Apprenticeship was also the model used for vocational training, of which teacher 'training' was once considered one among a range of other vocations. In other words, novices learned exclusively from observing an experienced master teacher in the classroom until they were deemed to have learned what they needed in order to assume independent teaching duties. Hence, there existed, and sometimes still does, the tradition for certain professions, such as teaching, to pass from one generation to the next of the same family. This was very much the medieval model of education in Britain, and later, 'in the twentieth century, apprenticeship forms of training for entry to some professions – school teaching is but one example – gave way to degree-level qualifications awarded by an institution of higher education' (Aldrich, 2006: 9). In the American context a similar trajectory emerged, and according to Johnson (2015: 515), 'the responsibility for preparing teachers in the North American context moved from normal schools to and within universities in the mid-20th century.'

Indeed, the relationship between higher education and what were, and sometimes still are, considered apprenticeship domains is both complex and contentious, although national frameworks of qualifications nowadays attempt to be inclusive of all such endeavors at a range of levels, from entry right up to PhD qualification.

For this reason, teacher education, or training, as it was more often known (see Widdowson, 1984 for a discussion of the different nuances and connotations inherent in the terms teacher education and teacher training), was often confined to specific teacher training institutions, or schools, rather than universities. In the American context, Labaree summarized how education schools were generally viewed when he said, 'institutionally, the ed school is the Rodney Dangerfield of higher education: it don't get no respect' (Labaree, 2004: 2). These views and divisions can still be found in many contexts and countries and are reflective of social and political trends throughout the history of teacher education. However, this is not our current focus. Instead, we intend only to link current practices with some of their historical roots to help us understand relevant evolutions. In any case, English language teacher education often followed rather different and circuitous developmental paths, which led to it finding a home just as easily in schools of modern languages, applied linguistics, or even English studies, rather than schools of education.

In contemporary education, some of the affordances and benefits of apprenticeship models have been acknowledged through the inclusion of experiential learning in what is known by different names in different contexts and disciplines. Terms such as internship, service-learning, cooperative education, and clinical placement, are commonly used. However, in contemporary contexts these are also very often different from apprenticeships. To understand this, it is important to note a distinction made originally by Dewey, between apprenticeship and laboratory (or scientific) models of approach to the practical aspects of teacher education. His preference was for the more forward-looking laboratory approach, and this is also more in keeping with a research-led orientation favored within academic contexts. 'Dewey then asserts that there are basically two positions regarding the goals of practical preparation. We can seek to develop those practical skills needed to do the job smoothly and capably on a daily basis. This he calls the apprenticeship approach. Alternately, we can design practical experiences to inform and "make real and vital" the two components of theoretical work – subject matter knowledge and knowledge of educational principles and theory. This second perspective he identifies as the laboratory view. Clearly the two perspectives are not exclusive and will interact' (Shulman, 1998: 512).

Periods which student teachers spend observing and practicing are called school placements, or teaching practice, or a practicum, or a teaching internship. These different terms often denote subtle practical and contextual differences, but in our experience are also used interchangeably in many cases. In this book, we interchangeably use the term practicum and practice, and in our context, this means the teaching practice that our MA in TESOL students engage in on-campus where they teach English to our international exchange and full-time students, under the guidance of the class teachers, as well as teacher educators from the teacher education program (often the same people performing a range of these roles). We saw in Chapter 1 that a key initial step in the practicum process is the observation of other teachers, and, after a contextualization of the practicum in social theories of learning, this is one of the two main focuses of the present chapter. The roots of observation practices are in the apprenticeship approach. The sections on observations explore the affordances of such experiences from students' perspective, drawing on examples from the PENSER corpus. Each of these will be discussed in practical ways to uncover how they can help a novice teacher to understand teaching in general, and more specifically their own teaching. The second substantive focus of Chapter 3 is on representations and approximations of practice (Grossman, Compton, et al., 2009; Grossman, Hammerness, & McDonald, 2009) as supportive simulations in advance of real classroom teaching practice. Such experiences align more with the laboratory approach advocated by Dewey and provide a more active engagement on the part of the student following, or in parallel with, classroom observations. Together these two approaches aim to provide more holistic transitioning support for teachers as they near their time to engage in real professional classroom practice. Throughout the chapter, the potential of complementary dialogic reflection with other participants such as mentors, cooperating teachers and peers, is explored to uncover the ways in which novice teachers can co-construct knowledge in collaboration with others.

SOCIAL LEARNING

Socio-Cultural Theory

Learning from practical and experiential contexts was a significant discussion in Chapters 1 and 2 in relation to the roots and reasons for RP. A key component of practice-based learning is social engagement, or interacting with others, to facilitate learning. Many teacher education programs and approaches base themselves on such models, formally attributed to Vygotsky and his Socio-Cultural Theory (Vygotsky, 1978). Vygotsky (1896–1934) was a seminal Russian psychologist best known for his theories on the psychological and cognitive development of children. Although he published his major works from 1920, originally in Russian and later translated into English, his contribution really only began to have an impact in the English-speaking world from the late 1970s through the influence of some of its main proponents such as Wertsch (for example, Wertsch, 1985, 1998).

Although Vygotsky never met Piaget, he is said to have been influenced by his work and commented on it, originally disagreeing with him but later lauding his conclusions. Equally, Piaget only became aware of Vygotsky's commentary after Vygotsky's death, and at that point responded to much of it, agreeing with certain points and disagreeing with others (Zavershneva, 2010: 78). Vygotsky has had a lasting influence on psychology and theories of (language) acquisition and there is a sense that this may have been even more profound were it not for his premature death at the age of 37. This also seems to have been his own self-assessment in one of his private notebooks where, just before his death, he wrote: 'This is the final thing I have done in psychology – and I will like Moses die at the summit, having glimpsed the promised land but without setting foot on it. Farewell, dear creations. The rest is silence' (Van der Veer & Yasnitsky, 2015: 88). We will now explore his main theoretical contributions related to learning and cognitive development and the practical implications they have for learning to become a 'mindful' teacher (Johnson & Golombek, 2016).

As the term socio-cultural suggests, there is a sharp focus on the roles that society/social engagement and cultural context (and history) play in the learning process. And while many of us now take such beliefs and their aligned approaches as a given in current educational contexts, this was not the situation in 1920s and 1930s Russia when Vygotsky was writing his pivotal works. The focus at that time was on the delivery of content by an expert, in what are known as directive or transmission-based models. A key to Vygotsky's approach is 'that the development of an individual's mental processes is social in origin' (Golombek & Johnson, 2019: 26). What does this mean in practice? To understand how this works, we look at some of his ideas which are most relevant to the practicum context: the social nature of learning, mediated activity, and the zone of proximal development. These ideas are very much interlinked, although we discuss them separately for the purposes of clarity in the following brief subsections (for a more detailed theoretical account see Golombek & Johnson, 2019 or Farr et al., 2019: Chapter 2).

The Social Nature of Learning

The main premise here is that the social nature of learning is primary as learners interact with each other, particularly those who may know more than they do: for example, mentors or teachers. Joint efforts are believed to add to the quality of each individual contribution (Mercer, 1995: 2), akin to the notion that the whole is better than the sum of the individual parts. It has been suggested that any activity is a socially constructed event, even those which happen alone (Walsh, 2001). Language is a means by which people can think and learn together, but also alone, with many of us reasoning things out by talking to ourselves quietly or out loud when trying to solve a puzzle, for example. In psychological terms, language is used to mediate what is known as intrapersonal cognitive activity, that is, to clarify and make sense of what we have learned through interactions with others and to then store that to our own cognitive understandings (Ahmed, 1994; Walsh, 2001). It is the tool we use to represent our own thoughts to ourselves and others. The most obvious way of sharing and passing on knowledge is by talking, but observing others in their professional contexts can also be deemed to be a type of social learning, and by extension socialization into the profession (Freeman, 2016).

Mediated Activity

If development is primarily social and cultural then all humans construct their knowledge based on artifacts such as tools, symbols, and signs (Lantolf & Appel, 1994: 7). In other words, learning is mediated, or facilitated in a range of ways by both physical tools, such as books or computers, and by what Vygotsky called 'signs' which support 'psychological activity in a manner analogous to the role of a tool in labor' (Vygotsky, 1978: 52; see also Lantolf & Appel, 1994: 8). One of the primary mediational signs at the disposal of socio-cultural groupings such as teachers, is language. Words help the teaching profession to articulate their experiences, thoughts, and feelings.

The Zone of Proximal Development

We have seen the importance afforded to the social nature of learning and the notion of mediated learning, with language having much to contribute within both dimensions. It is therefore unsurprising that Vygotsky also proposed a theory on how learning is assisted by those more capable of providing support. The idea behind his concepts is that the normal intellectual capacities of individuals can be improved through additional supports from those more capable at any particular undertaking. The role of individuals as mediators is central and has led to conceptualizations such as the mediated learning experience (MLE) perspective of Feuerstein (Kozulin, 1998: 59–79). From this perspective the learner has an actual and potential performance level and this is known as the zone of proximal development (ZPD). Vygotsky (1978: 86) defines the ZPD as 'the difference between the actual development level as determined by independent problem-solving, and the level of potential development as determined through problem-solving under adult guidance, or in collaboration with more capable peers.' In teacher education contexts, this suggests that there is a gap between what the student teacher knows and can do alone, and that which they could do with the support of more qualified and experienced teachers, mentors, lecturers, and others, who are deemed more capable and knowledgeable about teaching. This support will be necessarily social and cultural (in the sense of professional culture), and will provide the necessary mediation for novice teachers to develop within the ZPD.

As can be seen from discussions so far, Vygotsky, during his short life, achieved much by way of formulating an approach and theory to explain how human functioning relates to and reflects its socio-cultural and historical context. Despite criticisms of his theories for being underdeveloped and lacking a practical dimension, Vygotskian constructs have gained 'increasing prominence among scholars seeking to understand human development at the intersection of the personal and the social worlds' (Kinginger, 2002: 243; see also Warford & Reeves, 2003), and in particular the ZPD is seen as 'the framework, par excellence, which brings all the pieces of the learning setting together – the teacher, the learner, their social and cultural history, their goals and motives, as well as the resources available to them, including those that are dialogically constructed together' (Aljaafreh and Lantolf, 1994: 468, cited in Kinginger, 2002: 243). Specifically in a teacher education context, Johnson (2009) suggests that a socio-cultural orientation has changed the way teacher learning is conceptualized. It means a primary focus on the fact that education occurs 'in specific settings or contexts that shape how learning takes place' (Richards, 2008: 165) and 'is based on the assumption that knowing, thinking, and understanding come from participating in the social practices of learning and teaching in specific classroom and school situations' (Johnson, 2009: 13). Experiences and understandings of these contexts are primary then for prospective teachers. In this tradition, 'we see knowledge as constructed among members of learning communities...' (Hawkins, 2004: 89). This idea of communities will be the focus for the next and related section.

Communities of Practice

'Becoming an English language teacher means becoming part of a worldwide community of professionals with shared goals, values, discourse, and practices but one with a self-critical view of its own practices and a commitment to a transformative approach to its own role' (Richards, 2008: 161). This was articulated as one of the core concerns of contemporary teacher education approximately 15 years ago and holds even truer today based on our experiences during Covid lockdown periods, although many of these communities moved online during such periods (see Hanson-Smith, 2006 for an account of communities of teachers for the purpose of supporting the integration of technology). Lave & Wenger

(1991) are often credited with elaborating and evolving the idea of communities of practice, social groups who share common goals, practices, orientations, and even linguistic jargon which is specific to their own context but also partially shared among professional colleagues in local, national, and international contexts. Those outside of the profession may or may not share such understandings of how these things work: for example, we are not privy to professional processes or understandings of the legal profession unless and until we are peripheral or central participants in it. In relation to English language teaching, at one point or another in the past we were much less knowledgeable about, for instance, what a curriculum was, or classroom interactions, or that the past perfect progressive existed, much less how it is used. It is only through formal learning and experience and being part of a university-based community of professionals in the areas of applied linguistics and language teacher education that these learnings, understandings, and connections have developed. Recently, one of my students asked me what 'office hours' were, and it struck me how many assumptions we make when we use context-specific language in ways that imply a common understanding which may not actually exist in reality.

There is a much-cited necessity identified in the literature about the need for professional communities, one which relates to ongoing professional development and support after the completion of formal teacher education programs. The idea of a learning community is paramount here (Talbert & Mclaughlin, 2002) in a context where it is widely acknowledged that teacher education programs form only the basis for ongoing and continuous learning which necessarily takes place over the professional life-cycle of a teacher. This will be discussed further in Chapter 8 of the current volume. What is more relevant to the discussion in this chapter is the way in which student teachers can begin to socialize into the profession through interaction with and observations of qualified teachers, mentors, and peers. At first all student teachers feel like outsiders to some extent, but the more they engage with local and even online communities of other teachers the more they will begin to feel part of the profession. This socialization process takes time and is closely related to notions of identity and imposter syndrome (see Farr et al., 2019: Chapters 5 and 6 to learn more about how this socialization process is manifested in the discourse produced by student teachers), for example, but the process can at least begin during formal initial teacher education programs.

Pause for Reflection

1. Can you think of two successful examples of social learning in which you have been a participant? Deconstruct them to try to understand what made them successful.
2. Can you identify any potential disadvantages to socially-focused learning and engagements?

MENTORS

As well as contending with the cognitive/practical divide, there is an equally, if not more daunting demand when moving to classroom practice for the first time. This happens at the psychological level and involves a deep and reflective consideration of one's identity, including aspects related to culture, background, personality, as well as the more obvious components of teaching and learning (Barkhuizen, 2017, 2021; Donaghue, 2020b; Farr et al., 2019; Farrell, 2017). It involves asking the searching question: Who am I as a teacher? For some, this question is reasonably easily answered as they have considered it in the past, they have identified role models and they have made decisions about how they want to play the teacher role. For others who may not have given the question any deep consideration, they are suddenly confronted with questions which are not always easy to answer, such as: How do I see myself? How do others see me? Do I want to or need to make changes to how I present myself as a teacher? Are there aspects of my natural personality that I need to augment, or indeed hide? How do I play the part that I think is required of me when I stand in front of a group of real learners? There are no easy answers to these questions and the answers change and are influenced by experiences within the profession over time. However, during a teacher education program, and especially when in preparation for teaching practice, the thought processes around these questions must necessarily begin in earnest. In fact, so crucial are these processes, that it has been suggested that 'depending on the sort of experiences gained and the emotions felt during this period, preservice teachers start to form a clearer professional mental image of the teacher they are and will be. The more positive their mental images are, the more likely they are to stay in the profession' (Izadinia, 2017a: 66).

The demands are high of student teachers on teaching practice and this brings stress. In Chapter 1, we saw some of the concerns of our teachers as part of the PENSER cycle. In a larger-scale study of 300 teacher education students in the Australian context, Murray-Harvey et al. (2000: 25) summarize issues relating to teaching practice that are of most and least concern to the students. Table 3.1 illustrates these issues.

Table 3.1. Items of most and least concern to students on teaching practice (adapted from Murray-Harvey et al., 2000: 25).

Of Most Concern
Having high expectations of my teaching performance
Coping with the overall teaching workload
Being evaluated by my supervisor
Striking a balance between the practicum and personal commitments (e.g., family)
Being observed by my supervisor
Managing time
Managing the class and enforcing discipline
Of Least Concern
Relating to Principal/Vice-Principal
Relating to teachers in the school
Relating to my cooperating teacher(s)
Establishing rapport with pupils
Relating to my supervisor
Marking pupils' written work
Managing the individual seatwork

We can see from Table 3.1 that, as well as individual student teacher variables and expectations, there are a number of other key participants in the context of teaching practice. And while some of those who perform a more formal assessment role, such as supervisors, can be a cause for stress, many others can in fact be sources of support. So, despite the many challenges, so too are there supports provided to facilitate the transition to teaching practice. Teachers are not generally thrown in at the deep end of the classroom. As well as supporting modules/courses in the teacher education program which focus on content and pedagogy, there are many individuals, often performing multiple roles, who can provide different kinds of mentorship to novice teachers.

Pause for Reflection

1. How do you identify with and align yourself with the items in Table 3.1?
2. Are there other issues that are of concern to you which are not mentioned? What are they and why are they troubling?

Teacher Educators as Mentors

Although institutional requirements dictate that teacher educators must perform formal and formative evaluative roles, this is a part that many play reluctantly (as discussed in Chapter 2). However, key to the development of teachers during practicum periods is the way in which teacher educators can provide advice, support, and direction with insights that few others have in terms of academic, experiential, and context-specific knowledge. This may take place more formally when they are assigned roles of TP supervisor or TP mentor, but also informally through engagement in lectures, tutorials, and even during office hour chats. We strongly encourage student teachers to avail of all of these opportunities during the lead up to and roll out of teaching practice classes. Farrell (2021) has even argued that this mentoring role of a teacher educator should continue formally into the period of the first professional job of a newly qualified teacher. As Baguley (2019: 129) puts it, 'the importance of dealing with the issue of disparity between "learning to teach" and "teaching in the real world" cannot be underestimated.' Farrell convincingly argues that instead of what he calls 'teacher abandonment' (2021: 27) at the end of a teacher education program, we should engage in a 'novice-service framework' (2021: 29), as discussed in Chapter 2.

Cooperating Teachers as Mentors

Qualified classroom teachers are important mentors especially when teaching practice takes place in a school context which may be at a distance (culturally, geographically, and in other ways) from where the student teacher is enrolled in their education program. These teachers, often known as cooperating teachers during the practicum, will be able to offer insights which are not readily available to a novice teacher coming into the school for the first time. They can be an essential support to help student teachers make the challenging transition to a real teaching context (Beck & Kosnik, 2002), and can even contribute to a strong sense of achievement on the part of the student teacher during practice periods. An interesting study by Izadinia (2017b) examined the metaphors used by both cooperating teachers and student teachers to describe the relationship between them. The metaphors used by the mentor teachers and pre-service teachers fell into two broad categories: firstly, those referring to the interpersonal nature of the relationship, for example, dad and son, master and apprentice, and older sister; secondly, a group of metaphors associated with providing direction and support, for example, coach, guide, and lifeguard (Izadinia, 2017b: 510–511). In addition, this study found no considerable difference between the beginning and the end of the placement in terms of the metaphors used. All of this points to the deeply personal and supportive roles of cooperating teachers, who seem to provide a level of comfort and confidence to novice teachers during their school placements. However, the converse can also be true, and a related study identified 'the powerful role of mentor teachers to facilitate or inhibit the process of learning to teach for preservice teachers' (Izadinia, 2017a: 75). (For a fuller review of the literature in relation to teachers as mentors see Ambrosetti & Dekkers, 2010.)

Peers as Mentors

A much more symmetrical, and therefore less threatening, relationship exists between peers on a teacher education program, and indeed other programs. For this reason, as well as being perceived to have more in common with each other, peer mentors or peer buddies have been used frequently in educational contexts for some years, especially in relation to facilitating the transition from secondary to tertiary education (for example, Heirdsfield et al., 2008). Despite potentially having different backgrounds and levels of experience, all students on a teacher education program identify as such, students in education with much to learn before becoming qualified teachers. They are, however, knowledgeable novices, with opinions, observations, and previous life and learning experiences to draw on when interpreting or enacting teaching roles. The role of peers in formal teacher education contexts has become more prevalent over the last number of years with the move to social constructivism and the acknowledgment of the power of teacher thinking and cognitive processes (see, for example, several chapters in Nguyen, 2017 devoted to a discussion of both formal and informal roles associated with peer mentors in language teacher education programs). This, in some cases, has been in response to a concern about transmission-based models of learning on the practicum as a result of traditional models which position supervisors as authority figures and therefore limit opportunities for true reflective practice on the part of the novice teacher. A relatively recent study in the Vietnamese context highlighted the affordances of peer-mentoring in the practicum context and 'the important role of peer mentoring in promoting reflection on teaching while the pre-service teachers showcase the value of the peer-mentoring model for facilitating their engagement in reflection. There was evidence that peer mentoring not only creates opportunities for pre-service teachers to evaluate their own practice, but also enhances their professional knowledge. Peer mentoring was not only used for sharing, it also served as a tool for reflection on teaching' (Nguyen & Ngo, 2017). Effectively, it shifts the responsibility for reflection to those who have most to gain from engaging in reflection, and removes any authority-induced stress that may exist when traditional supervisors are involved.

We would argue that there is a place for all three types of mentoring discussed in these sections as complementary approaches during the practicum. Each has its own limitations and affordances but together they can provide the student teacher with excellent opportunities for a range of different supports to engage with. These mentoring relationships will be more and less prominent at different stages of the practicum, depending on how it is structured: for example, teacher educators may have a bigger role to play at the pre-practice stage, while cooperating teachers may come to the fore during a school placement, or indeed during classroom observation periods, which is the focus for the next section.

CLASSROOM OBSERVATIONS

As mentioned in the introduction to this chapter, observing others, especially more qualified and experienced others, aligns well with an apprenticeship approach to learning and reflecting. This is one important side of the coin of looking backwards and looking forwards at models of practice, and it does have limitations. Nonetheless, especially for the uninitiated student teacher, classroom observation provides a risk-free way for them to experience the social realities of the classroom without having to take a participatory role in the interactions that unfold. This section highlights the awareness-raising that can occur during periods of observation. It draws on excerpts from the PENSER data produced by student teachers as reflections during Stage 3 of the process, *Noticing*, which involves observing classes taught by qualified teachers and reflecting on identified *Puzzles* (Stage 1) student teachers may have had before the observation in relation to their own practices in particular (see Chapter 1). In total, eight insights or themes emerged from the PENSER reflections, written in TP portfolios following observations. These are detailed and exemplified in the following sections, some of which inevitably overlap. These sections do not intend to go into in-depth discussions on any of the specific focal points for the observations as these are covered in more detail in the relevant later chapters of this volume. For now, they merely illustrate the affordances and insights which engagement in an observation and reflection cycle can offer in advance of actual classroom teaching practice.

Learning about the Learners

Some of the student teachers chose to focus on the EFL learners during their classroom observation. It is clear from the commentary in Extracts 3.1 and 3.2 below that they are not overly familiar with the language levels of the learners. They are also somewhat surprised at the positive predispositions and motivation of the learners.

Extract 3.1 (Online TP Portfolio – PENSER Cycle 1)

ST Caitlin: What surprised me most was that they all knew the rules, so they had clearly learned them before. It reminded me that non-native speakers who learn English formally have a better knowledge of the rules of English than native speakers. If I am honest, it was a bit intimidating especially as I am a novice and I am still learning the rules myself. I was also surprised that they seemed to enjoy focusing on accuracy in their pronunciation whereas I would have thought they would find it boring. I suppose the fact that they are university students is important here because they are probably more motivated and disciplined than other learner groups.... I also have a better sense of what they can do at intermediate level.

Extract 3.2 (Online TP Portfolio – PENSER Cycle 1)

ST Shona: Asking the students to speak in front of the class can be daunting and shut them down, but in pairs and small groups they have less anxiety and inhibitions and gain confidence as L2 learners.

There are so many facets to the interpretation of learner interactions and behaviors in the classroom and it is interesting to note that both of these student teachers homed in on affective and psycholinguistic factors such as interest, enjoyment, motivation, and confidence. The EFL learners are mainly from European backgrounds and, culturally, we have observed over the years that they have tended to be more motivated, confident, and participatory in class than Irish students tend to be, particularly at undergraduate level. It is perhaps these differences that draws the attention of the student teachers as part of these observations. In both cases, it is clear that they have gained new and somewhat surprising insights which will inevitably help them to prepare better for when they themselves will be teaching these learners a few weeks later.

Learning about the English Language

Although ostensibly this student teacher is commenting on learning something new about the English language, Extract 3.3 actually hints strongly at identity issues also. It is clear that they position themselves as a native-speaker teacher who still needs to learn technicalities about the English language for teaching purposes. This will be discussed further below.

Extract 3.3 (Online TP Portfolio – PENSER Cycle 1)

ST Mary: My observation was with the upper-ints (intermediates) and the lesson was on collocations with the central word LAW. To be honest, I never even knew what a collocation was before so it was a learning curve for me too, as well as the students. I liked the way the teacher explained the term first and then did some brainstorming and wrote up examples on the board, and then she got the students to do the tasks in the course book.... So, the observation was really useful as it raised my awareness of collocations, showed me how to teach this kind of input.

The double advantage of being able to learn about collocations and to be able to see how to teach them being demonstrated at the same time in a real classroom situation is a relatively unique affordance of engaging in classroom observations. It is also a credit to the student teacher that they have managed to focus on both teacher content and pedagogic knowledge building simultaneously in this particular case. Although collocation is something that the student teacher will learn in a coming module on their program, its salience is likely to be much heightened as a result of this observational experience.

Learning about Pedagogy

This is a relatively broad section on increasing pedagogic awareness, inevitable as this is one of the main aims of classroom observations. We have divided it into more focused subsections below.

1. Instructions and teacher talk

Despite theoretical discussions with the support of illustrative examples in pedagogy modules, it seems that there is no replacement for first/second-hand experience of seeing how this works in practice. Extract 3.4 illustrates this well. The student teacher not only notes teacher language and clarity in instructions but appreciates the positive impact this has on student success.

Extract 3.4 (Online TP Portfolio – PENSER Cycle 1)

ST Darragh: From the observation, I have learned the importance of clarity in instructions, stating the purpose of tasks and providing a high quality of interactional teacher talk overall. The class teacher articulated the instructions very clearly and clarified the purpose of each task and this was important to the outcomes and student achievement. During my observation, I became aware that the students were successful in developing answers as they were given time and space to process and collaborate and there was a clear understanding of what was needed from them as students.

2. Classroom organization and learner groupings

Student teachers often struggle conceptually and practically with organizing learners into appropriate groupings for collaborative activities. They also sometimes struggle with assuming the authority it takes to do this and feel impolite when they have to direct learners to such an extent. This again relates to their emerging teacher identities and shaking off the imposter syndrome, which many new teachers find difficult at first. Extract 3.5 clearly illustrates that this student teacher has developed a new-found appreciation for the importance of directing and appropriately conducting pair and group work in the classroom (see also Waring & Creider, 2021 for a detailed account of micro-reflection on classroom communication).

Extract 3.5 (Online TP Portfolio – PENSER Cycle 1)

ST Sarah: When I was observing the lesson, what struck me was that the learners were given plenty of time for pair and small group classroom discussion and I saw lots of examples of good practice in this area. Integrating pair and small group discussion increases learner interest and engagements and helps the students maintain focus. They also learn from each other and hear and gain new and different perspectives.

3. Corrective feedback

Extract 3.6 is a really good example of a student teacher having a light-bulb moment which allows them to bridge theory with practice through observation. They even draw on the research from second language acquisition and error correction in an example true of Jay & Johnson's comparative reflections (Jay & Johnson, 2002). What is most interesting is that fact that this realization seems to have somehow liberated them with respect to their own practice. It has given them the much-needed permission to take action to change their own corrective techniques, which they now realize are not conducive to the promotion of learning.

Extract 3.6 (Online TP Portfolio – PENSER Cycle 1)

ST Mairead: I found that observing the teacher give feedback, and especially corrective feedback really helped me to understand what was involved and how to develop an approach I was comfortable with. Before, I just used to listen to the students' contributions and say 'perfect' to everything they said, which I know was wrong but I didn't want to appear negative or to be putting them down. I know this was wrong and it wouldn't help them learn. Research in L2 teaching proposes that teachers need to understand what is an important error and what is not, and they need to develop a range of corrective feedback strategies and use them in every lesson at an appropriate time, like using the whiteboard as a tool, and highlighting a common error in grammar and getting the learners to work together on corrections (Farr, 2015). The teacher demonstrated expertise in this area by actively monitoring the class during group discussions and taking note of any errors overheard. By allocating sufficient time at the end of the lesson to write these spoken errors on the board and through eliciting corrections from her learners, the teacher showed good practice in this area. Corrective feedback is an important aspect of L2 teaching as it encourages learners and helps develop their proficiency in English but it needs to be implemented in an informed way. This area of teaching is one that I have not felt confident about, but I now aim to practise these skills and incorporate them into my future lessons.

Interestingly, this also works in the opposite way. The student teacher in Extract 3.7 seems to have gleaned a lot from the observed lesson about what not to do when correcting students' errors. Their understanding is facilitated through a triadic discussion with the cooperating teacher also.

Extract 3.7 (Online TP Portfolio – PENSER Cycle 1)

ST Jean: I watched my team teacher teaching a lesson on grammar and I learned a lot from what she did well, as in she knew the grammar and explained it well, and from what she didn't do so well, as in when she was correcting the students where I think she overcorrected and was a bit harsh in tone.... I feel more confident about corrective feedback – at least I have a better sense of options and strategies. It was good that we got to do this in pairs with the class teacher as it made it less awkward talking about it.

Materials and Resources

The two student teachers represented in Extracts 3.8 and 3.9 choose to focus on the materials that the teacher selected to use, adapt, or design for the lessons they observed. They become aware of the range of resources available to the teacher outside of the course book and that these could be successfully used to engage the learners. ST Laura in Extract 3.8 appears to already have some teaching experience but interestingly situates her identity on the novice end of the scale as part of her reflection, and provides a really relevant link to how we can all learn from each other as parts of communities of practice. For ST Pauline in Extract 3.9, the observations around materials have prompted a renewed commitment and motivation for detailed and creative lesson planning.

Extract 3.8 (Online TP Portfolio – PENSER Cycle 1)

ST Laura: From my observations, I have learned that good teachers take what they need from the book and adapt it with online resources to make it interactive and fun for the students. When you're having fun with the students, they're more relaxed and learn more. You can take anything from the internet like a TED talk, songs, podcast, Youtube videos and make it into a lesson as long as it's relevant to the lesson and the learners. I can see that good teachers know and use a wide range of online resources like film, ads, games. Overall, it's a learning curve and I'm definitely not confident but I'm more open now to suggestions and trying out web resources. If any new teacher is feeling nervous, they needn't worry as even though I am experienced, I feel like I'm starting out too. In terms of technology and teaching, I think online teaching is growing and evolving so all we can do is our best and share our knowledge and skills with our colleagues so we can learn together in a community of practice.

Extract 3.9 (Online TP Portfolio – PENSER Cycle 1)

ST Pauline: I found it really interesting as to watch Adam teaching the advanced students as he's had some experience of teaching before. He designed a very engaging lesson because he chose a really current theme that the learners were genuinely interested in (smart city design in the Gulf region) and he integrated video clips to illustrate it – so climbing gardens on the sides of skyscrapers and green transport/infrastructure that is making cities greener. I never would have thought of building a language lesson around this type of content. It has given me ideas and made me put more effort into my lesson planning, which is something I have struggled with.

Professional Socializing with Teachers

Previous sections in this chapter discussed the process of socialization and becoming members of the professional community of teachers, as well as the roles that cooperating teachers can play as mentors. Extracts 3.10 and 3.11 illustrate how this can operate in practice. In Extract 3.10, ST Jean seems to have created or availed of the opportunity for a fairly elaborate discussion about the issues that occurred in the classroom around corrective feedback, which they had deemed not to have worked very successfully. The debriefing with the teacher seems to have provided some space for professional dialog and resulted in deeper clarity and an appreciation of the sensitive and real-time issues at play in real classrooms. ST Shona in Extract 3.11 seems to have a less formal but no less valuable discussion with the class teacher which results in a proposed solution that they can implement in their own future teaching.

Extract 3.10 (Online TP Portfolio – PENSER Cycle 1)

ST Jean: We had a feedback discussion with the class team teacher afterwards and it was interesting to hear her comments. I liked the fact that her feedback was constructive – it wasn't personal in any way, but rather focused on the incidents in the lesson, which we broke down step by step and then we discussed the types of errors that occurred, whether they were important and if they needed to be addressed, and alternative ways of dealing with them that didn't make the learners feel they were being judged or embarrassed. It showed me that it is not black and white and that as teachers we have to make on the spot decisions which can be difficult. Making sure learners keep their dignity is also so important and this part of the discussion was really useful.

Extract 3.11 (Online TP Portfolio – PENSER Cycle 1)

ST Shona: I also got a chance to discuss why we need to teach this kind of input and to anticipate any potential difficulties and how they can be planned for.

Debunking Assumptions

This short section raises a simple but significant issue for student teachers. Student teachers come to the practicum with a range of assumptions based on their own prior world and pedagogical experiences. Sometimes they don't even realize that they have implicit assumptions about the teaching context and its many diverse scenarios. Through direct observation of the learners they themselves will be teaching in later weeks, these assumptions are made explicit and highlighted as either being true or false. This came to light for ST Caitlin through part of their reflective account in Extract 3.12.

Extract 3.12 (Online TP Portfolio – PENSER Cycle 1)

ST Caitlin: I suppose the observation has made me realise the need to be careful about making assumptions about what learners want to learn and their knowledge and interests.

Teacher Identity

The notion of emerging teacher identity and choices to be made about the directions that this takes has been highlighted in relation to some of the previous extracts. In Extract 3.13, the student teacher has explicitly chosen this as the focus for reflection as part of their observation. They have learned from the positive qualities displayed by the teacher being observed, which in turn seems to have triggered a thought process about their own teacher identity and how this needs to develop.

Extract 3.13 (Online TP Portfolio – PENSER Cycle 1)

ST Darragh: The teacher was very professional and also very enthusiastic throughout the whole lesson and this, I think, this was important as it gave the learners confidence in her as a teacher in terms of her abilities, and her enthusiasm was infectious. It made me think more about the kind of teacher I want to be and trying to ensure that learners enjoy the lesson. In my follow-up discussion with the class teacher, she told me that when she started out as a teacher she used to get really nervous and she was so worried about appearing unprofessional in the learners' eyes that she was too strict and a bit impatient and snappy at times, but as she became more confident, she relaxed and became more aware of the learners' needs. So, it was a good lesson learned from my perspective.

In this extract, we can see the student teacher making two very pertinent observations about novice teacher identity: first talking about what is known as 'assigned' identity, which is effectively an identity promulgated by others rather than oneself (Buzzelli & Johnston, 2002), in this case the learners; then alluding to the very formal teacher identity in the early stages of being a novice. This has been theorized in the published literature by Zimmerman (1998: 90) who suggests that new teachers adopt a 'situated identity,' which is close to what they have experienced or observed as traditional or formal teacher roles in the classroom.

Affective Factors

Although woven through each of the previous sections and extracts, we thought it important to highlight how much student teachers focus on affective factors and how much they can learn about this most intangible of concepts through observation and reflection. In Extract 3.14, ST Joanna has an explicit focus on factors that fall under the umbrella of affect, including trust, rapport, emotional awareness and intelligence, amongst others. The importance of such qualities in a teacher have been highlighted for a great number of years as being key to enjoyable and even successful learning and as such merit explicit consideration and reflection before embarking on classroom practice.

Extract 3.14 (Online TP Portfolio – PENSER Cycle 1)

ST Joanna: I have developed a greater understanding of the importance of developing a good rapport with learners. Mutual trust and a good rapport between students and their teacher is a key element to a successful lesson. By taking time at the beginning of the lesson to introduce herself to the students and the students to one another, the teacher I observed demonstrated good classroom management skills and good emotional awareness and intelligence. This led to a high level of student engagement, which is essential in an EFL classroom as the learners were more eager to contribute in class discussions. Developing a comfortable and stimulating learning environment is essential. As a future teacher, I am motivated to replicate this enthusiastic, friendly energy in my lessons. This observation proved to me that a positive attitude between students and their teacher resulted in a more successful and enjoyable lesson.

In this section we have illustrated how useful classroom observation can be as a focus and trigger for reflection. There are a number of structured templates and aids to help focus such reflections which can be used on teacher education programs (see Farr, 2015: Chapter 4). In this chapter we have been speaking thus far of one model of classroom observation whose aim it is to encourage a less experienced teacher to learn from watching a more experienced teacher in a formative way. One caveat to be aware of in any discussion of classroom observation is that it can become problematic when we start to talk about good teachers or models of good practice, because, as Wragg maintains, 'mostly when we talk about a "good" teacher, an "effective" strategy or a "bad" lesson, we are referring to our own subjective perception' (Wragg, 2012: 60). In other words, subjective evaluation can impede interpretations. This is not such an issue in formative observations, but can become one when observations are used to evaluate teacher performances in more summative approaches such as can happen in primary and secondary schools under different models of observation for assessment (see, for example, O'Leary, 2012, 2013). This may also be a model that you will have to experience during your practicum if you are to be observed and evaluated by a supervisor or someone else in a formal position to assess your teaching practice. The next section briefly explores such an approach to observation.

Pause for Reflection

1. From all of the things that the student teachers learned about teaching through their classroom observations above (the learners, the English language, pedagogy, materials and resources, professional socialization, assumptions, teacher identity, and affective factors), are there any that you think are more important than others for you personally and why?
2. Are there any alternative interpretations to any of the extracts above that could provide different insights into the student teacher's cognitive processes in each case? What might these be?

BEING OBSERVED BY OTHERS

An unfortunate truth about the practicum, particularly if it occurs as part of an academic program of study, is that needs to be formally assessed by those charged with this role, often the same teacher educators who lecture and mentor the student teachers. Part, if not all, of that evaluation will come in the form of being observed and evaluated by a TP supervisor, or someone who performs a similar role and goes by a similar title. There are two considerations to help with a student teacher's readiness for such observation. The first is more affective and psychological, and the second is more pragmatic and strategic.

In Table 3.1 we saw that three factors which cause most anxiety among student teachers while on the practicum part of a teacher education program are: being observed by a supervisor, being evaluated by a supervisor, and concerns about one's own teaching performance. It is difficult for anyone in any career to be evaluated by another, particularly when that other is deemed to be more expert, but this is even more intensified during a teacher education program where the novice teacher is still at the early developmental stages of acquiring the classroom skills and dispositions for which they are being assessed. This means that student teachers need to prepare as well as possible, psychologically, to ensure that the natural stresses and tensions of the context don't negatively impact their performance. There are a number of pieces of advice that we often give to our own students to help with preparation for assessed teaching and to reduce stress as much as possible:

- If you don't already, get to know your supervisor and talk to them, if possible, to establish a positive relationship with them in advance

- Prepare to teach a lesson that is relevant and creative but not too complicated (this is not the lesson to take major risks with)
- Be fully prepared to teach the lesson and have all the necessary contingencies in place
- Have additional materials prepared in case you have time to spare at the end of the planned lesson
- Engage in any type of relaxation techniques that work for you, for example, mindfulness, meditation, visualization, music, etc.
- Arrive in plenty of time to chat with the learners and create a positive atmosphere for the lesson
- Avail of all of the support you can from peers, mentors, cooperating teachers, and anyone else who might be able to advise you, review your materials, help you through a dry run and in any other appropriate ways in advance of the assessed lesson.

In terms of the assessment focus of the observation, you can be as strategic as you need to be to increase your chances of getting a good grade. It is important to know and understand the assessment criteria being used and the weighting that each one carries. This will help you to design your lesson in a way that makes it easy for the supervisor to score you well on all or most of the pre-set criteria. If you do not fully understand how the assessment works then talk to your supervisor or course tutor well in advance, and avail of any shared wisdom of your peers who might have already been through an assessed lesson. It is also really important to ensure that you are fully aware of options that are open to you if you do not pass the assessment in terms of opportunities to repeat or compensate for any failed grades. Unfortunately, grading is a serious business, especially on the practicum, and this one grade alone may determine your future career opportunities and salary bracket in some cases. Employers place a high value on such evaluations, so it behoves you to do everything which is ethical and reasonable to increase your chance of a high grade.

Pause for Reflection

1. Which pieces of advice offered in this section do you find particularly practical and helpful and why?
2. To what extent does your response to the previous question relate to you as person and to what extent does it relate to your context?

SUMMARY

This chapter has aimed to explore some of the more well-established ways that student teachers can be supported and helped in the period up to and including live classroom practice with real learners of English. Following a brief historical contextualization, as a backdrop to the more practical discussions, relevant theoretical explications of socio-cultural approaches and communities of practice are presented. Three key enablers are then detailed in the remaining sections of the chapter. Firstly, mentorship from teacher educators, cooperating teachers and peers are presented as vital sources of supports for novice teachers preparing for teaching practice. Next, the potential of classroom observation of qualified teachers as a formative support and lens into the reality of the classroom is discussed and exemplified with numerous extracts from the PENSER corpus. This section is capped with a brief account of student teachers being observed and evaluated in summative ways as part of the practicum component of teacher education programs. We are now at a point in this book where we are ready to discuss the preoccupations of the actual teaching practice component where student teachers engage in a process of real practice in real classrooms.

Chapter 4
Reflecting on Preparation and Planning

INTRODUCTION

This is the first of four chapters that will draw on the PENSER data to trace the reflective thinking and professional development of a group of ten student teachers of EFL over the course of their TP journey. The discussion in each chapter will be informed by the spoken and written reflective data sourced from teacher educator-guided classroom discussions, dialogic discussions with mentors, and individual reflective writing in online TP portfolios over the course of three PENSER cycles, with the student teachers involved, referred to throughout by pseudonyms to protect their identity (see Chapter 1). In this chapter, we will meet the group as they grappled with challenges associated with the preparation and planning of lessons in the early days of TP. At this stage, it is useful to pause to reflect on your own concerns as a novice teacher as you prepare and plan for teaching at the start of your own TP journey.

Pause for Reflection

1. How well do you cope with the workload and requirements of lesson planning?
2. What issues arise for you in identifying suitable materials and resources?
3. Do you feel well supported by mentors and peers at this stage?
4. How do you overcome any inadequacies you may feel?

Returning to our group of novice teachers, in the first reflective cycle, which coincided with the first semester of TP, issues relating to preparation and planning featured saliently in the PENSER reflective data and they were present in the second and third reflective cycles also, albeit to a lesser degree. Table 4.1 sets out the six specific issues of concern identified by the novices in this area over the course of their TP journey.

Table 4.1. Specific issues identified relating to lesson planning.

Main Area of Challenge	Specific Issues
Lesson Preparation and Planning	• Workload • Identifying lesson aims • Writing the lesson plan • Understanding learner abilities • Constraints of the course book • Selecting suitable materials and resources

Before we explore the experiences of the student teachers as they set about preparing and planning for TP, it is useful to review the relevant academic literature from the fields of applied linguistics, SLA, and TESOL as this will provide important insights into the nature of the challenges that novice teachers can expect to encounter in this area of pedagogy, from which we can gain a better understanding of their perspectives, as well as the role played by RP in supporting their professional development in this area.

PLANNING FOR TEACHING

The ability to plan effectively for different learner groups is a key professional requirement for all teachers and involves complex decision-making. Lesson planning is the process of deciding, in advance, what and how to teach according to the aims of a particular lesson. This involves a wide range of factors relating to the syllabus, materials, activities and resources, learner knowledge and characteristics, and institutional requirements and constraints (Farr, 2015; Scrivener, 1994). In recognition of the importance of this knowledge, and the complexities involved, teacher education programs usually include lesson planning and preparation as a core element of the curriculum. This involves novices being required to write detailed lesson plans which identify and specify the learning aims and intended outcomes of the lesson, with a particular learner group in mind, and which provide a step-by-step description of the stages of the lesson. The value of RP at all stages of the TP experience has been highlighted by Farr (2015) while Crookes (2003: 101) has noted the support it can offer for novices as they design and plan lessons, in the sense that 'detailed lesson planning provides a concretization of practice, or at least of intended practice, and as such is also a tool for distancing oneself from practice so as to reflect upon it.' This suggests that providing opportunities for novices to engage in RP around the processes of planning and preparing to teach, can play a useful complementary role in their professional development.

Core to the planning process is the selection of suitable content for the target learner group. Here, teachers must avoid the twin pitfalls of demanding too much or expecting too little of learners, which requires a critical understanding of the background knowledge of learners and their prior learning. It also assumes a knowledge of the linguistic and cognitive abilities of learners at the various proficiency stages, and the ways in which they can vary from one group to another, and within groups. The ability to select suitable language content and to identify realistic language aims and outcomes also relies heavily on the teacher's knowledge of the subject, which in the case of the EFL teacher means a formal understanding of the workings of English at the levels of syntax, morphology, and phonetics and phonology. A further key area of knowledge that student teachers need to acquire if they are to make good choices and decisions in this area is a theoretical knowledge of how second and foreign languages are acquired, and the implications this carries for their lesson design and planning.

As far as student teachers are concerned, this knowledge base is usually gained over time through their engagement in modules in language systems, Second Language Acquisition theory, and EFL classroom pedagogy, which typically provide the foundation of the curricula of MA programs offered in universities, and also through their engagement with the related academic and research literature from the fields of applied linguistics, SLA, and other language-related disciplines. Meanwhile, at a practical level, TP creates opportunities to apply this newfound knowledge and to gain an understanding of the classroom environment and the backgrounds, abilities, and needs of learners. In their planning for classroom teaching, student teachers are usually guided by well-known pedagogic frameworks that set out detailed descriptors of language proficiency levels such as the *Common European Framework of Reference for Languages* (CEFR) (Council of Europe, 2001). Course books also offer accurate indications of what learners at different proficiency levels can reasonably be expected to know, as they are designed with this in mind. Over time, this enables student teachers to develop an understanding of learners' abilities at a given level, and on the basis of this knowledge, they can decide how best to break up the subject area being focused on into smaller units of learning, how it should be presented to ensure maximum clarity, and the types of tasks and activities they will build into the lesson to ensure that learners have sufficient practice in order to reinforce learning.

Lesson planning also involves decision-making around how the lesson should be structured and how to balance individual work with more active pair and group tasks, all the while ensuring that the lesson remains focused on its aims and intended outcomes rather than being aimless and confusing. Teaching can be unpredictable and even the best planned lessons can take an unexpected turn. It is vital, therefore, that teachers build some flexibility into their lesson planning to allow them to respond to learners' needs as they arise. This is also important to be able to exploit unexpected opportunities for teaching and learning. Good planning, therefore, also means anticipating where problems may arise and developing strategies to address them. For instance, it is not unusual for language learners to ask questions and request clarification and explanations around language points, and these are therefore key considerations that teachers need to take account of. This suggests that lesson planning is a complex process and that novices can benefit from guiding principles in this area, to help them to develop the expertise required, alongside the insights they gain from their own classroom experiences.

Murray & Christison (2011: 20) provide a list of the fundamental principles on which all lesson plans should be based, which can serve as a useful guide for novices during the early days of teaching practice:

- Find out, and build on what learners already know
- Present new information in chunks that learners can digest
- Include teacher input that is comprehensible to learners
- Challenge learners to move beyond their current level of language
- Include opportunities for learners to practice new skills and knowledge
- Provide feedback (from teachers and/or peers)
- Provide a supportive environment
- Be responsive to learning opportunities that occur in the classroom.

Having mastered the initial challenges of structuring the lesson and establishing its aims and content, the attention of novice teachers typically turns to activities and materials that will engage learners and maintain their interest and motivation (Farr, 2015). As we have gained in knowledge about the affective dimensions of SLA, there has been a consistent move towards developing learning activities that can enhance learner motivation and which are better targeted to their diverse interests and learning styles. Learning style refers to the preferences that individuals display in terms of being predisposed to the ways in which they think about, process, and understand, in this case, language. Research suggests that learners perform better and are more comfortable when they learn in ways that fit best with their own style, and models have been developed to explain and categorize learning styles. The most well-known of these is probably the sensory style model proposed by Dunn (1999) which specifies visual, auditory, and kinaesthetic preferences. Today, it is generally understood that learners can be anywhere on a cline between styles, and that they may change styles in different contexts. Meanwhile, as far as learner motivation is concerned, strong links are assumed between high motivation and language learning success (Gardner & Lambert, 1972; McCarthy & Farr,

2022). In this regard, both learner needs and learner wants are crucial factors that teachers must consider when choosing themes and topics for the lesson, and it can be challenging to balance these (Farr 2015). In addition to taking account of the range of learning styles, experiences, and interests that learners bring with them to the L2 classroom, underlying cultural dimensions must also be understood for the effective planning of topics, activities, and pedagogical materials to ensure that lessons are relevant, that there is maximum inclusion and participation, and that broader societal norms are respected.

A crucial part of planning is the selection of suitable course books, and supplementary materials and tasks that are appropriate to the capabilities of the target learner group and relevant to their interests and needs. In this regard, Mishan & Timmis (2015) have stressed the need for pedagogic materials to be principled, motivating, affectively and cognitively engaging, challenging, and that teachers provide suitable input and opportunities for appropriate output. In the English language teaching world, teachers are more often engaged in evaluating and selecting appropriate materials rather than creating them from scratch, due to the availability of an abundant range of high-quality materials, either commercially, or freely as open educational resources. It is also common practice for English language teachers to follow a set textbook which they supplement with authentic and pedagogically designed materials, depending on the learning context and institutional requirements. On pre-service teacher education programs that offer TP, novices usually begin by planning lessons that are based primarily on designated units/pages from course books selected by TP supervisors. This is considered necessary to provide the support that they need at this early stage and to ensure that learner needs are being met. As they become more familiar with different learner groups and their abilities, and as their pedagogical knowledge develops, they are gradually encouraged to integrate supplementary materials into their lessons, whether authentic in nature, or pedagogically designed, and to create suitable tasks around these. This requires a more sophisticated level of lesson planning in terms of the ability to critically evaluate the suitability of such materials and tasks and how they can be combined with appropriate methodologies and effective teaching practices (Tomlinson, 2012).

As novices progress on their TP journey, they begin to develop expertise in materials development, which is essential given the limitations of EFL course books (Riordan & Farr, 2015). While international course books largely remain the mainstay of EFL pedagogy and the main vehicle through which the English language curriculum is taught across different language proficiency levels, they have come under increasing scrutiny and are found wanting on several grounds. For instance, Mishan (2005) has highlighted their uniformity, the blandness of the topics included, and their lack of focus on local needs, interests, and cultures. Similarly, Tomlinson (2012: 158) has argued that 'many global coursebooks are not considered to be sufficiently engaging or relevant for their actual users.' This has led to calls for them to be 'humanised' by incorporating 'activities which help to make the language learning process a more affective experience and finding ways of helping the learners to connect what is in the book to what is in their minds' (Tomlinson, 2003: 163). Moreover, in the light of corpus research findings in the applied linguistics field over the last few decades, there have been increasing objections to their narrow linguistic focus, and in particular, that they still prioritize the teaching of either British or American Standard English despite upward global trends around the use of English as an international language (A. Farrell, 2019). This is notwithstanding the progress more recently with course books now increasingly informed by corpus research and featuring a greater representation of global Englishes (Mishan & Timmis, 2015). However, amongst critical linguists in particular, criticisms remain of the cultural and ideological agenda promoted in EFL pedagogy, which they argue is to advance neo-liberal western values and attitudes associated with globalization (Cunningsworth, 1995; Pennycook, 2000). This criticism also extends to the widely used international English language testing systems which operate in conjunction with the main academic publishing houses, as they are seen to maintain the 'prestige' and currency of Standard British English and Standard American English, and their continued promotion in EFL pedagogy, to the detriment of other varieties (Jenkins, 2009; Matsuda, 2012).

While in some countries there has been a growing trend towards localization in course book design, which typically involves national governments working with the main ELT publishing houses to produce course books that reflect local needs and practices, there generally remains an absence of locally produced EFL course books in many parts of the world (Tomlinson, 2012). This means that EFL teachers often rely on locally sourced authentic materials and adapt them for their own classroom context, particularly when they seek to bring a local cultural dimension to the lesson, where this is permitted. This is also the case for EFL teachers from Ireland, which is a context where international course books still prevail due to an absence of locally produced course books (A. Farrell, 2019; Murphy, 2011; Wallen & Kelly-Holmes, 2006). Accordingly, in Ireland, as in many EFL contexts, there is a conflict between the variety taught in the course books, which is largely Standard British English, and the variety used outside the classroom, namely Irish English, and the culture that EFL learners are exposed to in the published materials used in the Irish context is more often British than Irish. In the light of these limitations, Tomlinson (2001: 67) has advised that 'no course book can be ideal for any particular class and that an effective teacher needs to be able to evaluate, adapt and produce materials to ensure a match.' He also highlights a positive development in EFL pedagogy which is that 'teachers seem to be more constructively critical of their course books and more willing, confident and able to localise and personalise their course books for their learners' (Tomlinson, 2012: 170). To guide teachers in these initiatives, Tomlinson (1998: 7–21) has provided a useful 16-point framework that they can draw on to evaluate, select, adapt, and design materials for L2 pedagogy, and this also serves to underscore the complex range of pedagogical factors involved, as Figure 4.1 illustrates (note: TL = target language).

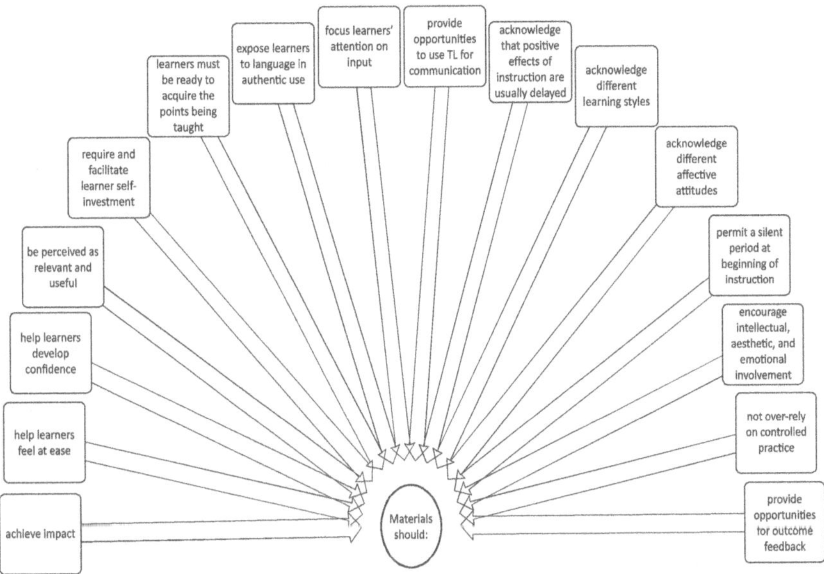

Figure 4.1. Principles of materials development (adapted from Tomlinson 1998: 7–21).

The ever-increasing array of digital and corpus-based materials and resources available for L2 pedagogy in more recent times has enabled teachers to bring greater diversity and creativity to their lessons (Levy, 2009; Wang & Vásquez, 2012; see also Mishan, 2013 for a detailed and useful account of specifically designed Computer-Assisted Language Learning [CALL] packages for English language learners; and Chinnery, 2006 for a review of the growing field of Mobile Learning and Apps [iOS and Android]). Moreover, the move towards data-driven learning (DDL) has created increased opportunities for learner-centered approaches and self-study with a wide range of resources and materials now available for learners at different proficiency levels (see Chambers, 2010 for a history of DDL; and Boulton, 2017; Chambers et al., 2011; Farr & Karlsen, 2022; Flowerdew, 2015;

Mishan, 2004; Reppen, 2010 for how to use DDL in language teaching). Walsh (2010: 342–343) has highlighted the multiple benefits that digital resources can bring: for instance, they can aid the development of language skills, as well as the acquisition of grammar and vocabulary across a range of varieties and registers of English (see Brezina & Flowerdew, 2017; McCarten, 2007; O'Keeffe et al., 2007). Meanwhile, the use of multimodal corpora (such as *Backbone*, *Sacodeyl*) with learners can improve speaking and listening practice (Farr & Karlsen, 2022; Walsh, 2010), teach listenership, increase students' interactional competence (Braun, 2005), and raise awareness of online discourse and paralinguistic features (Riordan, 2012; Riordan & Murray, 2010). Notwithstanding these obvious benefits, the use of digital and corpus resources in the L2 classroom has brought a whole new host of challenges for teachers, not least how best to integrate them into the lesson. This underscores the importance of training in technology for teachers which is now widely offered as a core component of teacher education programs (Abdel-Latif, 2020; Farr, 2007, 2008, 2010, 2022; Farr & O'Keeffe, 2019; Leńko-Szymańska, 2017). In Chapter 5 of this book, we explore how our student teachers engaged with online and digital pedagogical materials and resources in their classroom teaching, as reported in their reflections, but in the following account, our interests lie more in tracing the challenges they experienced in the early days of TP when issues relating to preparation and planning were uppermost in their minds, as well as the role played by TP in helping them to address these challenges. While reading their accounts, keep in mind your own challenges in this area in the early days of teaching and the ways in which you overcome them.

THE PENSER FINDINGS: PREPARING AND PLANNING FOR TP

As part of the TP module, the student teachers were required to design a 50-minute general English lesson for a group of EFL learners at intermediate, upper-intermediate, or advanced levels of language proficiency, with the process repeated going forward with different learner groups. Prior to this, they had engaged in classroom teaching observations and team teaching under the guidance of teacher educators and class teachers acting as mentors. Over the course of TP, they also continued with observations of experienced teachers, participated in TP preparation classes, and received feedback from TP supervisors. In order to support their professional development throughout the TP experience, they were encouraged to reflect on their TP experiences and challenges in teacher educator-guided group discussions, individual e-portfolios, and in dyadic discussions with

TP supervisors and mentors, and to share their thoughts and any newfound insights gained in the spirit of collaborative learning. We join the student teachers at the start of the first reflective cycle, when they were designing lessons for their first 'solo' teaching experience.

Problem 1: Workload

As Extract 4.1 from the initial teacher educator-guided group discussion in the first PENSER cycle illustrates, concerns about the unexpectedly high workload involved in lesson planning featured uppermost in the novices' minds at this stage, suggesting that many had underestimated the time and effort this would require as well as the complexities involved.

Extract 4.1 (Guided Group Discussion 1 – PENSER Cycle 1)

1. **TE:** So, how are you getting on?
2. **ST Sarah:** I'm really struggling with the workload involved in lesson planning. I just didn't think it would involve so much.
3. **ST Caitlin:** It's taking me absolutely ages to plan my lesson too and I'm still not sure if I'm doing it right. I actually had no clue it would be so demanding.
4. **TE:** So, it seems that many of you are finding lesson planning more challenging than you had anticipated. Would that be fair to say?
5. **ST Sarah:** I never really thought about teachers having to write formal lesson plans the way we are doing it.
6. **ST Darragh:** It isn't straightforward because you first have to do research about the learners to be able to find out key information.
7. **ST Shona:** One of the biggest challenges for me has been trying to work out exactly what I'm supposed to be teaching language-wise because I've been told to focus less on the topic and more on the language by my TP supervisor.
8. **ST Sarah:** I think it's the same for us all.

As indicated, the guided group discussion provided a useful, shared space for the novices to identify and explore the ways in which they felt most challenged at this early stage of the TP module, under more expert guidance. Having identified and articulated that lesson preparation and planning were key problems that many were experiencing, and with a new understanding that these were shared issues, they were guided towards hypothesizing the causes, as a key stage in the process of moving towards generalizing the problem, as Extract 4.2 illustrates.

Extract 4.2 (Guided Group Discussion 1 – PENSER Cycle 1)

1. **TE:** Why? Can you think of some reasons why this might be?
2. **ST Shona:** Well, I can only speak for myself. I don't come from a language background and this could be why I am finding it so hard to identify the language aims because I don't really know what this means.
3. **ST Caitlin:** I think if you're good at languages you would definitely have an advantage with this.
4. **ST Mary:** Well, for me, as we're doing more of the language systems module I'm finding it's helping me to get a better sense of what the language focus means, but it's also telling me how little I know about my own language, which was not what I expected because I actually thought the opposite would be true. You know, the fact that English is my native language would make it easier for me.

In the previous interactions, there is evidence of an important realization emerging amongst the group, which is that the difficulties that they were experiencing in identifying the language aims of lessons, might be related to their prior lack of a formal education in the language systems of English, as often arises for novice EFL teachers from a native speaker background (see Chapter 6 of this book where language teacher knowledge is explored as a main theme). Moreover, as Extract 4.3 illustrates, they were also now beginning to gain a deeper sense of the professional requirements around lesson planning for teachers, which many were surprised to learn about, as this seemed to contradict popular myths they had heard about the informal nature of EFL teaching in many parts of the world.

Extract 4.3 (Guided Group Discussion 1 – PENSER Cycle 1)

1. **ST Sarah:** It's not like what most people think about TEFL... you know... that you just go in and teach conversation without really having to prepare in advance.
2. **TE:** Is that what the rest of you expected too?
3. **ST Joanna:** Well, no, obviously with an MA you are expected to know how to plan a good lesson, but I personally didn't think there was so much to it. I mean, that you would have to spend days planning a one-hour lesson.
4. **ST Laura:** Yeah, it's definitely not a piece of cake like a lot of people think.

From this, the group was guided by the gentle probing of the teacher educator to move away from viewing lesson planning as a personal challenge towards understanding it as an aspect of professional development that brings challenges for all novices, as Extract 4.4 illustrates. This led them to a growing realization that the ability to plan effectively lies at the heart of the professional practices of teachers and that it involves knowledge and skills that take time to learn.

Extract 4.4 (Guided Group Discussion 1 – PENSER Cycle 1)

1. **TE:** And do you think that it is something that all new teachers struggle with?
2. **ST Mary:** Yeah, you have to learn your trade like everyone else.
3. **ST Sarah:** Yeah, but obviously it depends how much time and effort they put in and how much guidance they have.
4. **ST Caitlin:** You need a lot of knowledge, not only about the students but materials and resources.
5. **ST Mary:** But you would expect it to get easier as we start making the connections between theory and teaching.
6. **TE:** So, how do you see planning in relation to the teacher's professional role?
7. **ST Mairead:** I think schools would expect teachers to know how to write a lesson plan, whatever the subject.
8. **ST Shona:** I would think that teachers have to follow the same way of doing it, so it complies with the regulations, but they don't expect us to be experts overnight.
9. **ST Jean:** But I think students can tell if a teacher has prepared their lesson or not. I know I could in secondary school, and I appreciated teachers who planned their lessons because their teaching was always better. I respected them more for it.

From these interactions, it is clear that the novices were beginning to embrace the problem and that they were moving towards a deeper understanding of its relationship with other experiences and ideas, which is the aim of the second stage of the PENSER reflective process. At this point, they were also encouraged to think proactively about the knowledge and skills they would need for good planning practices going forward, and to report back to the group with specific strategies. This marked the beginning of the noticing, solving, and experimenting/exploring and research stages of the PENSER reflective process which took place over the following two-week period.

In Extract 4.5, which is sourced from the second teacher educator-guided discussion which took place a few weeks later, we find the group sharing their newfound insights and offering each other tips and advice. This suggested a growing understanding of their role as language teachers, and a willingness to take charge of the problem in hand.

Extract 4.5 (Guided Group Discussion 2 – PENSER Cycle 1)

1. **TE:** So, you have identified lesson planning as a challenge in terms of workload and the knowledge and skills needed to be able to plan effectively. How then can you develop this expertise?
2. **ST Joanna:** I found it useful to go back over the lecture slides.
3. **ST Sarah:** And we have the sample lesson plan. I followed the way it was worded when I was writing the different parts.
4. **ST Caitlin:** Getting the language aims right is really the starting point.
5. **ST Shona:** Yes, I agree and it's always a good idea to run things by your team teacher and read each other's lesson plans to make sure this is right.
6. **ST Mary:** And the teachers' book is very good for identifying the language aims of the lesson and what learners are likely to know or not from a language point of view.
7. **ST Sarah:** And it gives indications of the sorts of problems they could have in the lesson.
8. **TE:** So, there is a great deal of information you can draw on and you know where to access it. Does this reassure you?
9. **ST Mary:** Well, it feels less daunting than at the start when I felt like I was drowning.

We find further evidence of their commitment and the endeavors made to improve their lesson planning skills in their online TP portfolios over the following weeks, as in Extract 4.6.

Extract 4.6 (Online TP Portfolio – PENSER Cycle 1)

ST Caitlin: I've completely changed the way I'm planning my lessons and have a system I follow. So I start by getting an overall sense of the theme and the language points, and then break it down into parts and steps. I have a long journey home and use my driving time to go back over what I have done. I find it helps me rethink what will or won't work and come up with any changes I can make. You do need to think long and hard as there's such a lot involved. So, I've come to realise that it's a process that you have to keep revisiting. You can't get it all right in one go.

This is a more mature reflection, suggesting a growing sense of self-efficacy which Riordan (2018: 60) reminds us is vital for student teacher professional growth.

Problem 2: Understanding and Engaging Learners

In this subsection, we explore a second area of challenge in the area of lesson planning that was also identified in the teacher educator-guided discussions in the first PENSER reflective cycle. This related to the difficulties that the novices were experiencing in relation to understanding the varied needs and abilities of EFL learners, as Extract 4.7 illustrates.

Extract 4.7 (Guided Group Discussion 1 – PENSER Cycle 1)

1. **ST Darragh:** I'm finding it really hard to understand what they (the learners) do and don't know. I watched one intermediate class and they were really good and had loads to say and then another class where they just sat there and virtually didn't speak. So, how are we supposed to plan for the different groups when they're so different even when it's the same level?
2. **TE:** And would the rest of you also find this a challenge?
3. **ST Mairead:** Definitely.

Having established that this was a common problem within the group, as a crucial starting point to encouraging them to embrace the challenge, the novices were guided towards articulating the precise nature of the difficulties they were experiencing, and their significance, in terms of the impact they had on teaching and learning.

Extract 4.8 (Guided Group Discussion 1 – PENSER Cycle 1)

1. **TE:** Could you explain in a bit more depth what happened and the consequences?
2. **ST Darragh:** Well, I had planned to teach new words that were in the reading text but they already knew them all when I asked.
3. **TE:** So how did that make you feel?
4. **ST Darragh:** Er... stupid. Plus, they whizzed through the exercises and I ended up with an extra fifteen minutes at the end of the lesson with nothing to do. The TP supervisor had to take over and give them an extra task. It was very stressful because I could see it coming but I couldn't do anything about it.
5. **TE:** So, you felt you had lost control of the lesson?
6. **ST Darragh:** Exactly.
7. **ST Jean:** I actually had the opposite problem. I was told to challenge them more by my TP supervisor but I ended up making it too difficult and some of them started turning round looking at the TP supervisor for help.

8. **TE:** And how do you feel about teaching the group again?
9. **ST Jean:** Well, more nervous obviously because after that they probably won't have much confidence in me as a teacher.
10. **TE:** Okay, do you all think it is important that we explore why these incidents happened to help the teachers involved to move forward and regain their confidence?

This exchange highlights the anxiety and loss of control that some of the novices felt when their teaching didn't go according to plan, which was often due to their lack of understanding of the learners, and how this impacted on their confidence and ability to teach. It also shows how through skillful questioning, the lecturer was able to raise the group's awareness of the significance of the problem, as an important first step towards encouraging them to embrace it. In the following extract, we note how the teacher educator gently guides the novices involved towards hypothesizing the possible causes involved in order to move them towards generalizing the problem rather than seeing it as a personal failing, which was vital if they were to regain their sense of confidence and self-efficacy.

Extract 4.9 (Guided Group Discussion 1 – PENSER Cycle 1)

1. **TE:** So, let's think about why these types of incidents happen.
2. **ST Pauline:** I think it could be for lots of reasons. I suppose the group dynamic is important. Some of them might know each other very well so that could be a reason why they don't respond in one group while they do in others.
3. **ST Caitlin:** I think intermediate is quite a broad level and there are different levels within it.
4. **ST Shona:** I also think some of the students shouldn't have been in intermediate. They were too good, but it could have been the activities that were too easy.
5. **ST Pauline:** Well, I think I just totally underestimated their English. I suppose I thought that intermediate was lower than it actually is.
6. **TE:** So how can we make better-informed judgements about what learners at different levels are likely to know or to struggle with?
7. **ST Mary:** I think it's something we definitely need to work on because it influences everything else we do.

More focused now on finding solutions, the group moved towards the solving, experimentation and research stages of the first PENSER cycle, where they actively explored how they could improve their knowledge of EFL learners' needs and abilities to aid their lesson planning. Extracts 4.10 and 4.11, from their online

TP portfolios over the following weeks, illustrate the various approaches that were taken by the individual novices to enhance their insights in this area and the deeper level of understanding that was gained as a result.

Extract 4.10 (Online TP Portfolio – PENSER Cycle 1)

ST Joanna: I found it useful to go back to the CEFR framework we met in the first week of the TP module. To be honest, at the time it went over my head because I had never taught before and it was just too much to take in. But now that I have taught different levels, I can see that it gives really accurate information about what we can expect learners at different proficiency levels to know, although it's not an absolute. So, I've started to consult it more when I'm planning my lessons especially for the language items because that's where we have to be well-informed.

Extract 4.11 (Online TP Portfolio – PENSER Cycle 1)

ST Mairead: One of the best ways of gauging what students know in terms of their English is by observing the classes taught by the experienced teachers. It has made me more aware not only if they have met a word or grammar point before, but how well they actually know it. Before, if they had said they knew something I wouldn't have checked this. Now, after seeing the way the experienced teachers probe this, I can see that they might only have a vague knowledge and that they need to go back over it. Or they might think they know something when this isn't the case. So, it's helping me to get a much more accurate sense of their knowledge which I didn't have before.

These extracts provide us with evidence of student teaching learning, and with this, an increasing confidence in their ability to plan lessons more effectively with specific learner groups in mind.

Problem 3: Selecting Suitable Materials and Resources

We move on now to discuss a third area of challenge that was also salient in the reflective data in the first PENSER cycle and which related to the materials and resources that the student teachers could draw on in their lesson design. As Extracts 4.12 and 4.13 from the online TP portfolios illustrate, there were mixed views about the requirement to use a designated course book as the basis of their lesson as, on the one hand, they welcomed the support it offered, while on the other they were uncertain as to how much they should be relying on it, and some were also starting to question its relevance and suitability.

Extract 4.12 (Online TP Portfolio – PENSER Cycle 1)

ST Jean: We're teaching from a course book for most of the first semester which I must admit I'm relieved about as I feel I had a road map. In the TP preparation class, we looked at the pages from the book that we're teaching next week. I was surprised to see how much information is provided for teachers in the course book, which is helpful for me as an inexperienced teacher but I'm not sure how much I should be using the course book and if I should be bringing in other materials.

Extract 4.13 (Online TP Portfolio – PENSER Cycle 1)

ST Joanna: I like the fact that it (the course book) gives us the bones of the lesson, but I find the themes a bit boring and even cringy for adults.

The teacher educator-guided discussion offered the group a valuable space for the student teachers to collectively explore their experiences of using the designated course book during TP with a view to developing a critical understanding of both its advantages and its limitations.

Extract 4.14 (Guided Group Discussion 1 – PENSER Cycle 1)

1. **TE:** So, how are you finding the course books so far?
2. **ST Laura:** Well, the most important thing for me is that there's an answer key at the back which is a relief (laughs).
3. **ST Sarah:** I think they are laid out well and there's an index at the front which breaks each unit down, which helps because I found it really confusing at first just looking at the pages because they're very busy.
4. **ST Caitlin:** It's good to have the tape-scripts for the listening texts at the back so you know exactly what they're saying and how long it'll take to do it, which is helpful.
5. **ST Sarah:** Yeah, but it's good to listen to them too, you know, for the speed and accents.
6. **ST Laura:** To be honest I never really know how far we can stray (from the course book).
7. **ST Shona:** I don't really like being tied to a course book.

This exchange suggests that as the student teachers were becoming more familiar with the course book, they were also beginning to question its limitations. At this point, the teacher educator guides them towards developing a more critical understanding of the issues involved. This began with a more in-depth exploration of how the requirement to use a course book might relate to their novice stage of professional development, as Extract 4.15 illustrates.

Extract 4.15 (Guided Group Discussion 1 – PENSER Cycle 1)

1. **TE:** So, why do you think novices are often required to use a course book for TP rather than just finding their own materials?
2. **ST Mary:** I suppose we don't really know enough about what's out there and we might not be confident choosing the right things.
3. **TE:** Any other reasons?
4. **ST Sarah:** It would take us longer to find our own materials for every lesson.
5. **ST Caitlin:** Yes, but we could swop ideas and materials when we're teaching the same level.
6. **TE:** Can you see any disadvantages to that?
7. **ST Sarah:** Well, what someone else thinks is good might not be what the rest of us think and most student teachers would prefer to use a course book because we know they've been designed by experts, and we can trust them.

This extract would seem to indicate that some of the novices were more confident in their lesson planning than others, and so were keener to become more independent and creative. However, their comments also suggest that, as yet, they were lacking in awareness of the additional demands this would bring. In order to continue the process of meaning-making in relation to this challenge, they were asked to hypothesize what the advantages and limitations of using a course book might be, and to come up with ideas as to how they might explore this issue further over the course of the following weeks, using their e-portfolios as a space for individual reflection. This moved them to the noticing, solving, exploring and researching stages. Their individual reflective writing over the course of the following weeks reveals the different ways in which the novices engaged with the problem, and the understanding they gained as a result, as Extracts 4.16 to 4.18 from the online TP portfolios illustrate.

Extract 4.16 (Online TP Portfolio – PENSER Cycle 1)

ST Pauline: When I spoke to friends who are teachers, they mostly thought that novices would feel relieved to have a course book rather than having to go off looking for materials because they're still getting used to teaching the lessons in the book and there's a lot of guidance in the teachers' book. They also thought it was important for learners to have structured lessons around course books and that they might not appreciate teachers doing their own thing especially student teachers.

Extract 4.17 (Online TP Portfolio – PENSER Cycle 1)

ST Mairead: I talked to the class teachers about it because I know they still use course books even though they supplement them. So, I found out that one of the reasons for this is that there's an exam for the learners at the end of the semester and some of it is based on the book. So, teachers need to be aware of how the book fits in to the curriculum. This made me think about how teachers need to put the learners first and not our own interests or vanity.

Extract 4.18 (Online TP Portfolio – PENSER Cycle 1)

ST Darragh: I get it that we need course books when we are starting off and that we'll never learn if it's all done for us. For me, the best way forward is to gradually phase in more of our own materials as we become better at evaluating them, which is what I think is expected as we're doing an MA.

These reflections demonstrate that the student teachers were developing a more critical awareness of the complexities involved in teacher decision-making in this area, as well as a growing realization on their part that good lesson planning should begin with an evaluation of learners and their needs. They remind us too of the vital role that mentors can play in student teacher awareness-raising in relation to specific aspects of classroom pedagogy, and the complementarity of action research involving mentors as a further aid to their professional growth.

We turn next to the second teacher educator-guided group discussion in the first PENSER cycle, where the novices were now focusing on the challenges involved in designing lessons without the use of the course book, as this was a requirement for the last two lessons they were to teach. As Extract 4.19 illustrates, they were mostly excited at the prospect of selecting their own materials and resources, and keen to have a go, but at the same time, feeling daunted by the additional planning this would involve. This prompted the teacher educator to engage the group in a review of the criteria and guidelines for good planning practices.

Extract 4.19 (Guided Group Discussion 2 – PENSER Cycle 1)

1. **TE:** So, next week you'll be designing your own lesson. How do you feel about that?
2. **ST Mary:** Well, I'm glad we're getting the chance to be more creative and use different materials.
3. **ST Sarah:** Yeah, I agree there's a lot out there, but the problem is they're not all good.
4. **TE:** So, what does that mean for you as teachers?

5. **ST Caitlin:** Obviously, more work in terms of sourcing the materials and evaluating them.
6. **ST2 Mary:** Yes, more than with the course books where it's pretty much done for us.
7. **TE:** So, what should you keep in mind as you are selecting materials and resources?
8. **ST Joanna:** Well, the level of the learners is important.
9. **ST Mary:** And having a theme that they like and that challenges them intellectually.
10. **ST Sarah:** What will be tricky in our own lessons is making sure there's a strong language focus and that it's the right level.
11. **ST Mary:** Knowing what resources we have is important too if we want to bring in film or music.
12. **ST Caitlin:** I really want to bring in some music to lift the mood and maybe use the lyrics to teach vocabulary. Maybe a Christmas carol?
13. **ST Mary:** Yeah, but it might embarrass them if you make them sing (laughs).
14. **ST Pauline:** And how do you know they're Christian?
15. **ST Caitlin:** That's true. It's important to think about the culture when we're selecting materials and themes.

From the previous exchanges, it is evident that the guided classroom discussions offered the novices an effective forum in which to identify and explore challenges involved in selecting suitable materials and resources to integrate into their lessons, guided by a more expert other, and that this enabled them to develop a more principled pedagogical approach.

These new insights were articulated in the dyadic discussions between the novices and mentors at the end of the first semester of TP. By this stage, they had engaged in guided RP and shared learning around a range of issues relating to preparing and planning for teaching, and they had developed action plans and undertaken related research. As Extracts 4.20 and 4.21 exemplify, this process helped them to crystallize their ideas and understanding, bringing them a greater sense of professional confidence and enrichment.

Extract 4.20 (Dyadic Exit Discussion – PENSER Cycle 1)

ST Laura: It's really good to have someone to bounce ideas off and it's definitely helping me to think more creatively and be a bit more adventurous, which I wouldn't normally be. Yeah, it's definitely more enjoyable and less stressful than doing it on your own and it makes me think more about if the materials are suitable for the level and how the two halves of the lesson fit together and flow, because we discuss it and go through our lesson plans together.

Extract 4.21 (Dyadic Exit Discussion – PENSER Cycle 1)

ST Mairead: I've watched lessons where the teacher used so many resources like the PC, slides, YouTube clips and Menti (the mobile phone application). It was great to see them all in action so to speak but I've also seen a lesson where only the board and the course book was used and it was equally good. So, it's not only about the materials and resources but how you use them and if it adds to the lesson. So, you really do need a good theoretical knowledge of SLA when it comes to selecting suitable materials and resources so you can really target the needs and interests of different groups which can vary a lot in terms of terms of level, age, interests and cultural make-up etc. You also have to keep up to date with the all the new materials and resources available to make your lesson relevant but the most important factor in the equation is the ability of the teacher to get the level right.

The previous extract also reveals a developing critical awareness of theories and principles that underpin effective lesson planning, with the novice in question now better equipped to make more discerning judgments, having gained a deeper understanding of the criteria involved.

Pause for Reflection

1. As a language learner, how well were your needs understood and met?
2. How suitable were the course book/materials used when you learned a language?
3. What did the choice of materials reveal about the knowledge of the teacher?
4. What was the impact of the course book/materials on your learning experience and outcomes?

SUMMARY

In this chapter, we have endeavored to provide a snapshot of the challenges faced by novice teachers of EFL in the early days of TP, in the area of preparing and planning, and we have traced their developing confidence and abilities in this area, drawing on their spoken and written reflections over the course of the first PENSER reflective cycle. The empirical findings in this area were also positioned in relation to the relevant academic literature from the fields of applied linguistics, SLA, and TESOL to enable us to interpret their significance. In these ways, this chapter has demonstrated how the professional development of novice teachers at this early stage of their teacher education can be supported and nurtured by means of targeted and guided reflective practice with peers, mentors, and lecturers across a variety of RP modes, and it has also provided evidence of the value of this approach for the development of their reflective thinking. Having gained some valuable insights into the initial struggles of our group of novices as they prepared to embark on their TP journey, in Chapter 5 we meet them again as they assumed their new L2 teacher role and were confronted by a new set of challenges.

Chapter 5
Reflecting on the L2 Classroom Environment

INTRODUCTION

This chapter brings a focus to bear on the demands and challenges that arose for novice teachers as they assumed their new, classroom teacher role and began to familiarize themselves with the L2 teaching and learning environment, highlighting in particular issues in the area of classroom management and teacher/learner relationships. At this stage, it is useful to reflect on your own prior experience of learning a foreign language in a classroom setting.

Pause for Reflection

1. In what ways is the L2 classroom a different learning environment to other subject classrooms?
2. How confident did you feel interacting in the target language with fellow learners in the language classrooms that you have experienced?
3. How would you describe the rapport between the teacher and learners, and between learners in the language classrooms that you have experienced?
4. What role, if any, did the teacher play in motivating and engaging the learners in the language classrooms that you have experienced?

It is widely acknowledged that good classroom management skills are an essential requirement for all teachers; however the research literature indicates that it is a topic of enduring concern for practitioners in many educational settings (see Barnes et al., 2006; Boz, 2008). Classroom management (CM) also ranks as one of the main areas of preoccupation for new entrants to the teaching profession who often report a lack of confidence in this area and a need to be better prepared (Oliver & Reschly, 2007; Walsh, 2006). As is the case for teaching professionals more widely, EFL practitioners can be expected to face increasing challenges in their CM role due to ongoing developments in education that are changing how we teach and learn (Spiro, 2013). However, the precise nature of these challenges, and how novices are being prepared to address them on teacher education programs, remains unclear, with calls for more empirically-based research in this area in different contexts and settings (Spiro, 2013). The RP-oriented research highlighted in this chapter, which was conducted in the context of an MA in TESOL education program in Ireland, can thereby offer useful insights into the experiences of novice teachers of EFL in the Irish EFL classroom context, as well as highlighting the ways in which they made sense of their experiences. In so doing, it is also our intention that it can help to inform future directions in teacher education in the local context and add to the existing knowledge in this area more widely.

In the PENSER reflective data, classroom management was a recurrent and salient theme in the first and second PENSER cycles, which gives us a sense of the complexities it posed in the early days of teaching. However, it was not perceived as an area of concern in the third cycle, which suggests that the novices felt that they had managed to overcome some of the initial difficulties involved. In this regard, they identified six types of challenges over the course of PENSER Cycles 1 and 2, as listed in Table 5.1, and these formed the focus of their reflective group discussions and individual reflective writing during this period.

Table 5.1. Challenges and specific issues relating to the L2 classroom environment.

Main Area of Challenge	Specific Issues
Managing the L2 Learning Environment	• Teacher classroom anxiety • Poor teacher presence • Difficulties building rapport with learners • Low learner engagement • Uneven participation • Managing resources

CLASSROOM MANAGEMENT

As previously, we begin with a review of the related academic literature in order to contextualize the PENSER reflective data. Broadly speaking, CM has been defined as 'any action that the teacher takes to create an environment that supports and facilitates both academic and social-emotional learning' (Evertson & Weinstein, 2006: 3). This suggests that it is all-encompassing in nature in terms of the wide range of roles and functions that teachers are typically expected to fulfil. McNeely & Mertz (1990: 3) identified three main management roles, described as instructional management, people management, and behavioral management, which can be expected to vary in intensity from one educational context and setting to another. Meanwhile, Brophy (1986) listed sub-functions such as arranging the physical environment of the classroom, establishing rules, routines, and procedures, and maintaining a focus on lessons and learner engagement in academic activities. To this, Martin et al. (1998) added the management of time, tasks, materials and resources, social interactions, classroom relationships and classroom atmosphere, and more recently Tao (2010) pointed to cyclical aspects such as advanced planning, implementation, assessment, and evaluation. Today, CM is widely understood in educational circles as a multifaceted construct that involves cognitive, social, and affective dimensions. However, in public debates about education and in the academic literature, issues relating to classroom discipline in mainstream schooling still tend to attract the greatest attention and criticism (Yazdanmehr & Akbari, 2015).

When we consider the pedagogical approaches that have developed around CM, it is possible to categorize them into three main types, that is: the 'reactive' approach, the 'preventative' approach, and the 'combined reactive-preventative' approach. The first is directive in nature, and reflects behavioral management theory (Skinner, 1953); the second takes greater account of humanistic educational theory and affective influences on student behavior (Brophy, 1986; Stiffler, 2010); and the third combined approach seeks to involve students in managing and taking responsibility in relation to their own behavior, with Glasser's Choice Theory probably the most well-known (Glasser, 1986). Interestingly, research in the area of teacher beliefs informs us that teachers' decision-making in this area is influenced by factors such as teacher age, gender, cultural background, and the teaching methodology adhered to within a particular educational tradition, and that there is often a strong correlation between what they believe about CM and what they do in practice in terms of their CM performance (Martin & Shoho, 2000). Meanwhile studies which have explored teachers' CM practices has indicated that they tend to select and perform a range of preventative and reactive actions to develop appropriate student behaviors according to the challenges that arise in particular teaching contexts (O'Neill & Stephenson, 2012).

In this chapter, CM is explored through the lens of the experiences of novice teachers during TP with adult learners of EFL from a wide range of first language backgrounds. This will highlight the range of issues and concerns that novice L2 teachers are likely to share in common with all new practitioners, as well as those which are unique to this particular teaching and learning context. It will also allow us to explore how student teachers are prepared for their CM role, the role that individual and collaborative RP can play in this process, and the benefits that can be accrued. In the section which follows, we highlight the close assumed relationship between CM and learning in order to underscore the importance of good CM practices.

THE RELATIONSHIP BETWEEN CLASSROOM MANAGEMENT AND LEARNING

How well teachers organize classrooms and manage the behavior of their students is widely believed to have a crucial impact on learner engagement and educational outcomes (Oliver et al., 2011). In this regard, Emmer & Stough (2001) have observed that although good CM practices cannot guarantee effective instruction, they establish the classroom environment that makes good instruction possible; accordingly, well-managed classrooms are more likely to improve student performance and achievement while poorly-managed learning environments lead to less time being spent on academic work, with student performance negatively impacted (Patterson et al., 1989). Teachers can also be affected by their own poor classroom management performance in terms of morale and career progression, with some evidence that a teacher's success or failure to establish good CM practices can influence whether they choose to remain in the profession or to abandon it (Farrell, 2016b; Ingersoll & Smith, 2003). Teachers who struggle with behavior management and fail to establish good rapport with students are more likely to report higher levels of stress and symptoms of burnout, which, in turn, can impact negatively on their perceptions of teaching as a career choice (Berliner, 1986; Browers & Tomic, 2000; Farrell, 2016b), whereas teachers who are confident in their CM role have been shown to be more resilient to stress and 'burn out' (Parkay et al., 1988). Accordingly, developing effective CM practices is vital as it can lead to more positive educational experiences and outcomes for teachers and learners alike. Having established the centrality of teacher CM performance in the learning process, as well as for teacher professional development, we proceed to the crucial question of what *effective* classroom management means in practice.

WHAT IS EFFECTIVE CLASSROOM MANAGEMENT?

Educational theorists have identified a range of characteristics that can be associated with a well-managed classroom, which can serve as guiding principles for teaching professionals (see Evertson et al., 1983). For instance, it should involve high levels of student involvement; an understanding on the part of students of what is expected of them; relatively little wasted time, confusion, or disruption;

and a classroom climate that is work-oriented but at the same time, relaxed and pleasant. Teachers should also take account of the needs of different learner groups and contexts in their teaching methods and styles and ensure they are appropriate (Farrell, 2016b). Effective CM also means establishing good rapport with learners and ensuring a high quality of teacher-student and student-student interaction, as well as the sensitive, active monitoring of student engagement and progress (Walsh, 2006). This suggests that in order to become good classroom managers and maintain the confidence of those they teach, student teachers first need to develop a strong and 'alert' teacher presence. For Rodgers & Raider-Roth (2006: 266), this involves developing an awareness of what is happening in the classroom, and an awareness of the impact of their own behavior on the learning environment. Awareness-raising of this kind is a key area of focus on pre-service teacher education programs, for which classroom observations and RP can play an important complementary role, as has been highlighted in Chapter 3 of this book by the present authors, and more widely (Farr et al., 2019; Farrell, 2016b).

In the context of L2 teacher education, Farr et al. (2019) have highlighted the close link between CM performance and teacher identity, with novices found to become more confident and expert in their CM role as they gained an increased sense of being part of the teaching community. This initially involves becoming familiar with the norms and discourses that underlie the professional practices of teachers and then gradually developing a more critical understanding of what this might mean for their own classroom practices. Against the backdrop of new developments in teaching and learning, A. Farrell (2019) has also highlighted the importance of teachers keeping abreast of changing norms in education and engaging in critical reflection as to their implications for the local teaching context, and for teachers in other teaching contexts and settings given the global nature of the ELT profession and the fluid and evolving nature of teacher identity formation (see Farrell, 2017; Nunan, 2017; Richards, 2017; Sachs, 2005). As Richards (2001: 2–4) has observed, alongside their professional experiences, there are a myriad of additional factors that can shape teachers' professional development, including personal attributes, biography, gender, age, and culture. This underscores the importance of teachers at all career stages availing of opportunities to reflect on and explore their professional role in the context of the changing nature of teaching and learning today. In the following section, we explore recent and emergent influences that are impacting on the CM role of teachers, focusing in particular on the evolving L2 educational domain.

CLASSROOM MANAGEMENT IN A CHANGING EDUCATIONAL ENVIRONMENT

The shift towards learner-centered approaches in education over the past 50 years or so has brought about new CM requirements and practices (Howatt & Widdowson, 2004; McCarthy, 2020). Learner-centered teaching places an emphasis on the social, dynamic, and collaborative dimensions of learning, reflecting the growing influence of Vygotskyan socio-cultural theories of learning in western education systems (1978). This has led to a gradual move away from a traditional, didactic style of teaching to one in which practitioners are required to provide supported instruction, or scaffolded instruction as it is also called, and to create opportunities for learners to develop their own strategies and engage in self-directed study (Spiro, 2013: 27). Learner-centered educational approaches are now commonly promoted in the L2 classroom and have been reinforced by the wide-scale adoption of communicative/task-based language teaching approaches from the 1980s onwards (Oxford, 1997). These approaches place a newfound emphasis on learner participation and engagement, which are now considered vital for successful language learning (Allwright & Bailey, 1991). Within SLA, the work of Swain (1985: 146) has demonstrated the need to create opportunities for learners to become actively involved in both the negotiation of comprehensible *input* and the formulation of comprehensible *output* as essential elements for language acquisition, and this is now a widely held principle in the L2 educational domain. From this, a consensus has emerged in the ELT world that teachers must play a more central mediating role in the complex processes involved in learning a second or foreign language. This requires them to develop and integrate a wider range of skills and strategies to ensure a high level and quality of learner engagement and target English use. However, as Walsh (2006: 101) has argued, for this to occur, they must first become critically aware of the central role they play in managing and optimizing the classroom learning environment.

As far as the interactional practices of EFL teachers are concerned, they are expected to use elicitation and questioning strategies in conjunction with pair/small group work to encourage learners to contribute and actively participate throughout the lesson. However, getting students to respond and discuss their opinions and experiences can often be problematic, not least due to the psychological challenges that this can pose. There has been a growing interest in the affective dimensions of teaching and learning in the L2 educational domain in line with the advent and development of humanistic educational approaches since the 1970s. Studies in SLA which have explored the psychological challenges of learning a second or foreign language (Garrett & Shortall, 2002; Tsui, 1996) have highlighted the debilitating insecurities and anxieties that learners can experience when asked to speak in the target language in front of peers, due to inhibition or a fear of derision and making mistakes, which leads to a situation where they often dread being asked questions, and are reluctant to speak. As in other teaching contexts, this realization has led to an increased focus on the emotional well-being of learners in the EFL classroom and on the types of knowledge and skills that EFL practitioners need to acquire if they are to create a less stressful learning environment and reduce learner anxiety (Farrell, 2016b).

Pennington (1990: 134–135) has advised that for learners to fully engage in the language learning process, they must also feel that their ideas and opinions are valued and respected, which is more likely to occur when there is a positive connection and mutual trust and respect between teachers and learners. Similarly, Walsh (2006) and others since (Murray, 2010; A. Farrell, 2019) have called for teachers to develop a high level of socio-pragmatic sensitivity and skill if they are to maintain a positive classroom environment and relationships while at the same time navigating learners through the different stages of the lesson. This is considered of particular importance when issues of face and face management are at the fore, such as when instructions and corrective feedback are being given, due to the sensitivities involved (Walsh, 2006). Cultural linguists working in the EFL field (Kramsch, 1998) have cautioned, also, that problems of this nature can be exacerbated in multicultural teaching contexts where learners are more likely to come from fundamentally opposing educational cultures, as this increases the potential for misunderstanding and conflict to occur. This raises the critical question of how best EFL teachers can be prepared to manage the multicultural classroom context.

As the use of English continues to spread globally, the number of English language learners in many parts of the world has grown exponentially, including within native English settings, as a result of inward migratory trends (Farrell & Baumgart, 2019; Graddol, 2006). These developments have fueled the demand for EFL teachers worldwide, particularly teachers from native English backgrounds, who are now more likely than ever before to teach learners from a wide variety of L1 backgrounds. Differences between western, non-directive teaching approaches and more traditional and authoritarian eastern approaches have been well-documented in the academic literature in educational sociolinguistics and SLA. As a result, we now have a better understanding of the types of conflicting beliefs that can arise in areas such as teacher and student roles, teaching styles and approaches, and educational goals. Research by Garrett & Shortall (2002), for instance, has shown that some Asian students of English can find less directive socially-oriented lessons based on student-student interaction unfamiliar and confusing as they are used to seeing the teacher play a more central, authoritarian role. Learners from this background are also less likely to be familiar with the kind of 'confessional style' discussions that Prodromou & Mishan (2008: 196) have highlighted as typical of western Communicative Language Teaching (CLT) contexts, which they argue can be problematic in multicultural teaching contexts. This claim is supported by the work of A. Farrell (2019: 160–185) which revealed the kind of confusion and embarrassment that this can lead to, which makes these students less willing to participate in pair and group discussions. Moreover, it found that where teachers lacked intercultural sensitivities, they often mistook the silence of these students for boredom or indifference, which placed a further strain on teacher-student relationships.

To help avoid such problems, cultural linguists have called for EFL teachers to become better informed in relation to learners' expectations and opinions, and the ways in which they may vary from their own (Jenkins, 2007). They have also argued for more open and flexible teaching approaches that can take greater account of underlying cultural dimensions and allow practitioners to respond appropriately. This is with the ultimate aim of anticipating and avoiding potential issues of cultural conflict and fostering more open and inclusive classrooms while at the same time ensuring that important learning goals are met. Critical linguists (see Kumaradivelu, 1999; Pennycook, 2000) have argued that for this to be achieved, teachers need to develop a critical awareness of the ideologies that underpin the teaching and learning of English in different EFL contexts and settings as this will help them to avoid imposing their own dogmas on those they teach. Given the increasing diversification of the language as it spreads internationally, teachers also need to acquire an understanding of different English varieties and their similarities and differences with the main varieties taught, to be able to tailor their practices to local and international needs in terms of the target models they may be expected to teach and use with different learner groups (Matsuda, 2012; see also Chapter 7 of this volume where issues around teacher classroom language are discussed in greater depth). Developing the sociolinguistic knowledge of student teachers is thereby considered of paramount importance to enable them to work successfully in different teaching contexts and settings, each of which may have its own specific cultural, political, and social requirements (Spiro, 2013).

In line with these global trends and needs, researchers have turned their attention to identifying the types of challenges that can arise for EFL practitioners in different EFL learning contexts worldwide, including in the area of CM. The teaching of English to young learners in state schools in the Middle East and Asia has been found to be particularly problematic due to a host of factors; for instance, the unsuitability of imported, western-style CLT and TBTL (Task-Based Teaching and Learning) approaches, large class sizes, a lack of resources, fundamental differences in educational ethos, discipline problems, lack of motivation, and poor levels of learner engagement (Littlewood, 2007). Further challenges have arisen as a result of the transition to English medium instruction (EMI) across a wide range of academic disciplines in the higher education sector in countries in many parts of the world with a growing need for specialized English courses that can prepare and support L2 learners and L2 academics for this more demanding learning environment (Macaro et al., 2018). While developments of this kind are making TESOL a more attractive career option for graduates and are fuelling the demand for postgraduate-level English language teacher education (ELTE) programs, they have also created the need for a wider range of expertise and skills to be developed by new entrants to the EFL profession, and for greater standardization in teacher education in the interests of best international practice, including in the area of CM (Holliday, 2005: 385).

Alongside this changing global landscape, key advances in technology have been taking place which are also impacting on how teaching and learning take place and are viewed, including in the L2 classroom. The advent of digitized media and resources, and the ever-growing use of technology and computer-assisted language leaning (CALL) (Farr & Murray, 2016), has increased opportunities for self-access learning with more readily available resources for teachers and learners to draw on. These include mobile phones and applications, the Internet, Skype, blogs, podcasts, social networking sites, and a further expanding range of digital tools (Warschauer & Liaw, 2011). These technological advances are raising many new issues and questions in relation to how teachers manage the use of technology, and its impact on classroom practices, with calls for more extensive teacher training in this area, and for classroom-based research that can shed light on how these developments are impacting on teaching methods and teacher and learner roles (Spiro, 2013: 27). In this regard, research conducted by Riordan (2018) in the ELTE context in Ireland has revealed a pressing need for student teachers to develop a far more extensive knowledge of IT than their predecessors. Moreover, they must become adept at exploiting this knowledge and skill as well as being able to recognize when it may or may not be effective, and how it can be modified to suit different teaching contexts and settings (Spiro, 2013: 198). With these more complex professional challenges and requirements in mind, we turn next to the crucial question of how entrants to the EFL profession can be prepared and supported for their CM role in the more student-oriented, culturally diverse, and technologically advanced classroom.

PREPARING TEACHERS FOR CLASSROOM MANAGEMENT

In ELTE, as in teacher education more widely, there has been a growing recognition of the need to provide student teachers with greater professional development and supervised experience in CM to help them address the complexities involved (Baker & Murphy, 2011; Farr, 2015). This has led to the introduction of more systematic approaches to CM induction on teacher education programs, with a greater emphasis placed on guided practice and feedback in implementing different types of CM strategies with diverse learner groups (Oliver et al., 2011). From this, student teachers can be expected to acquire a common and comprehensive set of CM competencies as well as a growing ability to anticipate and address the particular CM issues that are likely to arise in different teaching contexts. Alongside this practical CM training, they are also routinely encouraged to reflect on their teaching beliefs and experiences in TP portfolios and diaries, with CM as a key area of focus. To facilitate this, video recordings of classroom situations are now often used as a basis for reflective analysis and discussion for awareness-raising purposes (Emmer & Stough, 2001; Farr, 2010, 2022). Case method of instruction is a further strategy that is becoming more popular as a means of enhancing teachers' problem-solving and decision-making skills in this area, and in general, whereby teachers apply their CM knowledge and skills to real-life situations. Farrell (in Farr, 2015) has welcomed the increased integration of knowledge and practical experience on pre-service teacher education programs, arguing that this development has led to an increase in the CM abilities and confidence of student teachers in relation to their multifaceted instructional role.

Meanwhile, a growing body of RP-oriented research undertaken in the ELTE context has highlighted the ways in which novices can be guided and supported in their CM role through both individual and collaborative RP with peers (Farr & Farrell, 2017; Farr et al., 2019). For instance, in their 2017 publication, the authors of this book demonstrated how student-teacher engagement in multiple RP modes including guided classroom discussions, online blogs, chat and discussion platforms, and individual TP diaries, created a valuable opportunity for them to explore CM-related issues and concerns that arise at different stages of their TP journey, and to develop strategies to address such problems. This research was instrumental in informing the design and implementation of the PENSER reflective model as a process that student teachers can engage in over the course of the teaching practicum in order to improve their practices, including in the area of CM. Before we explore the PENSER-related reflective data, it is useful to review the CM challenges that novice and early career teachers of English as a foreign language can typically experience in the early days of teaching, as have been documented in the related academic literature.

CLASSROOM MANAGEMENT CHALLENGES FOR STUDENT TEACHERS

Student, novice, and early career teachers tend to struggle with many aspects of their CM roles. For instance, they typically find it difficult to achieve a correct balance between maintaining good control of the class and establishing and maintaining good rapport with learners (Pennington & Richards, 2016). Many also tend to adopt a traditional or formal pedagogical role as their classroom 'default identity,' as this provides the type of safe structure or hierarchy they feel they need at this stage in their career, while conversely, a minority adopt a more informal, personal, and authentic teacher identity (Richards, 2006: 60). However, these styles may not be suitable for all contexts. Zimmerman (1998: 91) has observed that more informal styles may be less effective for an inexperienced teacher who has not yet mastered instructional content and pedagogical skills; however, this will largely depend on the age of the learners involved. This view is supported by corpus-based research conducted by Farrell in 2019 which found that when novices adopted an overly informal and indirect teaching style during TP, this often led to poor instructions and feedback (A. Farrell, 2019: see Chapter 6 for a fuller discussion of student-teacher interactional challenges). Similar findings were reported by Riordan (2018) and Farr et al. (2019) from their corpus-based research which revealed a range of CM issues experienced by novices during TP, as were identified either by their supervisors, or by student teachers in their reflections. These included a general lack of teacher presence and confidence, a failure to engage learners or to gain control over dominant students, difficulties in the planning and timing of tasks, and problems relating to the management and integration of technology and resources. The novices involved were also found to experience difficulties in establishing rapport with learners and in giving instructions and feedback to them, especially when they were of similar age to themselves, which highlights the psychological challenges that many novices experience in their new teacher role.

Student teachers from all backgrounds can feel challenged psychologically in the classroom, especially in the early days of teaching. Medgyes has observed that anxiety may be felt by any beginning teacher, whether native or non-native (Medgyes, 1994: 318), while Farr & Farrell (2017: 26) found that novices can experience poor self-esteem and fear being judged as inadequate by learners due to their perceived lack of knowledge and authority. Farr & Farrell (2017) also reported student teachers feeling stressed and overwhelmed by the responsibility of TP and the related workload. Interestingly, Farr et al. (2019) found that they were more likely to reveal the negative impact of TP on their emotional well-being in their online chats and reflective blogs, which led the researchers to conclude that these modes afforded them vital spaces to explore the affective demands of teaching, and for emotional release. Accordingly, there is a growing body of empirical evidence to suggest that TP can be a psychologically daunting experience for many student teachers, with fears and concerns relating to CM often uppermost in their minds.

Pause for Reflection

1. What are your own personal fears, if any, in relation to classroom management? Are you able to share these with peers?
2. As a novice teacher, were/are you concerned about how you would be perceived by learners, and how did you/will you overcome any insecurities you may have felt?

THE PENSER FINDINGS: CLASSROOM ENVIRONMENT CHALLENGES

This brings us to a snapshot of the CM issues that arose for the novices in our study over the course of their TP journey.

Problem 1: Teacher Classroom Anxiety

As the previous review of the literature has highlighted, the EFL classroom can seem a daunting and unfamiliar environment for student teachers and it is not surprising that emotions can often run high at the prospect of teaching a class of language learners on their own. Such fears were evident in the teacher educator-guided discussion in the first PENSER cycle, as Extract 5.1 illustrates. This coincided with the start of 'solo' teaching following several weeks of classroom observations and co-teaching with peers, and with class teachers acting as mentors.

Extract 5.1 (Guided Group Discussion 1 – PENSER Cycle 1)

1. **TE:** How are you feeling about teaching next week?
2. **ST Jean:** I am really dreading having to take charge on my own because up to now the class teacher has been there and I knew I could rely on her if anything went wrong. I feel sick with worry that I won't be able to do it.

3. **ST Sarah:** Yes, my mind keeps going over all the things that could go wrong.

These extracts are consistent with the observations made by Riordan (2018) in relation to the wave of negative emotions that novices often experience at the start of their TP journey. This is even the case when systems are in place to help ease them into their new teacher role, as was the case for our group of novices. However, Riordan's research also found that as TP progressed, a more even balance of emotions was observed, which led to the conclusion that as novices gain in experience, so too do they become more resilient and better equipped to deal with the psychological demands of teaching. The importance of reflective group discussions as a shared venue to explore the psychological impact of TP was a further key finding from Riordan's study, and that guided and collaborative reflection with peers and mentors created key opportunities for shared learning more widely. Evidence to support these arguments can be found in the previous extract and from Extract 5.2 which follows, in terms of both the emotional support and the professional insights that novices can gain from each other, and from mentors and TP supervisors.

Extract 5.2 (Guided Group Discussion 1– PENSER Cycle 1)

ST Caitlin: My TP supervisor said I should not dwell only what went wrong but write down three good things about my lesson, which I've started doing. This is more constructive instead of just beating myself up about it. And it's helped me recognise I have strengths too, which is comforting.

This comment highlights the vital role that dialogic reflection with the TP supervisor can play in helping novices to gain a more objective sense of their first TP and in guiding them towards actions they can take to improve their teacher presence and self-confidence. This is important given that their reflections during the initial weeks of TP showed that many of the group were struggling not only to establish a credible teacher presence but also to engage learners, as the following discussion will highlight.

Problem 2: Poor Learner Engagement

The greatest single concern reported by the group in the first semester of TP was their perceived inability to engage learners, which did little to help their self-esteem, as Extract 5.3 from the initial group discussion in the first PENSER cycle exemplifies.

Extract 5.3 (Guided Group Discussion – PENSER Cycle 1)

1. **ST Shona:** There was this silence when I asked them questions and I could feel that I was losing the class and it made me feel such a failure in their eyes and that they would lose faith in me as a teacher.
2. **ST Caitlin:** Yeah, I know what you mean. They just stared at me when I asked them a question; I felt so embarrassed... I just wanted to disappear.

Their reflections at this stage showed that the group had recognized this as a shared challenge and that they were beginning to open up about how it was impacting on them emotionally; however, as yet there was little evidence of any critical questioning of the factors that might be contributing to this problem, including their own behavior. This brings us to the key role that the teacher educator can play in scaffolding collaborative reflection in the classroom setting, in order to help student teachers move forward from articulating their challenges to rationalizing and generalizing more widely. For instance, in Extract 5.4, we find the teacher educator now beginning to prompt a deeper level of reflection around this issue as she asks the novices to come up with hypotheses as to why the learners were reluctant to respond to their questioning.

Extract 5.4 (Guided Group Discussion – PENSER Cycle 1)

1. **TE:** So, why do you think that the learners were reluctant to engage?
2. **ST Caitlin:** I think they didn't see us as proper teachers.
3. **TE:** Why might that have been?
4. **ST Caitlin:** Because we're more or less the same age and that made me feel awkward.
5. **TE:** What about the learners – how did they feel?
6. **ST Shona:** To be honest, my thoughts were not actually on them.
7. **TE:** Well, let's think about this a bit more. What have you noticed about how they engage in the classes you have observed?
8. **ST Shona:** Well, the students were a lot more vocal than in my class.
9. **TE:** Did they all engage to the same extent?
10. **ST Mary:** From what I saw, some contributed more than others.
11. **TE:** Why might that be?
12. **ST Pauline:** Personality maybe.
13. **ST Mary:** Different cultures I suppose too.
14. **ST Caitlin:** Better English maybe... this would affect their confidence, wouldn't it?
15. **TE:** So, how important is it for teachers to know about their learners?

16. **ST Shona:** Well, if we know what makes them tick, we can factor this into our teaching.

These exchanges underscore the benefits of guided collaborative reflection, which in the case of our group of novices, seems to bring an awakening sense of awareness of the need to understand their learners. This was achieved by probing questioning and encouraging them to reflect on their classroom observations. Interestingly, the previous comment also provides us with a sense that one of the novices is beginning to embrace her new teacher identity, as indicated by her repeated use of *we* which signals that she is positioning herself as a member of the teaching community. It also suggests that she has appropriated the challenge and is beginning to take responsibility for the issues in question. From this, the teacher educator skillfully moves the novices towards examining their own behavior and accepting that the challenge they have identified needs further investigation and understanding if it is to be resolved, as in Extract 5.5.

Extract 5.5 (Guided Group Discussion – PENSER Cycle 1)

1. **TE:** And what about your own behaviour as teachers? For instance, could we think about the questions you asked and how you went about this?
2. **ST Shona:** Well, they might have felt they were being put on the spot.
3. **ST Caitlin:** I might have come across as a bit too direct.
4. **TE:** So, do you feel that the problem may have something to do with the way teacher questions are being framed?
5. **ST Mary:** Probably.
6. **TE:** And so, what does this mean for you as teachers?
7. **ST Darragh:** Well, that we need to learn how to do it better (laughs).

Problem 3: Managing Learners

A further challenge raised in the initial guided group discussions in the first PENSER cycle related to behavior management. Extract 5.6 illustrates the types of struggles that some of the group were experiencing in establishing good control of the class, which they reported as a problem that was most acute with one EFL group.

Extract 5.6 (Guided Group Discussion 1 – PENSER Cycle 1)

1. **ST Joanna:** It's funny, I don't have any problems with the intermediate students, I mean they're nice and listen respectfully when I speak, but I'm finding it much harder to manage the advanced students because they just

ignore me or cut across me when I'm speaking, and a few are really dominant and take over.

2. **ST Laura:** Yeah, I agree, I sometimes feel like I'm going into battle when I teach them.

Having identified that managing the behavior of some of the EFL learners was a shared concern that needed to be addressed, the group was encouraged to reflect in their online TP portfolios on personal practice in order to gain a deeper understanding of the issues involved. In Extract 5.7, which was written the following week, we find that one of the novices is now questioning whether her own sense of insecurity about teaching might be impacting negatively on the behavior of the learners in question.

Extract 5.7 (Online TP Portfolio – PENSER Cycle 1)

ST Jean: I definitely feel less confident when I teach one group, so I think this probably affects the whole classroom atmosphere and makes them more bolshie and less willing to learn what I'm trying to teach them. Then I feel even less confident because I know they're not paying attention to me. So, I need to learn why this is happening and how to deal with it.

Extract 5.8 reflects a similar realization by another novice and that she is now moving towards generalizing the problem rather than seeing it as a personal failing.

Extract 5.8 (Online TP Portfolio – PENSER Cycle 1)

ST Mairead: I feel a bit intimidated by them because they seem so confident, even arrogant and I think they know I'm struggling. But it's something that I have to deal with, and I want to get better at reading the class and getting on with them.

These extracts provide evidence of progress in the reflective thinking of the novices as they were now moving towards embracing and investigating the problem.

In the second guided group discussion which took place a few weeks later, opportunities were created for the group to explore transcripts of lessons taught by experienced teachers to raise awareness of issues and strategies relating to teacher-learner relationships and role/s. From this, they moved on to the 'noticing' and 'research' stages of the PENSER cycle when they developed action plans involving tasks and activities they could engage in to strengthen their teacher presence and CM practices and to improve their rapport with learners. In Extract 5.9, from the third, and final, guided group discussion in the cycle, we note a growing sense of student teacher awareness and self-efficacy in these areas.

Extract 5.9 (Guided Group Discussion 3 – PENSER Cycle 1)

1. **TE:** So, what were your observations?
2. **ST Mary:** I've noticed that the experienced teachers looked like they were in control all the time but in a nice way. I mean, they did little things to relax the class like starting with small talk, you know, telling them what they did at the weekend themselves before questioning the students. And they gave them a chance to talk in pairs rather than expecting them to answer on the spot. So, it all seemed to flow seamlessly, but they were there going around the class keeping it going and focused.
3. **ST Sarah:** That's good to know and it's something I would like to try.
4. **ST Caitlin:** So, from my discussion with the class teacher I've learned that it's a completely new learning environment for some of them. I mean, the Chinese learners are just not used to giving their opinions so publicly and they don't like making mistakes in front of the class because it's shameful in their culture. So, I would be much more understanding than I was before and not take it to heart so much if they didn't answer.

Their written reflections at this stage also point to a growing interest in the cultural backgrounds of their learners more widely, which is further evidence that their focus is now moving towards a desire to get to know and better understand those they teach rather than being intimidated by them, as in Extracts 5.10 and 5.11.

Extract 5.10 (Online TP Portfolio – PENSER Cycle 1)

ST Darragh: There are so many different cultures and I've noticed that the German students are definitely more confident, and the Italians and Spanish are louder and more fun-loving, and they don't seem to get embarrassed when they make mistakes like the Japanese students, who need more encouragement (laughs).

Extract 5.11 (Online TP Portfolio – PENSER Cycle 1)

ST Joanna: I think that I've probably been too self-absorbed going into TP and not given enough thought to the learners and why they are here. I am much more aware of their problems and less nervous about teaching them and I will definitely try to make them feel more confident and encourage them more.

These extracts also provide evidence that the novices were becoming more emotionally aware and supportive teachers, and this is further reflected in Extract 5.12 from the dyadic exit discussions with mentors at the end of the first PENSER cycle, where we also find indications that the student teachers were becoming more confident in their ability to manage different learner groups.

Extract 5.12 (Dyadic Exit Interviews – PENSER Cycle 1)

1. **ST Caitlin:** I've realised that there are lots of things that teachers can do to make sure this type of behaviour doesn't happen in the first place, or to regain charge of the classroom. And every teaching context is different.
2. **ST Sarah:** Teachers need to really control who is sitting next to who, how much time students get to speak, while classes need less control of this kind. And teachers sometimes need to take troublesome students aside even when they are adults and tell them that their behaviour isn't acceptable if it is bothering other students and poisoning the atmosphere because they mightn't even be aware that they're doing this, but they can.

At this stage, one member of the group announces her intention to undertake research in the area of learner motivation as the topic for her MA dissertation, as in Extract 5.13. Her comment confirms that her attention is now directed towards learners and their needs, and it also reveals the type of supportive teacher that she is keen to become, as well as the insights she is developing as to how she can achieve this. This extract is further indicative of the ways in which student teachers' engagement in guided reflective thinking around specific issues and challenges can enable them to make important links between action research and improvements in their own teaching.

Extract 5.13 (Dyadic Exit Discussion – PENSER Cycle 1)

1. **TE:** What have you learned that you can carry forward?
2. **ST Pauline:** I've decided to research student engagement as the theme for my MA dissertation because I now know how important it is to have the right mental attitude and go into each lesson in an upbeat mood to set the right tone and make the lesson more enjoyable and engaging for everyone, and, I think that going forward, I would also openly discuss issues around dignity and respect to promote inclusive and holistic education, which we have been learning about, but I would do it in way that wasn't preachy or going to get their backs up.

Having provided a snapshot of the main issues of concern which arose for the novices in the first PENSER cycle in the areas of classroom management, learner engagement, and teacher-learner relationships, and the processes by which they were addressed, we turn next to problems that became more salient in their reflections in the second PENSER cycle, which related more to the management of teaching aids and resources in the EFL learning environment. As previously, we will pause at this point for your own personal reflections concerning this aspect of teaching.

Pause for Reflection

1. How much prior knowledge do you have of EFL teaching resources?
2. What criteria do you use to select and integrate suitable resources?
3. How would you rate your own technological skills for teaching purposes, and has this changed over time?

Problem 4: Managing Resources

We meet the group next as they are reporting back to their peers on the feedback they received from their TP supervisors concerning different aspects of their teaching. As Extract 5.14 illustrates, two of the group have been made aware of issues relating to their use of the whiteboard and PowerPoint slides, both of which are tools that teachers would be expected to routinely integrate into their teaching in order to support the learning process.

Extract 5.14 (Guided Group Discussion 1 – PENSER Cycle 2)

1. **ST Joanna:** My TP supervisor told me I should be using the whiteboard more to highlight key content for learners and that I should do this while drawing their attention to what I am writing so it should be more of a student-focused activity.
2. **ST Jean:** I've used the whiteboard, but I was told I was writing too much because I literally wrote everything, they (the learners) contributed, which took me ages and my writing was all over the place because I was writing so fast. It looks so easy when you're sitting at the back observing, but it's actually not.
3. **ST Joanna:** I was told to actually plan what I was going to write, which would help me to keep to the point, and that way the lesson would be better focused, which actually makes a lot of sense.
4. **ST Jean:** Yeah, and I am relying too much on slides too and it's stopping me developing teaching skills like giving instructions and explaining language points. I don't really feel comfortable giving instructions, so maybe I was subconsciously avoiding it because I didn't feel I had the authority.

Interestingly, in their comments, we find a willingness on the part of the two novices involved to share both the criticisms they have experienced as well as the new insights they have gained. This suggests they were developing a capacity for introspection and self-evaluation, which is important for teacher identity formation and professional growth (Riordan, 2018). In Extracts 5.15 and 5.16, we see further evidence of a growing sense of teacher self-efficacy within the group, as the novices go on to exchange further tips and strategies with each other in relation to the use of both traditional teaching aids and more recently available, digital teaching resources, including PCs and mobile phones.

Extract 5.15 (Guided Group Discussion 1 – PENSER Cycle 2)

1. **ST Darragh:** In some classrooms, the slides are projected on the whiteboard so you can't use the board at the same time, which is a big drawback for teaching because we need to be able to write new words and highlight pronunciation on the board in every lesson. We actually decided to bring in a small, portable board, so it wasn't ideal but at least we could still write up the key information for the students.
2. **ST Pauline:** I don't like using the PC for listening activities because the links don't always open first time and you can lose a lot of time waiting. Some of the classrooms have CD players on the desks so I try to use them instead and have it cued so there's no timewasting.

As far as digital technologies are concerned, a number of concerns were expressed by the group in relation to how best to manage the use of mobile phones by learners, as the following exchange illustrates.

Extract 5.16 (Guided Group Discussion 1 – PENSER Cycle 2)

1. **ST Caitlin:** I find they're (the learners) on their mobiles a lot during the lesson. It's hard to tell if they're actually working or just checking their messages. It's awkward because we can't really police it, can we?
2. **ST Shona:** Sometimes they use them to get the course book online, so they don't have to buy it.
3. **ST Pauline:** Have you noticed them taking snapshots of the board and the slides rather than writing it down?
4. **ST Jean:** Yeah, but I do that too, don't you?
5. **ST Caitlin:** Really? That's not good because I remember reading somewhere that physically writing it down helps to reinforce it in your mind.

This is an interesting exchange because it reveals that the novices were exploring the possible causes of the problem and its wider implications without the guidance of the teacher educator, drawing on their own learning experiences to try to make sense of the issue. As indicated, this led them to question how far their authority extended as teachers. Extract 5.17 provides further evidence that their reflections on such matters have now become more mature and considered.

Extract 5.17 (Guided Group Discussion 1 – PENSER Cycle 2)

1. **ST Caitlin:** And I wonder if looking down at their screens all the time is getting in the way of them talking to each other and developing fluency.
2. **ST Mary:** My students were looking up the meanings of all the new vocabulary on Google Translate, which made me feel a bit redundant when I was trying to concept check words which is what we're supposed to do but they were learning from it.
3. **ST Sarah:** It could be a good thing if they are using apps to become more independent learners but I'm not sure how accurate the translations are especially if the words have different meanings?
4. **ST Darragh:** And I think it could stop them working it out together, which is what we want to encourage as it gets them talking and interacting more.

As the discussion developed, they went on to explore the adequacy of their own knowledge and skills in this area as teachers, as in Extract 5.18, which is indicative of a growing ability on their part to evaluate their own professional needs going forward.

Extract 5.18 (Guided Group Discussion 1 – PENSER Cycle 2)

1. **ST Sarah:** To be honest, I feel I could be doing a lot more with technology as I've only got the hang of a few apps at this stage.
2. **ST Caitlin:** Yeah, I know what you mean, there's so much out there to keep up with but it would be good to know more about the different technologies we can use as they come onto the market, you know, for the future.

In this case, they were acknowledging their need for greater guidance and practical training in this area as an essential element of their ongoing professional development. This marked their move to the next stages of the PENSER process, which involved awareness-raising activities and targeted action research in relation to the problem.

In their written reflections in their online TP portfolios over the course of the following weeks, they were encouraged to continue to explore this theme, reflecting on their classroom observations and noting any examples of good practice they had seen relating to the use of different online tools and platforms, as Extracts 5.19 to 5.21 illustrate.

Extract 5.19 (Online TP Portfolio – PENSER Cycle 2)

ST Pauline: I liked the way the class teacher told the students about Duolinguo and got the students to practise it for minimal pairs. It showed me how it could be used to improve pronunciation.

Extract 5.20 (Online TP Portfolio – PENSER Cycle 2)

ST Mairead: In my last observation, the class teacher got them to use Menti at the start of the lesson to revise vocabulary, which worked really well, and they did it in pairs which made it more communicative. I think it was really fun and motivating.

Extract 5.21 (Online TP Portfolio – PENSER Cycle 2)

ST Mary: I'm someone who needs to see it done to get a real understanding of how it works rather than just hearing about it and I feel more confident about using it then. So, it was really good to observe the class teacher when he got the learners to use mobile phone applications at different points in the lesson to do language tasks instead of just using the course book. It showed me how I could do this to supplement it (the course book) in the future.

Spiro (2013) has stressed the importance of teachers being offered regular opportunities to upskill technologically and to discuss the pedagogical implications of the rapid advances being made in computer and mobile phone assisted language learning for their own teaching. To build on the progress made, the group went on to develop a targeted technology-oriented action plan that they could implement over the following two weeks. As a useful starting point, they devised an online survey in order to gauge the existing technological knowledge and skills within the group with a view to sharing them, and they then committed to actively exploring some of the pedagogical considerations around the use of different online tools and platforms through experimentation in their upcoming lessons. As a further awareness-raising strategy, they were directed by the teacher educator in question to the related research literature in SLA to find out more about recent trends in computer and mobile phone assisted language learning and to report back with their findings in the final group discussions. They were also asked to demonstrate a new language learning tool or application that they had discovered and used in their teaching for peer evaluation.

As Extracts 5.22 to 5.24 exemplify, there was a clear sense from their related written reflections that the group were actively seeking out solutions and developing practical insights to share with each other. There was evidence too that they were gaining a deeper understanding of pedagogical considerations surrounding the use of the various technologies they observed being integrated into lessons by experienced class teachers and learnt about from follow-up discussions with mentors, TP supervisors, and peers. This once again highlights the benefits of targeted observation, mentoring, and peer teaching within a supportive community of practice (CoP).

Extract 5.22 (Online TP Portfolio – PENSER Cycle 2)

ST Shona: I really focused in the observations on how much technology was being used. I noticed the parts of the lesson where it was being used, too. So, in the classes I observed, the teachers all used the PC and slides, but usually only a few, and only when they were focusing on language points rather than to give instructions. When I asked them afterwards about this, they said that it was important to give instructions orally to help learners develop their listening skills but that this would depend on the level as weaker students might need a few written cues as support. This is a good tip I'm going to pass on to the others.

Extract 5.23 (Online TP Portfolio – PENSER Cycle 2)

ST Jean: I read some articles about how mobile phones can be used to enhance language learning, so the short answer is that they shouldn't just be used randomly, and teachers really have to think about how they are going to integrate them. So, I've learned that it's ok for students to use them to check meanings but they should be encouraged to try to work them out first together from the context. Why is this important? Several reasons. It leads to higher levels of interaction and target language use and because it improves their vocabulary learning as they process the meanings more deeply. I discussed this with my teaching partner, and we feel more confident about how we can use mobile phone apps like Menti to teach vocabulary.

Extract 5.24 (Online TP Portfolio – PENSER Cycle 2)

ST Mary: I went to a great workshop about new mobile phone apps that was run by one of the EFL publishers. We tried out five different apps that have been designed for different areas of language work and age groups. Some were for vocabulary and pronunciation and others for practising reading and speaking skills. I'm going to try using some of them over the next few weeks. I also told the other students about them and offered to show them how they work once I've got the hang of them myself.

The benefits of active and collaborative learning were once again evident in the final group discussions in the second reflective cycle, when the group were asked to discuss their progress and to come up with a set of principles that could serve to guide them in their selection, use, and management of materials and resources, including online tasks and mobile phone applications, as Extract 5.25 illustrates.

Extract 5.25 (Group Discussion 3 – PENSER Cycle 2)

1. **ST Caitlin:** I feel I now definitely have a better understanding of the benefits of using a course book and how my lessons are part of a programme of study. So, they need to follow on logically and I have also learned how I can adapt the book content and integrate other materials.
2. **ST Mary:** Yeah, knowing what is suitable for different groups is vital and this applies to on-line tasks and activities as we should think about how much preparation learners need and how we can mediate the tasks and follow up.
3. **ST Darragh:** To me, making sure we plan for how we are going to integrate technology is really important and we need to ensure that learners understand the purpose of what they are doing and how they can benefit to keep them motivated.

Further evidence of their newfound insights in this area can be seen in their dyadic discussions with mentors at the end of the second reflective cycle. At this stage, the student teachers' proposed solutions to the challenges they had identified were critically evaluated to determine if they had been appropriately addressed, or whether further engagement was needed. Extracts 5.26 and 5.27 illustrate the fruitful outcomes that were achieved in relation to the range of concerns raised in this area.

Extract 5.26 (Dyadic Exit Discussion – PENSER Cycle 2)

ST Shona: I'm now much more aware of the criteria that teachers can use to evaluate them. Also, by using the course book I can see good models of how tasks are designed, and I have a growing understanding of how texts can be exploited for pedagogical purposes. Teachers are also expected to be familiar with different course books which is not something that I fully appreciated before. So, this is all adding to my professional knowledge.

Extract 5.27 (Dyadic Exit Discussion – PENSER Cycle 2)

ST Pauline: I've learned that teachers can integrate so many different types of technology in the language classroom so it's a really exciting time. However, we need to be able to evaluate the potential benefits and understand how to manage the various on-line tasks and activities as well as keeping up to date as technology is evolving all the time so we can't afford to be complacent.

These extracts underscore the benefits of guided reflective practice that encourages novices to make important links between action research and classroom practice in order to enhance their knowledge base and skills. Informed by the previous empirical account of the challenges that emerged for the novices as they assumed their classroom teacher role, and with their reflective observations and discussions in mind, we now invite readers to engage with the reflective task set out below which has related classroom-based issues as its theme.

Pause for Reflection

Select one of the classroom-based challenges that was discussed in this chapter that you can relate to as a teacher, and reflect on:

1. the possible causes in your own teaching and learning context
2. the impact of the problem on your own teaching
3. an action plan that you can develop to help you to address the problem going forward.

SUMMARY

This chapter has focused on the issues and challenges that novice teachers of EFL can expect to encounter in the early days of teaching as they grapple with the complexities involved in classroom teaching with different learner groups, as evidenced by the empirical findings from the PENSER research. The reflective data has confirmed that it is not uncommon for novices to struggle with both the emotional and practical demands of teaching, in particular achieving a correct balance between the need to assume the authority required to establish good teacher presence and classroom management, and the need to establish a positive and engaging learning environment. So too do many feel daunted by the need to address a wide range of practical considerations and challenges around identifying and responding to the differentiated needs of L2 learners, and the use and integration of suitable materials and resources in this teaching and learning context. By drawing on the PENSER reflective data, it has been possible to trace the changes that took place in the cognition, perspectives, and practices of our group of novices in relation to these challenges as they progressed through their first weeks and months of TP, and it has also highlighted the key role that individual and collaborative reflection played in supporting their professional development in these areas. In Chapter 6, we explore some of the uncertainties and concerns that arose for the group as they became more aware of their language teacher role, and expectations and requirements concerning the teaching of grammar, vocabulary, and pronunciation in the EFL classroom context.

Chapter 6

Reflecting on Teaching Grammar, Vocabulary, and Pronunciation

INTRODUCTION

In this chapter, we will trace the professional development of three of our student teachers as they endeavored to become more confident and expert language teachers focusing in particular on issues relating to the teaching of grammar, vocabulary, and pronunciation. As a starting point, it is useful for readers to reflect on their own confidence and expertise in relation to the teaching of the language content of the EFL lesson in the early days of TP.

Pause for Reflection

Reflect on your own prior, formal learning of English before you became a teacher.

1. To what extent were you familiar with the metalanguage and systems used to classify English for EFL teaching purposes?
2. Did you fear that learners might know more than you did and was this actually the case?

The case study approach used in this chapter will enable us to gain an in-depth understanding of the key difficulties that arose for the three novices whose experiences are explored, the methods by which they were addressed, and the outcomes achieved in each case. The choice of this approach here was influenced by its successful use previously by Bogdan & Biklen (1982), Farrell & Lim (2005), and Farr & Farrell (2017) in research which explored the professional growth of novices in the RP field. It should be noted also that the challenges around which the discussion in this chapter is framed, are representative of those experienced by the group as a whole and by novice EFL teachers more widely, as the review of the literature in this chapter will establish. Table 6.1 sets out the specific difficulties that arose in the PENSER reflective data in relation to the teaching of the three core elements of the EFL syllabus over the course of TP. Given the complexities involved, it was not surprising that this was a persistent theme in all three reflective cycles, but interestingly, it was most salient in the second cycle, for reasons which will be explored.

Table 6.1. Challenges and specific issues relating to teaching grammar, vocabulary, and pronunciation.

Main Area of Challenge	Specific Issues
Teaching Grammar, Vocabulary, and Pronunciation	• Lack of language awareness and knowledge • Unsuitable level of input • Poor explanations of language points • Overly didactic teaching approach • Lack of confidence teaching grammar • Fear of teaching pronunciation

As previously, we will begin with a review of the academic literature from the fields of applied linguistics, SLA, and TESOL with a focus on the teaching of L2 grammar, lexis, and pronunciation, which will serve to contextualize the PENSER reflective findings and help us to establish their significance.

TEACHING L2 GRAMMAR

There has probably been more academic discussion about the teaching of grammar in the L2 context than any other aspect of second or foreign language pedagogy, and yet many key questions remain unresolved, including the best pedagogical approach to take (Andrews, 2007). For instance, the debate continues as to whether it should be taught deductively or inductively, and the benefits and challenges in each case. The deductive approach is based on the premise that learners should be taught explicit knowledge of grammar, which means learning the rules that govern the use of the language, being able to compare and contrast the language system of English with that of their mother tongue using the appropriate metalanguage, and being assessed on the basis of their ability to produce the language accurately and 'correctly' (Ellis, 2002). Deductive teaching approaches have therefore been associated historically with prescriptive rules and norms and restricted versions of the language being taught. Such approaches were employed until about 50 years ago when inductive approaches to grammar teaching emerged, in line with the shift from deductive to inductive teaching more widely (Ellis, 2002).

Those favoring inductive approaches to grammar teaching have argued that while it is important for L2 learners to know the rules of the target language, such rules can be acquired by learners if they are exposed to the appropriate input. This leads to the view that the teaching of grammar should be implicit rather than explicit: that is, without overt reference to metalanguage or comparisons being made between the foreign language and the mother tongue, and with minimal explanations. This more natural way of language learning is influenced by theories of first language acquisition and has been associated with teaching methodologies such as Audiolingualism (AL), Communicative Language Teaching (CLT), and Task-Based Teaching and Learning (TBTL) although classroom practices differ in each of these methodologies (Howatt & Widdowson, 2004; Spiro, 2013).

One major area of confusion that has arisen concerns the place of formal grammar teaching in the CLT classroom wherein the emphasis is placed on developing the communicative competence of learners by means of exposure to authentic types of interaction and language use. Despite the widespread adoption of this approach, the extent to which grammar is taught either explicitly or implicitly in different contexts and settings is difficult to ascertain, and it is believed that in some, language teaching is still based on traditional grammatical analysis, the explicit learning of rules, and simplified explanations drawn from prescriptive grammar books which have not corresponded with the real language use (Carter & McCarthy, 2006). While the question remains as to whether grammar can be taught or whether teachers can only facilitate its learning, there is a general consensus amongst applied linguists and an expectation by learners and employers that language lessons will involve some teaching of grammar and that teachers will play a role in the learning process.

A second area of difficulty in the context of the teaching of grammar relates to the nature of the forms that learners are exposed to, and expected to learn, as part of the content of the lesson. One of the most important achievements of corpus linguistics is that it has led to revised pedagogical descriptions of grammar, which have changed the priorities set for the teaching of some grammatical structures, the range of meanings associated with particular forms, and the contexts in which they are presented. Corpus-informed grammars (see Biber et al., 1999; Carter & McCarthy, 2006) and course books which reflect real patterns of spoken and written English use have now become widely available. The development of learner corpora has also led to changes in the design and content of language courses, syllabuses, and examinations (Murphy & Riordan, 2016). This has brought spoken grammar to the forefront of language teaching, highlighting its role as a valuable classroom resource (Friginal, 2018; O'Keeffe & Farr, 2003; Reppen, 2010). However, corpus linguistics has also revealed the fragmentary nature, dysfluencies, and vagueness which typically arise in native speaker casual speech, by comparison with the more coherent structuring and precision used by speakers in more formal registers, which has brought new challenges in terms of the extent to which learners can and should be exposed to authentic spoken English, and how best this can be mediated (A. Farrell, 2019; Prodromou, 2008).

In addition to revolutionizing how spoken grammar is viewed and classified by comparison with written grammar, corpus linguistics has also brought new pedagogical perspectives on standard English which recognize diversity and variability (Biber et al., 1999; Carter & McCarthy, 2006). This signals a shift away from the rigid standard/non-standard dichotomy of the past to a more finely-nuanced approach which recognizes degrees of 'standardness' and formality associated with different types of written and spoken English. These developments are offering exciting opportunities in terms of the range of grammar that learners are exposed to, and formally learn, in the EFL classroom. However, they have also brought new dilemmas for teachers by bringing the tensions between what we know about language and the types of English we teach into sharper focus, as many have observed (see, for instance, Timmis, 2002).

Applied linguists have increasingly pointed to the complex sets of questions and dilemmas that EFL teachers must now address if they are to achieve a balanced approach wherein the input they provide for learners is both accessible and of practical value. Prodromou (2008), for instance, has stressed the importance of taking account of the proficiency level of learners when introducing naturally-occurring English into the classroom, given its complex nature, and the need to provide contextual cues to enable learners to determine the discourse and pragmatic dimensions of speech. Carter & McCarthy (1997: 154) have advised teachers to be mindful of the values that set the parameters for acceptable language use in educational and professional contexts, but to expose learners to natural spoken data wherever possible to raise awareness of real language use, all the while making them aware of sensitivities surrounding different types of spoken English. Timmis (2002: 243) has cautioned that practitioners should not ignore learners' preferences to be taught the types of English that feature in English language examinations which still mainly reflect SBE/SAE (Standard British/American English); and to this, Kramsch (1998) has added the need to give learners the opportunity to explore the cultural dimensions underlying different types of expression to help them develop intercultural sensitivities. This suggests a more complex pedagogical role for EFL teachers and learners than for their predecessors, with practitioners now required to carefully select and skillfully mediate a wider range of language content than was previously considered necessary.

The difficulties experienced by novice EFL teachers from native speaker backgrounds in relation to the actual teaching of grammar have been well-documented in the academic literature pertaining to the native/non-native English debate and research paradigm (Macaro, 2005; Medgyes, 1992, 1994; Nicaise, 2021). For instance, they typically struggle to offer good explanations of grammatical points, tend to focus more on communicative message rather than form, and ignore errors (Andrews, 2007). This has been linked to a lack of formal linguistic knowledge of English, with the teaching of grammar no longer part of the secondary school curriculum in most English-speaking countries (A. Farrell, 2019), and it contrasts markedly with the educational experiences of non-native English speaker teachers who have typically studied English grammar over many years and have a superior formal knowledge of the workings of the language as a result (Medgyes, 1994). It is also the case that most EFL teachers are unfamiliar with the mother tongue of those they teach or have only a superficial knowledge of the language and culture, the learning of foreign languages tending not be prioritized as a result of the dominance of English internationally (Graddol, 2006). As a result, they can find it more difficult to understand the linguistic and cultural challenges faced by learners, and so lack the ability to be able to scaffold them effectively, and to offer empathy. Problems of this kind can be exacerbated where novices are unfamiliar with the metalanguage used to formally describe the language systems of English and where there is a limited level of language awareness, which is often the case for those from non-language study backgrounds (Andrews, 2007), all of which can diminish their confidence in their language teacher role and thwart their ability to teach grammar and other areas of the language curriculum (A. Farrell, 2019; Walsh, 2011). We find evidence of these types of challenges in the three case studies that are presented next, following an initial account of the background of the novice in each case, and with pseudonyms used to protect the identity of those involved.

Case Study 1: Shona

Shona was a 22-year-old woman who had come to the MA program directly from an undergraduate university program, with a degree in Irish and History. She had grown up in the local community and worked part-time in a call center. She was keen to start a career as an English language teacher in the United Arab Emirates where many of her friends were employed in private schools. Like many of her counterparts on the MA program, she struggled with her confidence as a teacher, particularly in the area of grammar teaching. She initially attributed this to underestimating the complexities involved and was unhappy that she had not made sufficient progress despite her growing knowledge of English grammar.

We meet Shona in the initial teacher educator-guided discussion with peers in the second PENSER reflective cycle, where she describes the difficulties she has been experiencing teaching grammar to intermediate level EFL learners as part of the TP module, as she perceives it. By this stage, Shona and her peers are in the second semester of TP. Before we proceed, we would encourage you to reflect on your own challenges in this area of teaching and how you overcame them.

Pause for Reflection

1. To what extent have you struggled with the teaching of grammar?
2. What strategies have you used to develop expertise in this area?

Extract 6.1 (Guided Group Discussion 1 – PENSER Cycle 2)

ST Shona: Even though I spend a lot of time preparing my lessons I don't feel confident teaching grammar. I especially dread being asked questions about rules because I find it difficult to explain on the spot. I know that the students expect me to be able to give them good explanations and feel I am letting them down. I've been told by my TP supervisor that I should be guiding them (the learners) more so they can work things out for themselves which I get but I prefer to do it this way. I don't feel I can move on to teach the higher levels until I improve a lot more.

From this account, it is clear that Shona was experiencing several related problems, and that they were impacting negatively on her professional confidence and growth. Firstly, although Shona was a conscientious and hardworking student in terms of the efforts she was making in lesson planning and preparation, she continued to lack confidence in her ability to teach grammar effectively, which she felt was undermining her professionalism in the eyes of the learners. This feeling of inadequacy is not unusual amongst novices in the early teaching days when they are grappling with the complexities of teaching grammar and have yet to develop the required knowledge and expertise. In Shona's case, this sense of insecurity was exacerbated by a recommendation made by a TP supervisor that she should try to move away from the overly didactic approach she was using to teach grammar towards a more student-centered type of teaching, whereby the learners would be encouraged to explore and notice patterns of usage under her guidance. This had created a conflict for Shona, as her comment suggests, as she firmly believed that it was her duty as a teacher to use the more traditional approach and that she would be failing in her responsibility as a teacher if she moved away it.

Accordingly, although Shona was aware that a less direct, student-centered approach to teaching grammar would better align with the philosophy and goals promoted in the CLT classroom, she felt more comfortable and confident using a didactic approach. Previous studies of grammar teaching in the TESOL field have reported that it is not unusual for teachers to feel a powerful emotional attachment to direct grammar teaching even when they express enthusiasm on the surface for indirect methods (Farrell & Lim, 2005; Richards & Rodgers, 2001). This stems from several factors, not least their own prior educational experiences, which are likely to have shaped their beliefs about teaching and learning, and from this, their classroom practices (Borg, 2003). Within applied linguistics and L2 teacher education circles, this realization has led to calls for teachers to be given opportunities to explore their belief systems, which may be either tacitly or overtly held, as well as the underlying influences that shape them such as prior experiences, school practices, and individual personality (Kagan, 1990). This is vital given the widespread acknowledgment that these beliefs often serve to act as a filter through which instructional judgments and decisions are made (Farrell & Lim, 2005; Shavelson & Stern, 1981).

To enable Shona to begin to develop an understanding of the causes of the difficulties she was experiencing, and their relationship to her own prior learning, and her beliefs, she was asked by the teacher educator to hypothesize why she believed she was struggling with this area of pedagogy. Interestingly, at this stage, it was a peer who suggested that the answer might lie in Shona's prior experience of learning languages at secondary school where deductive teaching was likely to have been the norm.

Extract 6.2 (Guided Group Discussion 1 – PENSER Cycle 2)

1. **TE:** So, what do you think might be some possible causes for this problem?
2. **ST Mary:** It could be because of how we learned languages in secondary school. I mean, the teachers did all the work and we just wrote it all down and were expected to learn it off by heart.

Following this exchange, the group were asked to explore this hypothesis further in their written reflections in their online TP portfolios over the following weeks. Extract 6.3 highlights Shona's later questioning of her own prior experience of learning Irish grammar and how this might have shaped her beliefs about how grammar should be taught.

Extract 6.3 (Online TP Portfolio – PENSER Cycle 2)

ST Shona: I found it quite illuminating to look back at the way I was taught languages at school. I studied Irish at school and at university and it was my best subject. It's true to say that the way we were taught was completely different. We used to spend a lot of time studying the rules, which are quite complicated in Irish, and the teacher usually went through them. I can't remember being asked to work anything out with a partner or even to really discuss what we were being taught. We were tested though, quite often, on the grammar. So, I suppose I'm more used to this way of teaching. And because I did well at Irish in my exams it may have given me the impression that this was a good way to learn, even though it could be boring.

This suggests that she was starting to engage in the process of meaning-making in relation to this aspect of classroom pedagogy. In the second guided group discussion, which took place the following week, Shona had moved on to exploring why she felt reluctant to move away from a traditional teaching approach, of which she had become more aware.

Extract 6.4 (Guided Group Discussion 2 – PENSER Cycle 2)

ST Shona: I think I feel more in control when I'm giving the explanations and it's probably a way of avoiding questions because I could be asked anything and not be able to answer. But I suppose we all feel like that because we can't know everything and that's a scary thing to admit.

This is an open and frank disclosure. It reflects a developing sense of awareness on Shona's part that her insecurities are linked to her novice status, and with this, an appreciation of the vulnerability that all novices are likely to feel in the early days of teaching when their knowledge of grammar is as yet inadequate to be able to deal with all eventualities. Shona now recognizes and accepts that this vulnerability is an inherent part of the TP journey. From this new insight and acceptance, she is able to move towards generalizing the problem and developing a deeper understanding of its relationship with, and connections to, other experiences and ideas.

In the following weeks, Shona and her peers committed to actively embracing the reflective process with the intention of changing and improving their teaching practice in the future. From articulating and embracing the problem, this led them to the noticing, solving, and experimentation and research stages of the PENSER process.

During the 'noticing' phase, a series of awareness-raising activities were carried out by all of the novices to facilitate a better understanding of the challenges that had previously been identified in relation to the teaching of grammar. These involved classroom observations of experienced teachers followed by mentor-novice discussions which focused on the practices observed. These observations also provided the focus of novices' reflective writing in their online TP portfolios over subsequent weeks of the cycle. In the following extract, we note the crucial role played by the experienced teacher and TP supervisor as mentors at the 'noticing' stage of the process as they provided opportunities for Shona to question, compare, and rationalize her experiences in order to gain a deeper understanding of how best to develop a more student-centered approach to grammar teaching.

Extract 6.5 (Online TP Portfolio – PENSER Cycle 2)

ST Shona: I've found I've learned a lot about how to teach grammar inductively from doing focused observations of experienced teachers. I wanted to be able to really notice what it means in practice because we've heard so much about it, but it's actually very difficult to do. The first thing I noticed is that this way of teaching grammar creates a very different vibe. The learners are busy working away and chatting to each other and the teacher is moving around monitoring and giving help where needed. There was no sense of the teacher being in the spotlight like when I was teaching but she was still in control of the lesson. When students asked questions, she asked the others to come up with explanations and answers. What surprised me is that they really liked doing this. I forget sometimes that I'm teaching university students and that they're able for a challenge. They also obviously liked the more sociable atmosphere. When I spoke to the class teacher afterwards, she said that she uses the time and space when the students are working things out to work out herself how to bring it all together coherently on the board. This made me realise that there will always be moments in my lesson to gather my thoughts and reorient myself rather than having to be performing every minute. This is important because there will always be unexpected questions or points that need to be explained. So, going forward, I'm going to make an effort to throw it out and challenge the students a lot more. This will be a different way of teaching, but I feel more confident now I've seen how it can be done.

This detailed and mature reflection reveals Shona's commitment to proactively investigating the problem and the pedagogical insight she was developing as a result, all of which seems indicative of a growing student teacher self-efficacy. It also underscores the value of targeted classroom observations and RP for awareness-raising purposes amongst novice teachers, and the important cognitive and affective benefits that this complementary approach can bring.

We can gain a further sense of Shona's progress in resolving the problem she identified some weeks earlier from the dyadic discussion that took place with a TP mentor at the end of the second reflective cycle. As Extract 6.6 illustrates, she was now committed to finding out more about this key aspect of L2 pedagogy, announcing her plans to carry out more action research in this area for her MA dissertation. As she stated, this would involve an investigation of underlying factors influencing the approaches used to teach grammar, and their possible impact. This suggested that Shona was now more fully cognizant of the need to understand why teachers think and behave the way they do in relation to this key aspect of L2 pedagogy, and that she recognized the significance of this knowledge for novices.

Extract 6.6 (Dyadic Exit Discussion – PENSER Cycle 2)

ST Shona: I've had a few ideas about what to research for my MA dissertation and I was thinking of looking at the different factors that influence how we teach grammar because I think it would be very useful for novices to understand more about this when they start TP.

The previous account has highlighted how engagement in the PENSER process provided opportunities for Shona and her peers to develop a deeper understanding of the complexities involved in the teaching of L2 grammar as a starting point to building strategic competence in this area, and it has also underscored the key role that targeted and critically-oriented reflection can play in this process.

Pause for Reflection

1. In what ways did RP help Shona overcome her insecurities in relation to the teaching of grammar?
2. What opportunities do you have to reflect with peers and individually on this aspect of teaching?

In the following section we move on to our second case study which is concerned with challenges that arise in the area of vocabulary teaching, beginning, as previously, with a review of the related academic literature.

TEACHING L2 VOCABULARY

As with grammar, vocabulary teaching and learning is central to the theory and practice of ELT with interest in this area continuing to grow as it becomes more widely viewed as both the main task and the main obstacle in SLA (Carter & Nunan, 2001: 47). In essence, the teaching of vocabulary is concerned with the selection and presentation of words or lexis for learners. It is an area of pedagogy that for much of the 20th century was neglected; however, it has re-emerged since the 1980s as a central factor in language teaching (Johnson & Johnson, 1999: 68). In both earlier 20th-century teaching approaches such as Grammar Translation and the Direct Method, the teaching of vocabulary was largely subordinated to the requirements of grammatical pattern practice (Howatt & Widdowson, 2004). This was also the case for Audiolingualism which emerged in the post-war years when structural linguistic theory was influential in applied linguistic circles (Howatt & Widdowson, 2004). Similarly, in the early days of CLT also, no special priority was given to vocabulary in the new notional-functional syllabus designed by Wilkins that formed the basis of the communicative curriculum (Oxford, 1997). However, in the 1980s parallel developments in discourse analysis and corpus linguistics combined to reassert the importance of vocabulary in L2 language learning (Schmitt & McCarthy, 1997; Willis, 1990).

The application of CL to the EFL classroom has become increasingly significant in terms of its impact on how vocabulary is viewed and taught. From the 1990s, the increasing availability of computerized corpora of English has provided researchers and materials writers with access to powerful tools for vocabulary analysis. From this a growing body of research has emerged in the area of English language description which has revealed previously unavailable information about how words are used in a diverse range of spoken and written contexts, and the types of frequencies and patterns of expression and fixed usage that occur. This has led to an increased specification of the types of formal and informal lexico-grammatical usage on which teachers and learners should focus, with moves towards the development of a 'lexical syllabus.' This has seen a greater emphasis on the teaching of 'lexical chunks' and 'prefabricated phrases' in the more recent EFL course books in order to enhance learner communicative fluency, alongside the development of the Lexical Approach in the 1990s (Willis, 1990) wherein lexical patterns form the organizing principle of the whole syllabus (DeCarrico, 2001). Parallel with these developments, research into vocabulary acquisition in the field of SLA has given greater prominence to issues of learning word units as well as individual words, i.e., describing and accounting for the incremental stages of words, word families, lexico-grammatical phrases, and word networking which learners pass through as they gain greater L2 lexical competence (Schmitt, 2000).

The insights gained from corpus-based research in applied linguistics and SLA have challenged many previously held assumptions about the meanings and usage of words, and they have led to more complex decision-making around the selection and teaching of vocabulary. Word frequency is now a key criterion that is reflected in the priorities set in course books for the introduction of new lexis (see Grabe, 2010; Nation, 2001). Distinctions must also be made between words that are useful for everyday language and spoken contexts and those which are found in more specialized domains and contexts. Learnability and familiarity are further key considerations, as are decisions as to whether students will need access to spoken and/or written language, and whether lexical items need to be in the active/productive vocabulary which is always smaller than in the receptive/passive one. The issue of how much unknown vocabulary learners should be exposed to is also important to ensure that they are sufficiently challenged for learning to occur, but not frustrated or demoralized by lexical input that is inaccessible. Key questions also arise concerning how much naturally-occurring English learners should be introduced to, given the richness of vocabulary, idioms, cultural allusions, metaphorical turns of phrase, and variety of styles found in everyday spoken English, which make it difficult for them to engage with, particularly for those at lower levels of English language proficiency (Prodromou, 2008).

Accordingly, teachers face complex choices and decision-making around the selection of suitable lexis for different learner groups and how best it can be mediated strategically. For instance, there are various types of contextual cues they may need to provide to aid learner comprehension, for which a sophisticated understanding is needed of the complex processes involved in L2 lexical processing. In line with the development of student-centered approaches to teaching, L2 teachers are also expected to be able to skillfully guide learners and help them to develop inferential strategies for dealing with unfamiliar vocabulary to foster learner autonomy. As the English language spreads and becomes increasingly diversified, EFL teachers must also keep abreast of new vocabulary that is constantly being generated, some of which is shared through the cyber and digital world (Nation, 2001). As the previous discussion has highlighted, the teaching of vocabulary poses a number of complex practical challenges and requires a level of language awareness and pedagogical expertise that L2 teachers typically acquire over many years, and which is also continually expanding. It is not surprising therefore that for many novices, this is an area of pedagogy that is fraught with challenge. Before we turn to our second case study, which is concerned with challenges in the area of vocabulary teaching, we pause for reflection.

Pause for Reflection

1. What new words in English have you become aware of recently, and where did you first hear them?
2. How relevant are these words for learners of EFL, and how would you decide this?
3. How would you teach them?

In the following case study, we explore some of the challenges that were experienced by novice teacher Darragh in this area of pedagogy, beginning, once again, with some essential background information.

Case Study 2: Darragh

Darragh was a young man, 26 years of age, from the east coast of Ireland. He had a Bachelor of Arts degree in New Media and English and had previously worked in marketing for a local charitable organization. He had decided to study for an MA in TESOL because he was keen to teach English at a university in Japan where his partner was employed. We meet him in the first group discussion in the second reflective cycle, which coincided with the second semester of TP, as he recounts the difficulties he has been experiencing teaching vocabulary to a group of upper-intermediate level EFL learners. This brings to light a number of inter-related issues, as seen in Extract 6.7.

Extract 6.7 (Guided Group Discussion 1 – Reflective Cycle 2)

1. **TE:** So, how have you been getting on, Darragh?
2. **ST Darragh:** Well, I'm not happy with the way I've been teaching vocabulary. So, in TP I was with the upper-intermediate group and they have amazing vocabulary. So, I find it hard to know what I should be teaching them. I've made the mistake of teaching them words that I thought were really difficult, which they all knew, which was a waste of time and embarrassing for them and me. Then, I find they don't know a simple expression that I would never have guessed they'd find difficult. Also, when they asked me to explain the new expression, I found it really hard to give them the precise meaning and just rambled on, which confused them. I would like to be a lot better at teaching vocabulary because it comes up in each lesson and you have to be able to think on your feet and give good explanations.

While Darragh was cognizant of the central role that vocabulary occupies in the EFL curriculum, he felt he lacked the level of language awareness needed to be able to make discerning judgments about the suitability of different types of lexical input for different learner groups. We see evidence of this when Darragh was asked by the teacher educator to provide examples of the words and expressions that featured in the lesson where the difficulties arose, as in Extract 6.8.

Extract 6.8 (Guided Group Discussion 1 – Reflective Cycle 2)

1. **TE:** So, can you give us some examples of the types of words and expressions that have caused these difficulties?
2. **ST Darragh:** OK, so I didn't think they would know the word 'inoculation', which was coming up in a listening text, so I wrote it up on the board but none of them wrote it down, which made me realise that they knew

them already. Then, later on in the lesson, one of them asked me what the expression 'cosying up' meant, which I had definitely not expected, and I found it really hard to explain. I mean, I know what it means but trying to explain it to them was a different kettle of fish.

This comment prompted the teacher educator to move to a language awareness-raising activity with the group, as in Extract 6.9.

Extract 6.9 (Guided Group Discussion 1 – Reflective Cycle 2)

1. **TE:** I think it would be useful for you all to take a few minutes on your own and write down a definition of this expression. Then let's compare what we've written with a dictionary definition.
   (a few minutes later)
2. **TE:** So, what have we learned from this?
3. **ST Laura:** Well, we all know what it means but it's really hard to define it precisely like in a dictionary because we don't normally have to do this.
4. **TE:** Exactly, so why was this expression more difficult for the learners than the word 'inoculation'?
5. **ST Pauline:** Because 'inoculation' is a Latin-based cognate word so for most of the students, it's the same in their own language.
6. **ST Caitlin:** Plus, 'inoculation' is a well-known medical term.
7. **ST Mary:** And 'cosying up' is idiomatic and not likely to be the same in their language.
8. **TE:** So, are we saying then that the problems that Darragh experienced are likely to be common for all new teachers?
9. **ST Sarah:** I think it would depend on their backgrounds and language awareness.
10. **TE:** So, who might have an advantage here?
11. **ST Sarah:** Well, if they knew other languages, especially the students' L1.
12. **ST Darragh:** So, what it tells me is that we need to have good language awareness to be able to teach vocabulary well.

This guided and targeted awareness-raising activity within a reflective group discussion, helped to move the novices towards the realization that the problem that Darragh has identified has its roots in many different causes, at the heart of which is the teacher's understanding of the nature of the language items being taught and their relationship with the learners' first language. For Darragh, gaining this kind of awareness was a crucial initial step towards developing the knowledge and skills required to help address the problem, which he now understood, as his response indicates. It also suggests that he now saw that the problem he had identified was a shared one within the group and linked to their novice teacher status.

From identifying, articulating, and embracing the problem as an area in need of investigation, Darragh and his peers moved on to the following stages of the PENSER process where they committed to actions that would help them to begin to address it. This led to the group undertaking a series of language awareness-raising activities over the following weeks that were designed to enhance their knowledge of different aspects of vocabulary acquisition. In Extract 6.10, Darragh reflects in his online TP portfolio on what he has learned from this targeted language awareness focus and the implications for his own vocabulary teaching going forward.

Extract 6.10 (**Online TP Portfolio – PENSER Cycle 2**)

ST Darragh: I've come to appreciate that vocabulary and vocabulary teaching involves much more than I had previously thought such as the context of use, whether the meaning conveyed is literal or idiomatic, if it occurs in a collocational pattern, and whether it's being taught actively or passively. And there's also how words are spelt and pronounced which can be very different. What I've found very interesting is that the words I thought were easiest are often the most difficult for learners because they can have several meanings and could feature in lots of different patterns such as phrasal verbs, which learners find very confusing. I need to be much more aware of this when I'm planning my lessons and think about how I can direct my teaching to these areas of difficulty.

This extract reflects a growing sense of self-efficacy and pedagogic purpose. In the dyadic discussion with his TP mentor at the end of the second PENSER cycle, we find a more confident Darragh who was now focusing on developing strategies to improve his vocabulary teaching, as in Extract 6.11.

Extract 6.11 (**Dyadic Exit Discussion – PENSER Cycle 2**)

ST Darragh: What I now try to do is start by asking learners to brainstorm the meaning of any words that come up unexpectedly, and we check it in a dictionary together after they have made their suggestions. They seem to really like this approach because they get to show off their knowledge but leave at the end of the lesson with an accurate definition of the word from a dictionary. I also ask them to use the word as much as possible in the following days. I got this idea from one of the experienced teachers and I think it's a really good way to help them reinforce it, and then in the next lesson I ask them to tell each other where they used it and when. So, it's something that I'm building into my teaching because I think it works really well.

Moving on from Darragh's reflective journey, which related to the teaching of L2 vocabulary, we proceed to our third and final case study which centers on the teaching of L2 pronunciation and the experiences of Mairead, pausing for reflection first.

TEACHING PRONUNCIATION

Pause for Reflection

1. Do you think that novice teachers of EFL often avoid teaching pronunciation, and if so, why might this be?
2. What is your own experience in this regard?
3. How important is the teaching of pronunciation in the EFL learning context?

The ability to teach pronunciation is an essential requirement for EFL teachers. When talking about pronunciation in language learning we mean the production and perception of the significant sounds of a particular language in order to achieve meaning in contexts of language use (Seidlhofer, 2001: 134). In the CLT classroom, *intelligibility* is considered a vital area for learners of English to develop so as to be able to communicate effectively and confidently in the target language. Here, this term can be understood as both the extent to which a speaker is understandable and whether the particular words used by a speaker are successfully decoded (Seidlhofer, 2001: 138). The centrality of pronunciation in SLA is underscored by a body of research which has attributed the communication problems that many students experience to issues relating to pronunciation (see Derwing & Munro, 2005). However, despite widespread recognition of the importance of pronunciation, teachers routinely report it as difficult to teach.

In order to appreciate the types of challenges that learners and teachers face in this area, it is useful to briefly highlight the nature of English language phonology and phonetics as it relates to spoken communication. Phonetics is the scientific study of individual speech sounds, their physiological production and acoustic qualities, unrelated to any one specific language. Phonology, on the other hand, is a field of cognitive study within linguistics which is concerned with the study of sound patterns within a given language or variety of a language, and how they combine to form syllables, words, and phrases. It also considers the relationship between languages from the perspective of the sounds featured, how sound patterns within a language change diachronically or geographically, and how meaning is differentiated through sounds, silences, and patterns. This has indicated that pronunciation in any given language is highly complex, and that it can reflect emotional state and mood as well as being indicative of personal and group identity (Derwing & Munro, 2015). It has also revealed the types of pronunciation differences that can exist between one language and another as well as within varieties of the same language. This suggests that in order to be able to identify and address the challenges that learners from different L1 backgrounds experience in achieving intelligibility in English, EFL teachers must have at least a working knowledge of phonetics and phonology as well as the range of skills and resources needed to effectively teach pronunciation in different contexts and settings.

Before the advent of the Audiolingual approach to L2 teaching in the 1950s, little attention was given in the L2 curriculum to the formal teaching of pronunciation. This was despite the development of Phonetics and Phonology as a sub-field of linguistics from the late 19th century onwards and the subsequent introduction of the International Phonetic Alphabet (IPA) (Howatt & Widdowson, 2004). This represented a first attempt to classify the sounds of those languages with a common Latin base, and it has been regularly updated since. The English Phonemic Chart (EPC) was developed and introduced into the EFL curriculum in the 1950s and 1960s when Audiolingualism was in its heyday. This approach emphasized mechanical-style listen and repeat drills which teachers used to instill 'correct' pronunciation habits and eliminate errors which reflected the widespread acceptance of Behaviorist theory in L2 education at the time. Audiolingualism had stressed the importance of learners acquiring native-like pronunciation with Received Pronunciation promoted as the 'prestige' accent that all were expected to acquire irrespective of the context of learning. Hence, it was this restricted model of pronunciation that featured in EFL classrooms around the world where British English norms were favored, with Standard American English serving as a similar 'prestige' model in those contexts where this variety was preferred (Spiro, 2013). However, with the move towards the CLT approach from the 1980s onwards, pronunciation teaching became somewhat marginalized due to the commonly held belief that learners would acquire whatever skills they needed simply through exposure to the language (Jenkins, 2004). Moreover, in line with its overriding goal of developing communicative competence, the CLT approach brought a new emphasis on intelligibility rather than native-like proficiency although Standard British and American English accents continued to be prioritized in international EFL course books (Spiro, 2013).

Teacher beliefs and practices in relation to the teaching of pronunciation have been influenced by the development of new fields of linguistic enquiry in SLA. For instance, the advent of Contrastive Analysis and Error Analysis in the 1950s and 1960s highlighted the importance of understanding the relationship between the L2 learner's native language and the target language being learnt in order to be able to anticipate areas of either positive or negative transfer and to gain insight into L2 errors (Corder, 1967). From this, there was growing recognition that learner pronunciation and problems in intelligibility could be influenced not only by factors such as phonological 'distance' and phonetic transfer, but also by learner age and motivation, issues pertaining to learner identity, and the quality and quantity of exposure and instruction. Today, for instance, it is widely accepted that some learners may wish to maintain the phonological features of their L1 due to the fact that learner identity is closely bound to L1 accent (Rogerson-Ravell, 2011). A further research area that has had an impact on pronunciation teaching more recently relates to phonetic perception. From this perspective, it is proposed that learner intelligibility can be improved through strategic manipulation of input at both the segmental (individual sounds) and suprasegmental levels (Derwing & Munro, 2015: 14). Therefore, a teacher's ability to identify and prioritize what is necessary, impactful, or useful for increasing a learner's intelligibility in a given context is of paramount importance.

This suggests that teaching pronunciation for intelligibility requires teachers to prioritize the elements to be taught related to the context in which they and the learners find themselves. From this perspective, intelligibility is differentiated from accent in the sense that while an accent can remain, intelligibility can be improved specifically when there is instruction (Derwing & Munro, 2005). The growing phenomenon of English as a Lingua Franca (ELF) has added to the complexities involved in the teaching of pronunciation, as many researchers in the TESOL field have observed (Young & Walsh, 2010), since it has brought new patterns of English language communication worldwide. For instance, most communication in English is now predominantly between non-native speakers and this has led to different levels of tolerance for errors and distinct types of communication breakdown than those that arise in communication between native and non-native speakers of English.

As Derwing & Munro have observed (2015: 46), the development of computer-assisted pronunciation training (CAPT) and classroom technology in more recent times offers the potential for the teaching of pronunciation to regain its rightful place in the EFL classroom. A range of online resources has been developed by course book publishers to enable teachers and learners to use technology to enhance L2 learning both inside and outside the classroom, such as DVDs and software programs. Online applications have also been developed for L2 learning purposes, including new pronunciation training applications such as 'Say It' which was launched by Oxford University Press in 2019 (OUP). Students can also avail of CALL (computer-assisted language learning) platforms and tasks for autonomous pronunciation learning outside the classroom. These can be highly beneficial, as Mompean & Fouz-González (2016) have demonstrated with regard to the use of Twitter by Spanish learners of English. This underscores the importance of teachers keeping up-to-date with the new L2 learning technologies being developed, as well as developing a critical understanding of the ways in which they can be used with different learner groups to enhance opportunities for pronunciation teaching and learning.

However, teachers in this educational domain often report a lack of preparedness for this role, which may explain why many express a hesitancy if not a reluctance to teach pronunciation. Moreover, their attitudes towards the teaching of pronunciation can be complex. This realization has led to calls for research that can shed light on the underlying reasons why the teaching of pronunciation remains a neglected area (Derwing & Munro, 2015). There is also a need for empirical research that can add to our knowledge of pronunciation instruction in terms of the strategies that teachers use with learners to help inform the development of evidence-based teaching and teacher education in this area (Baker & Murphy, 2011). This is considered all the more important in TESOL pedagogy in the light of the increasing diversity in spoken English worldwide which has brought to the fore new issues and questions concerning the target models of pronunciation that are taught in different EFL contexts and settings worldwide. To enhance our understanding of how novice teachers view the teaching of pronunciation and the specific challenges they experience at the 'chalk face,' we turn next to the PENSER findings.

It is not uncommon for L2 teachers to avoid the teaching of pronunciation due to fear and a lack of confidence, as in the case of novice Mairead whose reflections in this area form the focus of the third case study. However, we still know very little about why the teaching of pronunciation is so feared by L2 teachers (Derwing & Munro, 2015). As previously, we begin with some important contextual information, before we explore the nature of Mairead's fears and the underlying factors involved.

Case Study 3: Mairead

Mairead was a 55-year-old woman from the southwest of Ireland who had returned to full-time education after a successful career as a hotel manager. Her motivation for studying for an MA in TESOL was that it would offer opportunities for her to travel and work part-time as an EFL teacher in different parts of the world. We meet Mairead in the initial group discussion in the third PENSER cycle, where she expresses her fear of teaching pronunciation, which has been her 'bete noire' since the start of TP, as in Extract 6.12. By then, Mairead and her peers had moved to the second semester of TP and had been teaching for several months.

Extract 6.12 (Guided Group Discussion 1 – PENSER Reflective Cycle 3)

1. **TE:** How has your teaching been going?
2. **ST Mairead:** To tell you the truth, I've been avoiding teaching pronunciation altogether since Day 1 because it just frightens the life out of me. We're now well into the second semester of TP and I really need to have a go so I can get over this stumbling block. It makes me feel so inadequate that I still haven't included it in my lessons when I see the others doing it. I feel it's my bete noire and I really need to conquer it.

Having made the frank disclosure to the teacher educator and the group that she has not been able to overcome her initial fears of teaching pronunciation, and is still avoiding teaching this area, she is encouraged by the teacher educator to articulate the precise nature of her fears as a crucial first step towards appropriating the problem.

Extract 6.13 (Guided Group Discussion 1 – PENSER Reflective Cycle 3)

1. **TE:** Can you tell us a bit more about why you still fear it so much?
2. **ST Mairead:** I suppose from the start I never gave it the attention I should have done, and it seems very technical which I think turned me off too. I also think I just don't have that developed a sense of hearing or perception that other people do.
3. **TE:** Can you give us some examples of this?
4. **ST Mairead:** Well, I find it difficult to hear word stress and even to work out how many syllables are in a word. I see that the others in the group don't have a problem with this so that makes me think it's just something I'm not naturally good at, which is odd because I love music and I thought I had a good sense of rhythm.

From Mairead's comments, it is clear that she still viewed the problem as resulting from a personal deficiency, and that this was impacting negatively on her willingness to actively seek out ways to improve the situation. At this stage, the teacher educator invited the group to reflect on their experiences in this area to help Mairead gain a more general perspective on the issue, as in Extract 6.14.

Extract 6.14 (Guided Group Discussion 1 – PENSER Reflective Cycle 3)

1. **TE:** How have the rest of you found teaching pronunciation?
2. **ST Sarah:** I've only really started to think about integrating it in the second semester of TP because it just wasn't on my list of priorities.
3. **ST Caitlin:** Me too, and I think I was confused for a long time about what exactly we were meant to do even though I know what all the sounds were technically.
4. **TE:** So, would you say you… many of you have found it difficult to apply what you have learned theoretically?
5. **ST Mairead:** Yes, definitely.
6. **ST Pauline:** Same for me.

Having established that several of her peers had also not given the same attention to the teaching of pronunciation as they had to other areas of the language curriculum, and that they had also felt confused as to how to approach it, the teacher educator set the group the task of reflecting on a point that Mairead had raised to explain her own perceived lack of progress in this area, which was that some people had a weaker innate ability to hear and process sounds, which could disadvantage them when teaching pronunciation, as Mairead believed was true in her case. In the follow-up group discussion held a few weeks later, we find the group exploring this question with reference to learning theories they had become aware of from other modules on the program, as in Extract 6.15.

Extract 6.15 (Guided Group Discussion 2 – PENSER Reflective Cycle 3)

1. **TE:** And what about the idea that some people are just better able naturally to teach pronunciation?
2. **ST Sarah:** Well, if you have a strong musical intelligence you'd be able to pick out sounds and patterns of sound more easily but that's not to say that we can't improve on our different innate abilities, as Gardner's theory of Multiple Intelligences proposes.
3. **TE:** So, what does this mean for language teachers?
4. **ST Mary:** Well, I think we can improve over time, you know the more you interact with the students, the more we get used to hearing their accents and the sort of errors they make.
5. **TE:** Mairead, would you agree, that student teachers can develop this kind of skill over time?
6. **Mairead:** But I think we would have to make a conscious effort to develop your perception to sound and want to do it.

7. **TE:** So, let's think of some practical ways that language teachers can improve their perceptual awareness.

This exchange encouraged Mairead to view the problem more proactively as an aspect of her professional development that she could work on, and it brought her to the realization that this would require both focused attention and a willingness to embrace the problem. From this, the group brainstormed plans they could put in action in order to develop their strategic skills in this area. This moved Mairead and her peers to the noticing, solving, exploring and research phases of the third reflective cycle. Over the following weeks, they committed to engaging with the research literature and undertaking focused classroom observations of more experienced teachers to gain awareness of the sound systems of English that were being taught to different learner groups, and the various pedagogical strategies used to do so. In Extract 6.16 from her online TP portfolio, we find Mairead reflecting on the new insights she has gained from classroom observations of intermediate level EFL groups being taught by experienced teachers, and from her engagement with research in the field of L2 pronunciation.

Extract 6.16 (Online TP Portfolio – PENSER Cycle 3)

ST Mairead: I suppose what I noticed first was that in the lessons there were usually only a few specific sounds that were focused on where the teacher wrote up words with the sound on the board and with the phonetic symbol. And she would usually model the sounds individually and then in the actual words and get the students to repeat them. What surprised me was that the words were often very basic like 'study' or 'live' which the students were very obviously mispronouncing to the point where it sounded very different. So, they probably weren't taught how to pronounce these words when they learned them and have been saying them incorrectly for years. This made me realise the importance of teaching the pronunciation whenever learners meet a new word, or otherwise they are going to end up pronouncing it wrong. And, because English spelling and sounds are sometimes very different, it can be almost impossible for them to get it right. And then, from the reading, I was able to connect this to the notion of fossilisation which I found very interesting because it explains why even when they hear the word pronounced correctly the error persists. So, making sure they get the chance to hear the word pronounced correctly at the time they meet is actually really important. And when I talked about this to the class teacher afterwards, she also said that teachers have to make this very overt like highlighting it on the board and repeating it several times because otherwise it can get missed by the student.

From a dyadic discussion with a TP mentor at the end of the third reflective cycle, we can gauge the progress that Mairead has made in her thinking and practical expertise in this area, as in Extract 6.17.

Extract 6.17 (Dyadic Exit Discussion – PENSER Cycle 3)

1. **TE:** From reading your more recent reflections, you seem to have come to a new understanding of the role of pronunciation teaching in SLA, and your relationship with it seems to have changed too.
2. **ST Mairead:** Well, it's made me much more aware of how much learners need to be shown how to pronounce different sounds because they can't work this out for themselves. And it can mean that they sound really strange and people can end up laughing at them which is horrible. Or people can't understand them at all, and they have to keep repeating what they want to say which is embarrassing for them. So, not teaching it means that we're actually making it harder for them to communicate in English.
3. **TE:** So, you seem to have much more of a sense of learners' needs in this area.
4. **ST Mairead:** Yes, I'd definitely approach my teaching a lot more from the learner's perspective which I didn't do enough before. When I'm planning my lessons, my first thought now is what will be useful for them (the learners). So, I know them quite well now and I feel I know what they'll need help with and where they'll probably make errors. So, I think I overlooked this before because, I just wasn't at this stage but now I can see in practice problems that come from interference from the L1.
5. **TE:** So, how do you feel about teaching pronunciation now?
6. **ST Mairead:** I'm definitely not so stressed and I think I'm getting there… you know making a conscious effort to bring it into all of my lessons. I now see that it's an important part of language learning and it would be neglectful not to teach it.

This exchange suggests that Mairead had successfully addressed her earlier fears and that her newfound confidence stemmed from her growing understanding of learners' needs, which were now at the forefront of her planning and teaching. From this account of the reflective journey of three of our novices as they assumed their language teacher role, we proceed to the reflective task. For this, we encourage readers to revisit the themes addressed in this chapter drawing on their own L2 classroom experiences as both language learners and language teachers.

Pause for Reflection

1. In what ways have the three case studies outlined in this chapter informed your professional knowledge and growth as an EFL teacher?
2. What advice would you give to a novice teacher who is struggling with her language teacher identity and role?

SUMMARY

This chapter has focused on issues and challenges that typically arise for novice EFL teachers in relation to the teaching of the language content of lessons, with specific reference to the teaching of grammar, vocabulary, and pronunciation, tracing the progress of three of our novices as they have developed critical pedagogical understanding and practical skills in these areas and highlighting the reflective journey of the group as a whole. The PENSER data has provided fascinating insights into the complexities involved in L2 language teaching, viewed from the perspective of novice teachers, and it has highlighted the ways in which they can be guided and supported by means of targeted reflective practice to enable them to assume a more confident and expert language teacher identity and role. In Chapter 7, our focus moves to the challenges that arose for the novices in relation to their teacher talk and interactional practices with L2 learners.

Chapter 7

Reflecting on Teacher Talk and Interactional Skills

INTRODUCTION

This chapter endeavors to highlight the ways in which reflective practice and corpus linguistics can be used in a combined and integrated way to raise novice EFL teacher awareness and skills in relation to L2 teacher talk and interactional skills. In so doing, we will provide empirical evidence to support the view that in the EFL context, teachers play a central role in the processes of SLA through their talk and interactions with learners. As previously, we will pause first for reflection in relation to this crucial area of EFL teaching.

Pause for Reflection

1. What is your understanding of teacher talk in the EFL classroom?
2. As an EFL teacher, how can you become more aware of your own use of English and its impact on the English language learning process?

The PENSER research revealed that challenges relating to teacher talk were largely absent from the reflections of the novices in the first and second cycles of the PENSER process, but featured more saliently as they moved through the third cycle, by which time they had gained valuable teaching experience. This suggested that their attention at this more mature stage of their TP journey was now more directed towards ways in which they could support the L2 learning process. Table 7.1 presents the specific issues that were raised by the novices in the spoken and written PENSER reflective data. Before exploring the issues involved, it is useful to review the relevant academic literature from the fields of applied linguistics, SLA, and TESOL from which we can gain essential insights into the role and features of L2 classroom discourse and the implications this brings for teaching professionals in terms of their own teacher talk and interactional knowledge and skills.

Table 7.1. Challenges and specific issues relating to teacher talk and interactional skills.

Main Area of Challenge	Specific Issues Identified
Teacher Talk and Interactional Skills	• Quantity of teacher talk • Quality of teacher talk • Suitability of teacher talk • Quantity of student talk • Quality of student talk • Questioning strategies • Poor instructions • Corrective feedback

THE ROLE AND FEATURES OF L2 CLASSROOM COMMUNICATION

As the classroom-based research of Walsh (2006, 2011), amongst others, has highlighted, communication patterns in the L2 classroom have changed considerably over the past 50 years or so, in line with the shift towards Communicative Language Teaching (CLT) and Task-Based Teaching and Learning (TBTL) methodologies. These more recent approaches view high levels of peer interaction and target English use as essential to help learners achieve communicative competence which is the overriding teaching and learning goal (Oxford, 1997: 443). As a result, the talk of both teachers and learners takes on a greater significance in the L2 educational context than is the case in subject-based and traditional L2 classrooms. Although this is now a widely accepted view in the ELT world, it represents a revised position from the early days of CLT where teacher talk was often viewed as inferior and to be avoided due to its lack of authenticity (Howatt & Widdowson, 2004). This fundamental change in perspective can be linked to a growing awareness of the unique and valuable dual role that teacher talk plays in the complex processes involved in learning a foreign language where it serves as 'both the goal of instruction, and the vehicle through which learning is managed and accomplished' (Allwright & Bailey, 1991: 71). Moreover, there is a growing body of research in SLA which has provided a wealth of evidence to support the view that teacher talk is multifaceted and complex. As Walsh (2011: 7) describes it: 'teachers use language in their teaching in order to facilitate and promote learning; to help co-construct new meanings, new understandings, knowledge, and, in a language classroom particularly, skills.'

This important realization has led to the expectation and requirement that L2 practitioners develop a high quality of teacher talk and interactional competence to be able to accommodate the diverse needs of learners in different teaching contexts and settings. This knowledge and skill is now widely viewed as essential if teachers are to provide the kind of target English input and supportive dialog that will enable learning to flourish. We now also know much more about distinct sets of linguistic features that L2 teachers use in their classroom interactions, and their impact on the L2 learning environment, as a result of the wealth of classroom-based research in SLA (Cullen, 2002; Nicaise, 2021; Thornbury, 1996; Walsh, 2013). For instance, Thornbury (1998: 218) highlighted questioning strategies including elicitation (drawing out learners' opinions and answers) through referential questions (genuine questions) and display questions (where the answer is already known); and the use of wait time, speech modifications, hesitation, rephrasing, clarification requests, and repetition. Cullen (1998: 182) expanded this list, adding form-focused feedback; teacher initiated and dominated feedback; echoing or rephrasing of student responses; sequences of IRF (initiation-response-feedback) discourse patterns; and teacher initiated and dominated talk.

Meanwhile, at the level of speech modifications, Cabrera & Martinez (2001: 287) have highlighted two types of linguistic adjustments that teachers make to address the diverse needs of learners. The first relates to the nature of the input provided at different proficiency levels, and in distinct learning contexts, at the grammatical, lexical, and phonological levels in order to facilitate learner comprehension; and the second, to adjustments made at the interactional level to further support the learning process. From this research, a general consensus has emerged in applied linguistics circles that L2 teachers need to combine linguistic modifications with interactional adjustments, as teacher talk is considered most conducive to language acquisition when both its linguistic and interactional features are fully exploited. Accordingly, to support and enhance language learning, L2 teachers must strategically control both the input they provide for learners and their interactional language use.

In the context of L2 teacher education, the extensive body of empirically-based research carried out by Walsh in the field of L2 classroom interaction (2006, 2011, 2013) has provided a further wealth of insights concerning the range of interactional strategies that L2 teachers can use to aid learner comprehension and enhance learning outcomes. These include comprehension checks; confirmation checks; rephrasing; reformulation; turn completion; backtracking; and back and front chaining (gradual build up). This research has added weight to calls for practitioners to be given opportunities to develop awareness in relation to key linguistic and socio-cultural considerations that arise in the L2 teaching and learning context, if they are to achieve the high level of strategic interactional competence that is required to successfully support the learning process. For instance, they must take into account the degree of complexity involved for learners from different types of language use, and the usefulness and relevance of the target forms for the context of learning, both specifically and in general.

Andrews (2007: 41–43) has stressed the importance of EFL teachers acquiring enhanced language awareness to ensure that the language they use is suitable and effective. This involves acquiring a deep understanding of the relationship between language form and language use as well as the type of systematic patterning that is found in different language genres. An awareness of the creativity and playfulness of language, the double meanings it can convey, and the embedding of language and culture is also considered vital for teachers to be able to identify and respond effectively to the difficulties that L2 learners experience in understanding different forms of grammatical, pragmatic, and lexical expression in written and spoken English (Andrews, 2007: 41–43). Such knowledge can enable practitioners to address the challenges that arise for learners from everyday English which typically involves the use of phrasal verbs, idiomatic expressions, slang, and non-mainstream grammar which carries culturally-rooted meanings.

From this, Walsh (2006, 2011) has highlighted the need for L2 teachers to acquire a deep understanding of the nature of their own language use to ensure it is suitable for different classroom micro-contexts; for instance, so that they can avoid using imprecise, ambiguous, and overly informal usages when asking questions to elicit answers, and when giving instructions, checking comprehension, and giving feedback on errors, which are pedagogical functions wherein the careful framing of language use is essential. In these ways, they can ensure that their target language is used in more meaningful and effective ways to reinforce understanding.

To facilitate the development of this superior interactional awareness, Walsh (2006) designed the SETT pedagogical framework (Self-Evaluation of Teacher Talk) which is now widely used on L2 teacher education programs for awareness-raising purposes amongst both novice and experienced teachers. Building on this body of corpus-based research, Angela Farrell's 2019 study of teacher talk amongst Irish EFL teachers has highlighted the types of face-saving strategies that practitioners can develop and draw on in their challenging CM role to ensure that positive social relationships and communication practices are maintained while at the same time attending to important pedagogic goals such as promoting a high level and quality of learner participation and engagement in the lesson. Moreover, it has shown how the development of socio-pragmatic expertise of this kind can help practitioners to become better prepared psychologically for their role in the classroom in terms of attending to their own face needs and learning to become more comfortable and confident with their position of authority and their professional role (A. Farrell, 2019).

Against the backdrop of the changing English landscape internationally, and growing challenges to the historic Anglo-American target model approach, there have also been calls for EFL teachers to develop enhanced sociolinguistic knowledge if they are to understand the relationship between their own varieties and those used by others, given the ongoing diversification of English worldwide (Jenkins, 2009; Kachru, 1992). Moreover, critical applied linguists argue that practitioners in this educational domain will now need to acquire multidialectal competence to be able to target their English language use to the needs of learners in diverse language environments (Matsuda, 2012). This suggests a move away from the restricted Standard English norms of the past whereby teachers have been expected to avoid the use of varieties other than Standard British English or Standard American English, even when teaching in the local context. However, a move towards a more flexible and finely-nuanced approach of the kind envisioned would require superior language awareness and target English skills on the part of all practitioners, with implications for English language teacher education at both the pre-service and the continuous professional development stages. In the previous discussion, we have highlighted the key role played by teacher talk in the L2 learning context and the expanding knowledge base and skills required of EFL practitioners if they are to address the complex range of demands that now arise across cognitive, socio-cultural, affective, and ideological dimensions. From this context, we review recent, empirically-based research in the L2 teacher education field to gain an understanding of the types of difficulties that novice teachers typically experience at the interactional level.

CHALLENGES IN TEACHER TALK FOR NOVICE L2 TEACHERS

One of the main areas of difficulty that typically arises for student teachers from native speaker backgrounds relates to their overly informal conversational style with learners (Walsh 2006, 2011). This has been found to occur even at stages of the lesson when key instructional functions are being expressed and the careful framing of language by teachers is essential, as when giving instructions and feedback or when checking comprehension. Walsh has attributed this to a lack of awareness on the part of many L1 speakers to the nature of their own language use. He has also linked the poor target English performance of novices to a limited understanding of the role played by teacher talk in SLA, and a failure to appreciate normative requirements in the EFL educational domain (Walsh, 2006: 112). This, he argues, hampers their ability to control and modify their speech so as to ensure that it is comprehensible and accessible for learners at different levels of English language proficiency, and that it is targeted towards the needs and preferences of different learner groups (Walsh, 2006: 117). As a result, they are often seen to speak at too rapid a pace, and with poor diction, and to resort to highly idiomatic expression, and slang and culturally-shaped usages that are difficult for learners to decipher and interpret, especially those at lower levels of proficiency. Walsh has raised this issue as a key area of professional concern, stressing that these practices are likely to confuse and frustrate learners. They may also lead learners to doubt the expertise and professionalism of the teacher, given the mismatch between teacher talk and the more formal varieties and registers found in course books which practitioners are expected to explicitly teach (Walsh, 2006: 118).

Similarly, A. Farrell's research (2019) has highlighted the failure of many novices to accommodate their speech to the proficiency level of learners, and the poor quality of teacher instructions and questioning this can lead to. These findings have added weight to the view that L1 competence in English does not automatically confer advantages in terms of target English use and instructional skills. Farrell (2019: 148) found that problems of this kind were linked to poor levels of novice teacher language awareness at entry level to MA programs, with some entrants lacking even a basic understanding of the formal linguistic properties and workings of English, as the previous chapter in this book has also highlighted. This was seen to impact on their awareness of the features of their own variety of English and its relationship with SBE/SAE. This led Farrell (2019: 152) to question how novices from native speaker backgrounds can best be prepared for their complex interactional role. In the following section, we review corpus-based studies undertaken for L2 education purposes, which highlight how corpus linguistics and discourse analytic approaches can be used to identify the educational needs of novice EFL teachers with an ultimate view to improving their classroom interactional performance.

THE ROLE OF CORPUS LINGUISTICS IN DEVELOPING L2 INTERACTIONAL SKILLS

Corpus researchers working in the L2 teacher education context (Boulton & Tyne, 2014; Breyer, 2009; Farr, 2022; A. Farrell, 2019; Leńko-Szymańska, 2017; Ma et al., 2021; Mukherjee, 2006; Nicaise, 2021) have demonstrated the valuable role that corpora can play in raising student teacher language awareness of issues relating to the quality and suitability of teacher talk and, from this, their strategic competence. For instance, corpora sourced from different EFL contexts and settings can provide novices with exemplars of real classroom interactions as a basis for analysis, and exploratory classroom discussions. Key findings from corpus-based research can also be highlighted, and their implications explored, such as the study by Nicaise (2021), undertaken in the Belgian EFL context, which found different types of grammatical patterning in the interactional teacher talk of native/non-native English speaker teachers (NEST/NNESTs). For instance, the speech of NESTs was seen to reflect a high use of modal verbs which led to a marked tentativeness and indirectness in their instructions and questioning, whereas that of NNESTs more obviously featured imperative forms which led to a more direct speech style (Nicaise, 2021). Similarly, at the lexical level, NESTs favored a more informal type of teacher talk which was typically expressed through phrasal verb usage and idiomatic lexical expression, while NNESTs more often used Latin-based words which created a high degree of formality. A. Farrell's corpus-based research (2019: 83–89) in the Irish English teacher education context also found a high level of indirectness and informality in the instructional speech style of student teachers from NEST backgrounds, which was found to impact on the quality of their questions, instructions, and explanations.

Corpus-based research of this kind which is pedagogically oriented has highlighted the potential value of classroom corpora as an educational resource to help teachers to critically appraise the acceptability and efficacy of teacher talk with L2 learners at different proficiency levels, and at different stages of the lesson when particular functions are being performed. In this way, they can become more critically aware of how teachers can accommodate their speech and scaffold learners through the linguistic choices they make, and from this gain valuable insights into the links between pedagogic theory and practice. Data-based approaches of this kind also provide an empirical basis for novices to explore alternative approaches and choices that might be more suitable in different teaching contexts and settings, with a view to enhancing their critical sociolinguistic awareness and skills. Accordingly, corpus-based approaches are being developed that can shape practical guidelines to help teachers to make more finely-nuanced judgments in relation to the suitability and the efficacy of their instructional language use, which is vital given the diverse and complex needs of language learners today. The work of Riordan (2018) and Farr et al. (2019) has further demonstrated the complementarity of corpus linguistics and reflective practice in L2 teacher education and the fruitful outcomes it can bring, as will be underscored in this chapter. In the following discussion, we highlight, in particular, how this combined approach can be used to shed light on, and facilitate, the developing interactional skills of student teachers as part of their TP journey. Drawing on the PENSER data, we will attempt to trace how the group dealt with the range of issues that arose in this area and the dual and complementary role played by CL and RP in the process.

Interestingly, the PENSER research indicated that the novices tended to ignore challenges associated with the quality of L2 teacher talk until the third reflective cycle when they featured more often than any other type. This suggested that the group were now making important links between the nature of teacher talk and learning outcomes.

Pause for Reflection

1. Compare and contrast the ways in which EFL teachers from a native and non-native English background might be challenged differently in relation to their teacher talk.
2. How do you think corpus techniques could be used to raise student teacher awareness of the role of teacher talk as different pedagogical functions are being performed?

PENSER REFLECTIONS: TEACHER TALK AND INTERACTIONAL SKILLS

We begin with Extract 7.1 from the initial teacher educator-guided discussion in the third reflective cycle, wherein issues relating to what constitutes suitable and effective teacher talk with different L2 learner groups are the focus of attention.

Extract 7.1 (Guided Group Discussion 1 – PENSER Cycle 3)

1. **ST Mary:** I didn't realise when we first started that when I was speaking it was going over their (the learners') heads because it was way too fast. I actually do speak really quickly so I have made a real effort to slow it down and speak more clearly. But it's hard to get the balance right. You know, I don't want to sound fake but they're not really able for real spoken English at intermediate level. This is where I struggle.
2. **ST Sarah:** Yeah, I know what you mean. We need to pitch it at a level they can understand but make it as authentic as possible at the same time which is really hard because we don't have that much teaching experience to go on.
3. **ST Caitlin:** So, it really is making us think about what I+1 (input plus one) actually means in practice with different learner groups.

This exchange is striking for several reasons: firstly, for the confident and authoritative way the novices have identified and articulated the challenges they were experiencing; secondly, because it demonstrates that they were moving away from viewing their challenges as personal failings, recognizing instead that they were commonly shared problems that stemmed from a lack of experience; thirdly, because it suggests they had appropriated the challenge and were willing to actively seek out ways to improve their pedagogical understanding and skills in order to solve it; and finally because it highlights important links they were making between theory and practice, all of which seems indicative of professional growth. As the discussion progressed, they began to explore how the quality of their teacher talk might be impacting on the learning experience of those they were teaching, drawing on their own prior language learning experiences to gain a deeper understanding of learners' needs and perspectives, as in Extract 7.2. There is evidence therefore, that the novices were now better able to connect at a personal level with their students and feel empathy towards their struggles.

Extract 7.2 (Guided Group Discussion 1 – PENSER Cycle 3)

1. **ST Mary:** I suppose we should be thinking a lot more about the language we use throughout the lesson from the students' perspective.
2. **ST Sarah:** Yes, I think it's easy to forget that everything is in the L2 for them, so it's really important that we get the level right and check that they understand.
3. **ST Caitlin:** I remember learning Spanish in Spain and not being able to understand the teacher. It was awful and I ended up giving it up because I just used to dread being asked anything and feeling stupid when I couldn't answer.
4. **ST Sarah:** There's actually nothing worse for your confidence is there when you're trying to learn a language so I get how the learners feel.

As the novices moved into the 'noticing' phase of the PENSER process over the following week, they committed to observing the ways in which teacher talk was used by the experienced class teachers to scaffold the learning process. In Extract 7.3 from an online TP portfolio, we find one of the novices commenting on a teacher's use of repetition in a lesson she has observed from which she feels she has gained valuable insights into the important mediating role that L2 teachers can play in the learning process. It has also made her more aware of the need for teachers to ensure that the face needs of learners were being met, particularly at sensitive stages of the lesson when issues of 'face' were at the fore.

Extract 7.3 (Online TP Portfolio – PENSER Cycle 3)

ST Mary: What I found useful from my observation was seeing how the class teacher used repetition throughout the lesson. She repeated key words to make sure that the students were following the lesson which was a much more natural and effective way of ensuring comprehension than constantly asking 'Do you understand?' This is something I have been doing even though I can see that it's a bit pointless because they (the learners) rarely reply. Maybe it's because they don't want to admit to not knowing in front of the class. It's making me think a lot more about teacher talk as a tool we can use to help learners. This is important because everything is done in the target language. And I also realise I should try to avoid asking them questions that embarrass them in front of the class.

Meanwhile, in Extract 7.4, also from an online TP portfolio entry, another member of the cohort is reflecting on her growing understanding of the importance of checking learner comprehension, and the types of pedagogical strategies that can be used to achieve this in an effective but adult-appropriate way.

Extract 7.4 (Online TP Portfolio – PENSER Cycle 3)

ST Sarah: I noticed how the class teacher used comprehension checks to make sure they had understood her instructions like getting them to tell each other in their own words. This was less face-threatening than making them repeat it individually in front of the class or as a group which is more suitable for children. This also increased the amount of student talk so there was a double benefit. And she gave them lots of chances to check their work with each to make sure they had the right answer, so they were obviously much more willing to contribute when she asked.

Following on from their classroom observations, the group was guided towards a series of targeted corpus-based initiatives that were intended to raise their L2 classroom interactional awareness. This involved the analysis of corpus transcripts of lessons taught by experienced teachers, viewings of recordings of the lessons, and follow-up group discussions. The analysis of transcripts of EFL lessons offered useful opportunities for finely-grained explorations of the appropriacy of different choices of expression, as a starting point to observing their use in practice, and the impact in each case. Extract 7.5, from the second guided group discussion a few weeks later, highlights the enhanced understanding this approach brought in relation to the linguistic choices and interactional strategies that teachers make, and the outcomes. In particular, it helped the novices to appreciate the ways in which the learning process can be supported, rather than inadvertently thwarted, at crucial moments in the lesson such as when instructions and feedback are being given, or when explanations and opinions are being elicited.

Extract 7.5 (Guided Group Discussion 2 – PENSER Cycle 3)

1. **ST Mary:** What it really brought to me was how precise the class teachers were especially when giving instructions. It made me think about how vague and rambling I sound which must really frustrate the learners.
2. **ST Sarah:** Yeah, there were times when the class teachers were more direct and precise but at other times they used more informal expressions and phrasal verbs, and even some slang. It depended on where the lesson was at the time and also the level. They definitely used less modal verbs too with the intermediate group when they were giving instructions and feedback to make it non-ambiguous.
3. **ST Caitlin:** Reading the transcripts made it easier to see the ways the class teachers elicited answers from the students and to gauge the level of student responses. I've also seen the different ways we can respond when an answer is either right or wrong. So, making it very clear but in a nicer, less threatening way so they say 'Exactly' or 'Yes, that's correct'. And when it's wrong they say 'Try that again' which is more encouraging and less embarrassing for learners than hearing 'No' or 'That's wrong'. I probably wouldn't have picked this up in this detail just from a teaching observation.
4. **ST Shona:** So, we can give encouragement by saying 'Have a go' and 'Try to work it out' which I think really took the edge off and made them feel less like they were being put on the spot and expected to get everything right.

This more mature and informed reflective discussion further serves to highlight the ways in which corpus linguistics and reflective practice can be used in a combined and integrated way to raise novice teacher awareness of the ways in which teachers can skillfully scaffold the learning process through the linguistic choices they make for teacher talk. The novices' reflections suggest also that they were becoming more aware of the socio-pragmatic dimensions of teaching and learning in the adult EFL classroom and the role that teachers and teacher talk can play in ensuring there is a positive and less stressful learning environment, especially at stages in the lesson when issues of face are at the fore. With a view to building on their progress in this area, the group were encouraged to develop and implement action plans for further investigation of the challenge over the following weeks. This included engaging with the research literature in SLA and watching video recordings of EFL teaching in different cultural contexts, from which they reported back to their peers on their observations and newfound insights. At this stage, in the third and final group discussion in the cycle, they were also asked to present a strategy that they had observed or read about which served as an example of best practice that the other novices could attempt to integrate into their future teaching. Extract 7.6 illustrates some of the contributions made, and the shared learning gained from the various targeted tasks.

Extract 7.6 (Guided Group Discussion 3 – PENSER Cycle 3)

1. **ST Jean:** I read a journal article by Steve Walsh which highlighted the importance of giving students sufficient wait time and interactional space to think when we are asking questions because teachers often forget that learners are processing everything in the target language which takes time and effort.
2. **TE:** So, how do you think this will this change your teaching approach?
3. **ST Jean:** It'll definitely make me more mindful of the need to factor this into my planning and teaching. I'll be making a conscious effort to allow them to have time to process the question and to think about their response whereas before I wouldn't have understood why they didn't answer sooner and I probably would have just asked another student when they didn't respond.
4. **ST Joanna:** I watched a video recorded of a classroom in China where there were about a hundred students and the teacher stood at the front with a microphone. The only speaking that the students did was to repeat dialogues that the teacher modelled. There was no authentic interaction at all, and the teacher only asked display questions that the students shouted out the answers to together. This made me realise how incredibly challenging it must be for Chinese students to be asked their opinions and to join in group discussions with European students who are often opinionated and uber-confident.
5. **TE:** And has this impacted on your teaching?
6. **ST Joanna:** Well, it makes me want to look out for them and to make sure they understand the purpose of what they're being asked to do. So, at the start of the lesson, when we are waiting for everyone to arrive and settle, I've started to have a bit of a chat with them one to one because it might be the only authentic interaction they have during the day. I can see they appreciate it and they're not as anxious because I'm not forcing them to speak in front of the whole class.

In the later dyadic discussions with mentors, we find evidence of a growing understanding of the ways in which L2 teacher talk can be used to support the learning process, as Extract 7.7 exemplifies.

Extract 7.7 (Dyadic Exit Discussion – PENSER Cycle 3)

ST Darragh: I never realised before that teacher talk is a tool for language teachers. So, making sure the pace is right and that everyone can hear and follow is really important. But this is just the starting point because everything we say is an opportunity for them to learn. And if the quality of our teacher talk is not what it should be, it's a wasted opportunity or even worse it can confuse students and put them off.

The previous discussion has highlighted some of the ways in which novice teachers of EFL felt challenged in their interactional language use with learners from the perspective of its quality and strategic effectiveness, and the more developed sense of teacher talk and its importance, that they have gradually gained. From this, we turn to issues of a more critically-oriented and normative kind, specifically the varieties of English that EFL teachers can and should use with learners.

Issues that were raised in this area stem from the historic requirement for EFL teachers to use SBE/SAE in their professional practices given that teacher talk is seen to serve as an implicit target model for learners alongside the models explicitly taught (A. Farrell, 2019; Mishan & Timmis, 2015) . As a result, practitioners in this field have been expected to align their professional language use to these 'prestige' varieties which continue to dominate the EFL curriculum and international examinations despite the growing calls by critical applied linguists for learners to be exposed to a wider range of Englishes to enable them to cope with the greater diversification of spoken English today, and to contest the existing Anglo-American target English status quo (Canagarajah, 2005; Matsuda, 2012).

Research by one of the present authors (A. Farrell, 2019) has highlighted the types of professional difficulties that can arise for novices from non-main variety backgrounds as a result of their lack of awareness of the need to avoid the use of the local variety with learners, even when teaching in the local context. These difficulties were found to be exacerbated when novices had only a superficial understanding of the relationship between the local variety and SBE/SAE, in terms of similarities and differences, and of the implications this carries for their classroom practices. For instance, it led to a tendency for some to favor a highly informal and overly 'laid back' instructional style which often featured non-standard grammar and highly idiomatic lexical expression. This was found to be inappropriate for the teaching context and confusing for learners. In Farrell's research, these failings were also linked to several additional factors including the lack of experience of the novices, their individual personalities, and their age, given that they were similar in age to the Erasmus students they were teaching, and cultural influences pertaining to the informal speech style of the Irish as a sociolinguistic group. More widely, the findings also highlighted the complex processes involved in becoming socialized into the norms and practices of the TESOL profession.

In the light of this research, and with growing calls for EFL teachers to be made more critically aware of the ideologies that underpin the global ELT profession and industry, and the implications of changing sociolinguistic trends in English use internationally for their own professional practices, our group of novices was encouraged to explore the practical challenges that target model change might pose for teachers and learners alike. This began with an initial critical awareness-raising focus drawing on corpora representing different English language varieties from Inner, Outer, and Expanding Circle settings, accompanied by targeted engagement with the academic literature from the World Englishes field (Kachru, 1992). The potential of corpus linguistics as an approach and a resource for critical awareness-raising in L2 teacher education has been recognized for some time, and this approach has been embedded into the MA TESOL program that forms the backdrop to this book across a number of core modules and electives. Accordingly, language corpora and corpus applications, corpus data, corpus techniques, and corpus-based materials and tasks are routinely used to extend the linguistic knowledge base and practical pedagogic insights of our novice teachers and also to raise their critical language awareness in relation to the diversity of English today, to enable them to develop flexible and critically-informed strategic responses. A complementary CL/RP approach can also be used to raise awareness of the particular challenges that EFL teachers from non-main variety backgrounds can face, as a result of the prevailing target English status quo, in order to help bring about a more finely-nuanced theoretical understanding of the supposed NESTs/NNESTs dichotomy and a transformation of ELT professional practices.

With these considerations and goals in mind, in the following discussion, we provide a snapshot of the more critically-oriented reflections of our group of novices as they engaged with the related themes of variation in English and suitable target Englishes for EFL pedagogy. This theme arose in the initial group discussion in the third PENSER cycle, as illustrated by Extract 7.8, and stemmed from an initial focus on their own variety, that is Irish English.

Extract 7.8 (Guided Group Discussion 1 – PENSER Cycle 3)

1. **ST Pauline:** I feel embarrassed to say it but I didn't even know there was something called Irish English until I started this course. When we started TP my TP supervisor told me that I use a lot of Irish English expressions in my lessons and that I needed to become more aware of this as it might confuse some learners, or they might not want to hear this.
2. **ST Sarah:** I think I would have been quite offended by that.

3. **ST Pauline:** No, I don't think she meant it like that. I mean I did feel it was a criticism at first. But I realise now that we have to know about the rules and regulations even if we don't like them and think they are discriminatory. So, it's good to have this pointed out and it doesn't necessarily mean that we have to agree with the system.
4. **TE:** I think this is a very good area for us to reflect on over the next few weeks as it's central to what we do.

This extract highlights the novices' awakening sense of critical awareness of the status of different varieties of English, including their own, and their willingness to explore what this might mean for their classroom practices in terms of the versions of the language that might or might not be suitable to use with different learner groups, as well as the types of constraints they needed to be mindful of, all of which is indicative of their increasing professional maturity.

In their written reflections in their online TP portfolios from the same period, we find a growing interest in, and knowledge of, the features of Irish English as a variety, as a result of the guided exploratory analyses they have undertaken of corpus data, as in Extracts 7.9 and 7.10. This kind of sociolinguistic understanding is now considered vital for all EFL teachers given the global nature of the EFL profession and industry, and the findings presented confirm that corpus linguistics can play a useful complementary role in targeted reflective practice around linguistic and ideological issues that impact on teacher identity and professionalism, by providing an empirical basis for critical reflection and discussion.

Extract 7.9 (Online TP Portfolio – PENSER Cycle 3)

ST Mairead: I suppose I am much more aware of using 'Ye' than when I started because I didn't realise we were the only ones who said it until it was brought up in TP feedback. This made me think about other forms of expression that we might have which are not used elsewhere. Now that I know a lot more about English from our corpus projects and how much variation there is, I understand that there have to be certain norms we follow, or it would be confusing for learners but there is the need for more flexibility depending on the context and who the learners are. I mean, it would be very useful to know about 'Ye' if you were coming to live and work in Ireland seeing as you'd hear it all the time. In fact, teaching students about it would reduce confusion and be useful for them culturally and linguistically.

Extract 7.10 (Online TP Portfolio – PENSER Cycle 3)

ST Laura: Since we started looking at different varieties of English using corpora, I've become a lot more aware of IE usages and how much we use colloquial expressions and slang when we speak and also how different it is to the kind of academic English we are expected to use in our assignments. It's the first time I've actually studied English which seems wrong because everyone needs to know about their own language style, and we are at a massive disadvantage as teachers if we don't.

The enhanced critical understanding that the student teachers have gained from this complementary CL/RP approach is further evident in Extract 7.11, which was sourced from the second teacher educator-guided group discussion a few weeks later.

Extract 7.11 (Guided Group Discussion 2 – PENSER Cycle 3)

1. **TE:** So, you've been reading quite a lot about Standard English and how it is changing and having seen evidence of it in your corpus explorations, what are some of the challenges this raises for you as EFL teachers?
2. **ST Mary:** Well, I am much more aware of language change and that applies to Standard English too but the problem how I see it is that linguists are much more tolerant of language use because they are only looking at it from a factual point of view but as teachers we still have to teach to certain norms and standards.
3. **ST Sarah:** Yeah, but it's who gets to decide the rules. Isn't that the point?
4. **TE:** Why do you think that most learners have been encouraged to learn Standard British or American English rather than local varieties?
5. **ST Mary:** I get that it's easier for learners to learn only one variety but there are so many varieties of English today that they have to get used to learning more than just the standard especially when they are living in countries where a local variety is the main form of communication.
6. **ST Sarah:** In fact, I think anyone coming to live and work in Ireland should be taught Irish English and we should speak naturally with them in a way that they hear outside the classroom.
7. **ST Darragh:** I think that in ESL classes in Ireland, teachers should be highlighting what people actually say and that they can do this by using Irish English.
8. **ST Joanna:** Yes, but you couldn't really use Irish English in say Dubai or China which means we can't really use it as we would be teaching one thing and saying another.
9. **TE:** So, how might practices in this area be changing in the EFL world?
10. **ST Pauline:** I don't think we are expected to change our accent anymore.

11. **ST Mary:** I think we would be expected to know more than just one variety; we might have to teach American English in one context and British English in another, but we wouldn't have to change our accents just tone it down if we had a strong regional accent and in Ireland, we could teach local expressions especially if the learners are interested.
12. **TE:** So, do you think teachers should consult learners about the variety of English they are exposed to in the classroom?
13. **ST Sarah:** I think they should have some say but it's probably got a lot to do with the exams they are taking too.

Accordingly, as illustrated, this approach has brought enhanced critical awareness of the kind of choices they will have to make as future practitioners, and the ways in which their decision-making may be influenced and constrained in different global contexts in terms of the suitability and acceptability of different varieties of English. Their growing ability to critically gauge the complex range of factors involved in their target English choices going forward, is further evident in the final dyadic discussions with mentors at the end of the third PENSER cycle when the second TP semester was coming to a close, as in Extracts 7.12 to 7.14.

Extract 7.12 (Dyadic Exit Discussion – PENSER Cycle 3)

ST Shona: I've learned a lot about the ways in which international EFL course books and examinations lead to restrictions around the types of English that teachers use with learners in different contexts but that there are developments around this with more varieties likely to be represented. In the future, we'll also probably see more non-native varieties being included.

Extract 7.13 (Dyadic Exit Discussion – PENSER Cycle 3)

ST Caitlin: Learners are most definitely influenced by exam requirements. They tie them to the varieties in the exam so I think most learners would question teachers it if they heard us using very different grammar or vocabulary to what's in the book or the exams. It's important to understand their attitudes and preferences so I'd like to have discussions about this with learners in the future but not impose my variety on them just for some ideological reason.

Extract 7.14 (Dyadic Exit Discussion – PENSER Cycle 3)

ST Laura: If the examinations reflected a wider variety of English, that would change the situation a lot, especially for teachers like us who are not from American or British English backgrounds. I think this will happen in the future and it's something I'll keep up with wherever I'm working to see how it pans out.

These more critically-oriented reflections confirm that the novices were gaining the wider, sociolinguistic understanding now required of future EFL teachers if they are to develop a more finely-nuanced target English approach in their future practices, as a crucial starting point to developing an enhanced range of interactional skills as will also be needed. From this snapshot of the challenges experienced by our novices in the area of teacher talk and teacher interactional awareness and skills, we move on to our reader reflective task which we hope will encourage you to explore your own perspectives in relation to some of the key issues that were explored in the previous discussion in relation to the complex, interactional role of teacher talk in the L2 learning environment today.

Pause for Reflection

Reflect on your own beliefs and practices in relation to:

1. the variety/ies of English that are suitable for (a) use by teachers in your own EFL context and (b) as models to be explicitly taught to learners
2. interactional strategies that can support the L2 language learning process
3. corpus techniques that can inform teachers in relation to the multifaceted role of EFL teacher talk.

As a starting point to your own personal reflection, we suggest that you record yourself teaching an EFL lesson and listen to it, noting the nature of your own teacher talk as you perform different pedagogical functions.

SUMMARY

This chapter has demonstrated some of the ways in which novice EFL teachers are challenged by the complexities involved in L2 classroom interaction, using an evidence-based approach. It has also highlighted the valuable role that CL and RP can play when used in an integrated and complementary way in enhancing student teacher language awareness, as a crucial first step towards improving the quality of their teacher talk and interactional performance, with a view to better supporting the learning process. The discussion has also shed light on both the new demands and the new opportunities that novice teachers of EFL must now become aware of, as a result of the changing English language landscape internationally, and the benefits that critically-oriented RP can bring in terms of preparing them for the more complex target English role that this sociolinguistic development will inevitably bring. In Chapter 8, we explore the post-TP reflective period. This is strongly supported by teacher educators in spoken and written feedback contexts, the former of which is the focus of our discussions.

Chapter 8

Post-Observation Feedback: A Tale of Two Teachers

INTRODUCTION

This chapter is designed to help prepare for and engage in any post-observation discussions that take place between student teachers and mentors or supervisors. This is known variously as TP feedback or post-observation feedback. This is a really significant part of the reflective process as it provides the opportunity for support, direction, and insight from those more experienced as a way to guide and deepen student teachers' own reflective endeavors. However, the teaching experience is always uniquely the teacher's so their interpretations are likely to be equally as insightful as those offered by others and such feedback encounters should therefore be seen as an opportunity for shared and collaborative reflection. The illustrative data that we use in this chapter does not come from the PENSER set, as has been the case in previous chapters, but from the Teacher Education Corpus (TEC) as outlined in Chapter 1. More specifically, it is a sub-corpus of TEC, consisting of post-observation feedback sessions between TP supervisors and our MA student teachers, which are conducted on a one-to-one basis. The data presented in the various sections below was collected in a pre-Covid world and therefore the feedback sessions took place face-to-face in the supervisor's office, usually within a couple of days of the TP class under review. In the same context, Farr (2011: 70–71) presents some diary entries and responses to a questionnaire from MA students which relate directly to predispositions towards the feedback experience. In general, the student teachers, although slightly anxious, easily identified the merits of engaging in feedback and anticipated a mixture of positive and negative feedback to help direct their future teaching. They also articulated how they felt about being praised and criticized, two of the most significant types of talk likely to occur in any feedback context. Table 8.1 shows some of the results.

Table 8.1. Student predispositions to criticism and praise (Farr, 2011: 71).

	How do you feel about being criticized?	**How do you feel about being praised?**
Jim	No problem, as long as there's a reason for it and it's constructive.	It helps, obviously.
Joanne	If it's constructive, I don't see it as criticism. Can be embarrassing.	Good – helps build confidence therefore making you more open and relaxed.
Lorna	I don't like it but know that in this case it's for my own good. I realise that it is not unfounded and is constructive.	It's a great confidence boost, encourages to try out new ideas and feel more assured about your teaching capabilities.
Michael	It's necessary. If it's put correctly it can be more encouraging/constructive than praise.	I'm not pushed about being praised, as I tend to relax a bit too much. Can make me feel lazy and uncomfortable. Still, I like it when it's due.
Petra	Not too bad. It will depend on the way it's done.	It depends. Sometimes it can be a bit patronising or not believable.
Roseanne	I don't mind, as I believe it's the only way to improve my teaching.	If I do well it would be nice to hear so. It helps my self-confidence.

There are mixed feelings about both being praised and being criticized. In the main, it seems that students can see the merits of critical discussions in helping them to improve but express a hope that it is communicated sensitively and constructively. In terms of praise, there are a range of feelings expressed. Some students seem to want and look forward to hearing positive comments to make them feel good and build confidence, while others feel that it could potentially be patronizing or instill a type of complacency. Only you will know how you tend to react to these types of interactions and how you might need to prepare for them so that you benefit most from the discussions (see Farr, 2015: 113–117 for a range of specific ways to prepare for TP feedback sessions). The remainder of this chapter will focus on an exploration of how TP feedback unfolds in practice through a narrated account of two cases of the discourse of teaching practice feedback from the TEC involving an experienced teacher, Maria, in one case, and an inexperienced teacher, Nina, in the other. We do this in the form of two accounts in each section below, which illustrate the different types of interactions that you might expect as part of the experience. The next section reveals how both feedback sessions begin, while the following one uncovers how the discussion unfolds in attempts at deeper and focused reflections jointly constructed between the teacher educator and student teacher in each case. Finally, we explore the conclusion of each session and how they terminate. These accounts are not intended to be exemplars of good or bad practice, simply of real practice. The stages in the PENSER framework are often apparent in the interactions, although this framework was not explicitly employed by the interactants.

Pause for Reflection

1. Think of previous instances when you have engaged in feedback interactions. How did you prepare for and behave in such interactions?
2. Will you engage differently in the context of feedback during the course of the practicum? Why and how?

STARTING GENTLY: ESTABLISHING COLLABORATION AND IDENTIFYING A PUZZLE

It is likely that when you start teaching, or indeed at the start of a feedback session, there will be a stage when you engage in a fairly descriptive narrative account of what went on in the lesson. This is useful for the teacher educator to remind them of the details of the specific lesson (even if they have notes or recordings), especially if the feedback is a few days after the event. It is also extremely beneficial for student teachers to be able to recount the event in some detail as a first step to noticing and commenting more critically on what went on. The idea is that such awareness will lead to reflections on how to modify and improve future practices, or simply put, learning from experience. From an interpersonal perspective, it is a non-threatening way to start the conversation as it generally doesn't involve much evaluation and is therefore likely to give both participants an opportunity to ease gently into the discussion. Extract 8.1 takes place between a very experienced teacher educator and a student teacher (Maria) who had some years of teaching experience before entering the MA program. She seems therefore to be less daunted by the whole experience and very much open to learning from it in a positive way. This is the second time that Maria has taught that particular EFL group and she begins in the second week by recapping a little on the theme of 'puns' which she had introduced in the first week. The interaction in Extract 8.1 takes place at the very beginning of the feedback session, which occurs just the day after the teaching practice lesson.

Extract 8.1: ST Maria (TP Feedback)

1. **TE:** Ok, so this was your second teaching session with that group, so how did you find it?
2. **ST Maria:** Mm, not as successful as the first one. I felt, mm, just because it wasn't as structured and I struggled to give the instructions successfully.
3. **TE:** Ok.
4. **ST Maria:** Mm, yeah so that was what I really struggled with...
5. **TE:** Ok, so would you think that would be a good area for us to focus on in feedback?
6. **ST Maria:** Definitely, yeah.
7. **TE:** Ok, and so did you bring a copy of the book with you?
8. **ST Maria:** Yeah.
9. **TE:** Well, keep it there until the specific things that went on in the lesson.
10. **ST Maria:** Yeah, yeah.
11. **TE:** Ok, so remind me then of the topic and of how you started the lesson.
12. **ST Maria:** Ok, so I wanted to just have an informal chat to start with, the first week or the second week.
13. **TE:** So, this is, we're talking about yesterday?
14. **ST Maria:** Yesterday, ok, so, mm, so, I just brought in a couple of puns because last week I wasn't as prepared with the idea of puns, so I wanted to just to get them talking about them again.
15. **TE:** Yeah.
16. **ST Maria:** And break the ice a little bit.
17. **TE:** So, yeah, so how did that go, the pun?
18. **ST Maria:** It went ok, I think, I clarified the idea of it a little and just to sort of get them laughing a little bit and stuff because I don't want it to be too formal in there.
19. **TE:** Ok.
20. **ST Maria:** So...
21. **TE:** I, I think it was nice to start the lesson with a reminder of what they did last week and I think puns, mm, are, you know...
22. **ST Maria:** Yeah.
23. **TE:** There's humour out of it.
24. **ST Maria:** Yeah.
25. **TE:** But, they're, they're really difficult, aren't they, to understand?
26. **ST Maria:** Yeah.
27. **TE:** You know, you need a high level of language.
28. **ST Maria:** Yeah.

29. **TE:** Mm, so remind me of the way that they that they… you did that task, so what did you actually get them to do?
30. **ST Maria:** I just got them to work on terrible puns mm and then…

From this part of the interaction, it is clear that both parties intend for this to be a collaborative engagement as there is an obvious willingness to co-construct the dialog. Initially, there is a general question from the teacher educator to glean overall reactions and impressions of the lesson under review. Maria immediately homes in on an aspect of the lesson which she feels was problematic, the way in which she managed classroom talk specifically related to instructions. From Turns 5–13 there is some organizational talk attending to the details of the lesson and then in Turn 11, the teacher educator brings it back to a discussion of the topic of the lesson and how it began, which is obviously something she wants to focus on. In this effective maneuver she quickly changes topic from the focus of instruction giving identified first by the student teacher, showing the implicit power attributed to and assumed by her. In Turn 17, there is an unambiguous focus on how the teaching of puns went during the lesson. In Turn 21, Maria articulates her satisfaction with achieving her aim of providing clarification and humor following on from a previous lesson. Interestingly, in Turn 19, the teacher educator uses the continuer 'ok,' which doesn't necessarily indicate agreement (Farr, 2003), and then agrees with Maria in Turn 23 that they can be humorous, before changing the direction of the commentary in Turns 25 and 27 to begin to indicate that there may be some issues which the student teacher may not have identified on first reflection. Having hinted at some sort of problem, or puzzle, the teacher educator then seamlessly reverts to asking a question designed at eliciting a descriptive account in Turn 29, to which the student teacher responds with a preferred response by beginning the narrative account. We will see how this interaction unfolds further in Extract 8.3 below.

Extract 8.2 is also from the very beginning of a feedback interaction, with an experienced teacher educator and a relatively inexperienced student teacher (Nina). This is quite a different beginning to the discussion than the one we just saw in Extract 8.1. It begins and continues in quite a negative vein and the teacher educator does not begin to take much control over the dialog until quite a way into the interaction, allowing the student teacher a lot of freedom in expressing their own thoughts and opinions first. The lesson under review took place in the second last week of the semester, late on a Monday afternoon during the dark winter months in Ireland. One of the topics for the lesson was vegetarianism.

Extract 8.2: ST Nina (TP Feedback)

1. **TE:** Ok, so, you, you, talk to me, so, this is Monday week eleven.
2. **ST Nina:** Week eleven, mmm, actually, I went, I didn't think this was going to be a good lesson.
3. **TE:** Mhmm.
4. **ST Nina:** And I had done a good bit of preparation with the slides, and I thought that this particular topic would be quite, mmm, energetic for them.
5. **TE:** Mhmm.
6. **ST Nina:** Plus, you know the way people are thinking more into the thing of being vegetarians and all this political...
7. **TE:** Yeah, mhmm.
8. **ST Nina:** You know you'd think of that, and I thought they would have been more responsive and, and when I came, as I was like 'god that's like drawing blood from a stone'.
9. **TE:** It was like pulling teeth, wasn't it?
10. **ST Nina:** It was. So, it was just, it was like they didn't even have an opinion.
11. **TE:** Mhmm, mhmm.
12. **ST Nina:** And even those who did answer, like Carl, I suppose was the only one who seemed to have any sort of opinion.
13. **TE:** He did. The guy at the front. Yeah. Yeah.
14. **ST Nina:** Yeah, and Marie, and what's his name? Rafael. They answered, I think, sort of out of duty.
15. **TE:** Mhmm.
16. **ST Nina:** Because they're just good students.
17. **TE:** Yeah. Yeah. Yeah.
18. **ST Nina:** But, like, I'll ask the question even, even, even ask them if they are vegetarian.
19. **TE:** Mhmm.
20. **ST Nina:** They still looked at me blankly, like as if they didn't even understand...
21. **TE:** Yeah.
22. **ST Nina:** ... me, you know? But I don't know whether they're just so into their meat that they don't even think either way on it.
23. **TE:** Yeah. Yeah.
24. **ST Nina:** But, it, it was just...
25. **TE:** Look.
26. **ST Nina:** It might, it, it, it, I think I just felt really bad after the lesson.

27. **TE:** Mhmm.
28. **ST Nina:** Cos I felt…
29. **TE:** You didn't get what you anticipated out of it.
30. **ST Nina:** I didn't get half of what I anticipated…
31. **TE:** Mhmm.
32. **ST Nina:** … out of it, because it just kept, mmm, it was like I was talking on deaf ears all the time.
33. **TE:** And what, what do you think? Coz if you can find, if you can try to figure out why, the reason, you know, the reason behind it.

Nina, the student teacher in the interaction in Extract 8.2, clearly has a negative impression of what went on during the teaching practice lesson, and we can almost feel her panic in the continuous flow of talk accounting for how she felt and what had gone wrong in the lesson. Most obvious is the fact that she doesn't seem to know the reason for the non-responsive nature of the students and this is probably causing her to fret even further during an interaction where she knows she is expected to be able to account for what has happened and why, especially at such a late stage in the semester when she will have already done several practice lessons. For the most part, all that the teacher educator can manage to do is respond briefly with various types of response tokens such as *Yeah* and *Mhmm*. In Turn 26, Nina openly admits what has been obvious from the first few utterances: that she feels very bad about what happened during the lesson. With this frank admission, the teacher educator finally takes the floor in Turn 29 to offer an empathetic response showing a level of human and shared understanding. Interestingly, this happened after a failed attempt in Turn 25 to take the floor through the use of the word *Look*, which was consciously or subconsciously ignored by Nina during her emotional flow. Only on Turn 33 does the teacher educator take more control of the interaction by starting to direct a focus in the talk towards a deeper level of reflection aimed at moving beyond the negativity and panic towards an understanding of what had gone wrong with the ultimate aim of trying to find a resolution. The emotional feel to the beginning of the feedback sessions represented in Extracts 8.1 and 8.2 is very different. 8.1 feels controlled with a level of maturity and understanding from the student teacher. In contrast, 8.2 displays a sense of negativity through panic and total loss of control on the part of the student teacher, which the teacher educator allows to run until its emotional conclusion, probably in the hope that having allowed the student teacher to articulate emotionally for the first few minutes, they can now transition to more mature and more useful reflections together. We will see if this is, in fact, the case in the next section.

Pause for Reflection

1. Do you agree with the interpretations we offered in relation to Extracts 8.1 and 8.2? Why/why not?
2. How do you think these discussions will progress to the next part of the feedback sessions?

MOVING DEEPER: EXPLORATIONS AND RESOLUTIONS

Having seen some of the ways that a feedback session can start, we will now look at how each of the two interactions under review progress to an intended deeper exploration of the particular puzzle identified jointly during the opening turns of the dialog. We saw that the teacher educator played an active role in helping Maria to identify and begin a descriptive account of the teaching of puns. In Extract 8.3, the teacher educator uses a range of elicitation questions to quickly focus the discussion on the more precise teaching point that needs to be addressed.

Extract 8.3: ST Maria (TP Feedback)

1. **TE:** Do you think they understood that pun?
2. **ST Maria:** I think so, because as I said it they laughed, mmm, but it would've, it probably would've been helpful to check it again, mmm.
3. **TE:** Yeah, so that came from the writing centre, didn't it?
4. **ST Maria:** Yeah, from the writing centre.
5. **TE:** So they all tore off...
6. **ST Maria:** Yeah,
7. **TE:** ... one pun and then they had time to...
8. **ST Maria:** To read it.
9. **TE:** Yeah.
10. **ST Maria:** And to make sure that they all understood them, mmm, just a couple of them, mmm, read them out to the class.
11. **TE:** Yeah, and do you think they all understood each pun?
12. **ST Maria:** Probably not.
13. **TE:** Yeah.
14. **ST Maria:** I realised that as they were reading them, that they might have been bit hard.
15. **TE:** Yeah. What would have been challenging, do you think about?
16. **ST Maria:** Mmm.
17. **TE:** You know, when you, if you were doing that as a native speaker.

18. **ST Maria:** Yeah.
19. **TE:** Sometimes you need to…
20. **ST Maria:** Yeah.
21. **TE:** … hear it…
22. **ST Maria:** Yeah.
23. **TE:** …more than once, but also sometimes you actually need to read it, because it's a play on…
24. **ST Maria:** Play on words, and then read it.
25. **TE:** And it could be, so could you think of way that you could have done it? Where you could have ensured that they really got the most out of that?
26. **ST Maria:** I think if I had put them in a power point that would have been the best way.
27. **TE:** Ok.
28. **ST Maria:** Have them on…
29. **TE:** Listed.
30. **ST Maria:** Yeah.
31. **TE:** And then?
32. **ST Maria:** Focus one by one, maybe a pun and then talk about it in class and…
33. **TE:** Yeah.
34. **ST Maria:** … and just discuss about and…
35. **TE:** I like the way you got them to tear one off though.
36. **ST Maria:** Yeah. Yeah.
37. **TE:** That made it real, but I think you could have actually got them to tear one off each.
38. **ST Maria:** Ok.
39. **TE:** And then in turns they could have explored the meaning of each one in their groups…
40. **ST Maria:** Mhmm.
41. **TE:** … because they are sitting in groups, aren't they?
42. **ST Maria:** Yeah.
43. **TE:** In that classroom, with those tables, round tables.
44. **ST Maria:** Yeah.
45. **TE:** I think they needed time discuss each one, and to actually say to each other 'ok, so what's the pun'?
46. **ST Maria:** Yeah, but I think I did rush through. It was just very…
47. **TE:** Yeah, it was just, I suppose it was coz you were trying to remind them of what they'd done before.
48. **ST Maria:** Yeah.

49. **TE:** But I think that... because it was actually a very nice task, when you obviously went to the trouble of finding the materials and thinking of, 'ok, this, this relates to my lesson', so it's a shame not to use it...
50. **ST Maria:** Yeah.
51. **TE:** ... in a way that they get the full benefit out of...
52. **ST Maria:** Yeah.
53. **TE:** So, perhaps in future it might be an idea to make it more of a task where they get the chance to explore the meanings.
54. **ST Maria:** Yeah.

The way in which this feedback session unfolds is interesting. It is clear that the teacher educator wants to elicit as much as possible from the student teacher and that Maria, in response, wants to engage fully and has ideas such as the use of PPT slides in Turn 26, which is not taken up much by the teacher educator who goes on to be quite directive in her talk in Turns 37, 39, 41, 43, and 45 where she shares her very specific ideas about what could have worked better. Maria simply responds *Yeah* to many of these turns, which doesn't really indicate a level of agreement but a level of acceptance that the teacher educator holds the power and the disciplinary knowledge in this context to offer advice and suggestions (Vásquez, 2004). To repair any damage that might have been caused by the directives, the teacher educator does some face-saving work (Edge, 1984) in Turns 49 and 51 before focusing clearly on the future in Turn 53. Despite that fact that many teacher educators articulate not wanting to be directive or prescriptive in these types of interactions (Farr, 2011), they very often fall back into this mode. Maybe this is instinctive, or perceived as being more efficient, or often it may be because it can be difficult to elicit what they want to from the student teacher and so they revert to actually directly articulating their thoughts on the matter. Both parties fall back into traditional student/teacher roles, which is probably their comfort zone in any case. It does beg the question however about the extent to which it promotes the acquisition of skills required for reflection and development on the part of the teacher on the cognitive level (Lasagabaster & Sierra, 2005). On the other hand, on the affective level, it keeps the feedback positive and supportive and in line with some of the expectations of both parties, as seen in the introduction to this chapter. There are pros and cons to all feedback approaches, and this is no different. The main advantages of this type of exchange sequence is that it is time-efficient, the student teacher probably feels well-supported, and the message is communicated in a fairly unambiguous way. Many student teachers actually like the type of certainty afforded by such an exchange and have a clear understanding of what went wrong and why as they leave the discussion. The disadvantages are that the student teacher doesn't contribute equally to the dialog and doesn't really find (or isn't given) the space needed to develop their own reflections and come to their own conclusions. This is not a criticism of either the student teacher or the teacher educator, and in fact the interaction is hugely variable at different stages, so this is not a consistent pattern for either party. It simply serves to illustrate one of the ways in which a feedback session can develop at some points in time and shows the versatility of the participants in negotiating in ways that work in these potentially tension-fraught discussions. Listening to the feedback segment there is no sense that there is anything but mutual respect and a cordial relationship between the parties from beginning to end.

The continuation of the discussion directly from Extract 8.2 with inexperienced student teacher Nina has a very different feel to it. The contrast between the two different teacher educators' discussions really highlights how different personalities and identities play a strongly influencing role in how feedback interactions unfold in such teacher education contexts and how this is apparent, and often constructed, through the discourse (see Barkhuizen, 2021; Farrell, 2017; Nunan, 2017; Richards, 2017; Riordan & Farr, 2015 for further discussions on language teacher identity). It quickly becomes apparent at the beginning of Extract 8.4 that the lesson under review took place immediately following the Paris terrorist bombings in 2015 and provides an excellent illustration of the classroom as a social context amid many other local, national, and international contexts.

Extract 8.4: ST Nina (TP Feedback)

1. **ST Nina:** I don't know what.... Maybe they were just tired. Maybe it was after the weekend of events in, in, in Paris, that maybe had some of them...
2. **TE:** And that's exactly what I was thinking as well, and, you know...
3. **ST Nina:** Coz...
4. **TE:** And yesterday was the first day in the class, I thought...
5. **ST Nina:** It seems it was actually dark...
6. **TE:** It was really dark.
7. **ST Nina:** ... before the class began, it was actually dark.
8. **TE:** Yeah.
9. **ST Nina:** And they seemed a little livelier in Evanne's half, and I thought, 'but her half seems to be sort of more positive'.
10. **TE:** Mhmm.
11. **ST Nina:** Maybe she, maybe she just got whatever was left in them. I don't know.
12. **TE:** Mhmm. Mhmm.
13. **ST Nina:** But, mhmm.

14. **TE:** Mhmm, I think you're right on both those. You know I think it could be either of those. Mmm is there anything that you would have done differently during the discussion task? Because remember, mmm, you did the advantages and disadvantages you tried to...
15. **ST Nina:** I, I, I, I tried... the advantages and disadvantages.
16. **TE:** On reflection...
17. **ST Nina:** And probably, on reflection, I, I was looking at it last night on the, on the thing...
18. **TE:** Yeah.
19. **ST Nina:** ... and I thought to myself 'I should have actually given them the disadvantages and advantages on each one more'. But they just didn't seem interested either way. Anything I...
20. **TE:** Mhmm.
21. **ST Nina:** ... seemed to have said on the advantages and disadvantages...
22. **TE:** Mhmm.
23. **ST Nina:** ... even the talk about health, I couldn't even, there was nothing...
24. **TE:** Absolutely.
25. **ST Nina:** A little bit down, and I know...
26. **TE:** Absolutely.
27. **ST Nina:** ... Rafael, he was he was dressed all in his black...
28. **TE:** Yeah.
29. **ST Nina:** ... and...
30. **TE:** And there's a lot of French students in that class.
31. **ST Nina:** There are a lot of French students...
32. **TE:** Yeah.
33. **ST Nina:** Like, yeah, Laura, mmm, and Floriane, and, and they're all friends.
34. **TE:** Absolutely.
35. **ST Nina:** And, mmm, they were very, mmm, because I spoke to a few of them beforehand...
36. **TE:** Mhmm.
37. **ST Nina:** And they were very, sort of ...
38. **TE:** Ok.
39. **ST Nina:** ... in touch with it, and then some of them had relatives in Paris...
40. **TE:** Mhmm.
41. **ST Nina:** And you can understand, I suppose, I said...
42. **TE:** And that's...
43. **ST Nina:** I know, I said to them all 'when you're away from home, these kind of tragedies really make you feel so isolated'.

44. **TE:** Mhmm.
45. **ST Nina:** And things like that.
46. **TE:** This is it.
47. **ST Nina:** You're not there with the comfort of your family and things like that.
48. **TE:** Yeah.
49. **ST Nina:** To talk with it and you're out on your own.
50. **TE:** Yeah.
51. **ST Nina:** And...
52. **TE:** And I think that you could be right there.
53. **ST Nina:** Yeah, it may have been...
54. **TE:** Yeah.
55. **ST Nina:** It may, was just late Monday afternoon.

At the end of the previous extract, the teacher educator managed to eventually make a fairly direct attempt to focus Nina in her efforts to understand the lack of response from the EFL learners to a discussion task that Nina had attempted with them. The frantic and emotional flow actually continues through to this part of the interaction, with Nina gasping (it literally can be heard on the recording) and grasping for an explanation. In Extract 8.4 we again see the student teacher dominating and controlling the floor throughout, with the teacher educator just managing to retain some agency through some backchannelling response tokens. This has also been seen in in-service feedback contexts, where 'power can shift between the interactants, regardless of institutional status' (Donaghue, 2020a: 1). What's more, one of the aspects of this interaction which we removed from the transcription for ease of reading is the fact that almost all of the turns overlap either completely or partly with other turns. In other words, Nina doesn't stop speaking even when the teacher educator tries to interject and take the floor. Nina offers any explanation she can think of on the spot for why the task didn't unfold as anticipated and for the learners' lack of participation. This moves from blaming it on extraneous factors such as the terrorist attacks to the winter evening darkness, to teacher-related factors such as inadequate scaffolding in Turn 19. It moves back to events in Paris before finally settling on the fact that it was 'just late Monday afternoon.' Nina's reflective efforts during the session seems to plateau at the level of what Vygotsky (1986: 193) would call spontaneous concepts. Her inability to progress her thinking to scientific concepts, which are abstractions, is notable. Such abstraction is deemed to be important in reflective contexts because it 'allows the learner to transcend the physical, visual situation of a particular context, and apply the concept to other situations and contexts' (Harvey & Vásquez, 2015: 92).

In practice, this means that all of Nina's efforts seem to be on narrating the events in the specific context rather than on abstracting to a higher level which would allow her to possibly find solutions to inform future teaching. She seems to be stuck on an emotional roller coaster of panic and lack of real theoretical insight or clarity about how to move forward. It is often the role of the teacher educator to model conceptual thinking (see Harvey & Vásquez, 2015: 95 for their data-informed taxonomy of conceptualization including: principles, generalizations, terminizing, analytic ideation, and ideation) for the student teacher. However, in this case, the teacher educator's apparent inability to interrupt the flow leads to a rather unhelpful discussion in terms of practice-focused development. On the other hand, an alternative interpretation may be that the teacher educator sees the need for this interaction to serve a cathartic purpose for Nina, and is allowing the conversational flow to continue. In other words, she may have felt that Nina needed to get it all off her chest.

Soon afterwards, the teacher educator makes two suggestions in the form of hedged questions relating to getting the students to work in pairs/groups and also diverging in topic from what was covered in the previous class so that the learners stay engaged. But even after this constructive direction, Nina is still preoccupied with the failure and concludes 'because the thing is I think, it's in my blog, I put, it took me about four hours to do the lesson plan and a few minutes for it to just fall apart, it's a bit like building a house and one thump of a thing and it's down.' This type of retroflection, while useful to a point can become very negative and unproductive for future-oriented action, which is essential to growing as a teacher. There is even a question as to whether the student teacher notices and absorbs the suggestions being offered by the teacher educator. Of course, these will be mentioned again in the written report but there is perhaps a missed opportunity for the student to use this precious time in the presence of the educator to fully explore, internalize, and take a sense of ownership over strategies to be implemented in the next practice session. Both feedback sessions continue in reflective cycles around different issues and parts of the lesson, but generally the same disposition is evident throughout from Nina. Maria, on the other hand, does become more involved in co-constructing the meaning and understanding of the practice lesson as the feedback unfolds further.

Pause for Reflection

1. If you had to identify with either Nina or Maria, which one do you think you would be most like in such an interaction and why?
2. Which feedback session do you feel is most useful or successful so far?

COMING TO A CLOSE: BACK TO THE BIGGER PICTURE AND FUTURE ORIENTATION

Towards the end of a feedback session, we would expect a return to a macro-level discussion and a look forward to future actions, particularly as student teachers progress in their teaching and the ways in which they interact in feedback (Vásquez & Reppen, 2007), and this is exactly what we find in the case of Maria. Extract 8.5 begins where the session is drawing to a natural close.

Extract 8.5: ST Maria (TP Feedback)

1. **TE:** I mean, perhaps because we dealt a lot with that (topic) today we could look at a different area next week and you might want to think about an area, or if you want to talk about it again that's fine, you know?
2. **ST Maria:** Yeah.
3. **TE:** Ok, thank you very much.
4. **ST Maria:** So...
5. **TE:** So, maybe just work on those points there. Is that alright?
6. **ST Maria:** Will I send it (the lesson plan) on to you then?
7. **TE:** Yeah.
8. **ST Maria:** Ok.
9. **TE:** Adding something to a lesson, oh, if we're adding something to enhance a lesson, I think I made that point in the...
10. **ST Maria:** Yeah, in the (TP preparation) class.
11. **TE:** So, it was just a general point I make it with everyone, not specifically about your lesson, but that we can supplement, and that's where we are adding to the lesson.
12. **ST Maria:** Yeah.
13. **TE:** Even bringing in the cultural dimension or sociolinguistic dimensions, something that's not in the book. So, often, that kind of fixed in a particular variety or, or the theme is not relevant or dealt with in a way that's not relevant and the age, so, is that ok? Ok, so I'll give this one (lesson plan) back, ok so you're teaching, so it's good that you've got the chance to teach that group again and then it would be nice, I think, it would be really relevant for you to move to another level.
14. **ST Maria:** Yeah, exactly.
15. **TE:** To get the chance to. So, I would definitely recommend to Fidelma that you get the chance to teach the intermediate level because I think

that's going to be... it, it throws up a whole new set of challenges but also opportunities so...

16. **ST Maria:** Yeah.
17. **TE:** ... you know, to show different skills and to learn different skills and to show you're developing your skills.
18. **ST Maria:** Yeah.
19. **TE:** So, kind of see it in those terms.
20. **ST Maria:** Yeah.
21. **TE:** Is that alright?
22. **ST Maria:** Yeah, yeah, definitely.
23. **TE:** Okay, so, good to talk.
24. **ST Maria:** Thank you.

This extract is rather like a long goodbye, trying to pack in all the information possible before terminating the discussion. In Turn 3, the teacher educator clearly, and politely but abruptly, signals that the session is coming to an end. It is perhaps a little unexpected that she is also the one to offer thanks, but this is just an ostensibly polite way of using her position to once again direct the discourse. This is followed by a number of turns mentioning some general teaching points and looking to the future. Turn 21 again signals an end to the discussion through the question 'Is that alright?' from the teacher educator, to which the only preferred response is 'Yes' and Maria obliges with this and a reinforcing 'definitely' before final niceties and thanks as required by the social conventions of such interactions.

The concluding turn in the second feedback session has a rather different feel. After finishing another rather frenzied discussion about how to give appropriate instructions there is a rather transactional and abrupt finish to the feedback, without any return to general issues and no explicit or repeated orientation to future teaching practice classes.

Extract 8.6: ST Nina (TP Feedback)

1. **ST Nina:** But, mmm, ok, so...
2. **TE:** Ok, and there we go.
3. **ST Nina:** Brilliant. Thanks so much.
4. **TE:** There you go. I'll write your report and send it to you.

Although polite, from listening to the recording, we get the sense that the teacher educator wants to draw the session to an end. It is unknown whether this is because of time constraints or because she feels a lack of productive and fruitful engagement in the discussion. After all, 'in feedback, there are rules to be followed' (Copland, 2011: 3835). We suspect it may be a little of both, with some underlying frustration that the core messages to be had from the session may not have been as apparent to the student teacher as they ideally should have been. Although not explicit in this case, there can be many reasons for tension in feedback sessions (Copland, 2010), such as non-cooperation, evaluation, lack of reflective skills, emotional incongruity, anxiety, and others (see Farr 2011: 24–30). It may be that the final mention of writing a report is the teacher educator's last hope of directly and explicitly highlighting some important aspects of the discussion, something which she may not feel confident has happened during the interaction. However, it is also worth noting that sometimes a more mature and prolonged reflection on what was said in the feedback session itself, without the urgency of having to engage in the discussion in real time, can actually lead to later realizations and insights on the part of the student teacher. As we have said many times, learning to be a teacher is rarely, if ever, a simple linear or sequential journey.

TYPES OF TALK IN A FEEDBACK SESSION

The previous three sections were concerned with narrating two feedback sessions sequentially in order to appreciate the way in which the discussion might unfold in two of many possible different ways. We could also look at the same extracts in a different way and categorize the discourse by way of a range of different (and overlapping) functions. In earlier, more elaborate research based on a corpus of 80,000 words of spoken TP feedback, Farr (2011: 73) developed a data-informed categorization of four general types of talk typically present in this kind of discourse: reflection; direction; evaluation; and cathartic and relational talk. These often overlap, but for clarity of understanding have been isolated here. Table 8.2 outlines these categories with some examples from the two cases we have discussed in earlier sections of this chapter.

Table 8.2. Types of talk in TP feedback (adapted from Farr 2011: 73).

1. Reflection	**TE:** Ok, so this was your second teaching session with that group, so how did you find it?
2. Direction	**TE:** More than once but also sometimes you actually need to read it because it's a play on...
3. Evaluation	**TE:** It was like pulling teeth, wasn't it?
4. Relational and Cathartic Talk	**ST Nina:** It might, it, it, it, I think I just felt really bad after the lesson. **TE:** Mhmm. **ST Nina:** Cos I felt ... **TE:** You didn't get what you anticipated out of it.

Of course, all of this type of talk could be categorized loosely as reflection in the broad sense of the word; however, here the category of reflection really refers to the ways in which events are narrated and described, or how this is elicited by the teacher educator, as in the example in Table 8.2. Such reflections can be fairly open and museful, often the case at the beginning of feedback, or can be more focused as the discourse develops around specific themes and sub-themes related to puzzles or issues with the practice lesson. For two reasons, the educator often elicits reflection from the student teacher: it is less face-threatening if one identifies their own issues than if someone else does it for them (Brown & Levinson, 1987); it helps develop the student teacher's critical thinking and awareness skills, which is part of the objective of such an interaction. Secondly, direction most often comes from the teacher educator and can either be explicit, as in the example in Table 8.2, or as is often the case, couched in a question such as 'Have you thought about...?' or 'Do you think... would work?'. Again, this is to scaffold and prompt teacher insight. The importance of questioning in feedback discourse cannot be overemphasized, for both pre- and in-service teachers. Display questions are used to help co-construct positive identities for student teachers: 'display questions give feedback participants the opportunity to voice their knowledge and expertise thereby enabling them to claim positive identities' (Donaghue, 2020b: 193).

Evaluation often comes in the form of praise or criticism, but in the example provided here it is nicely embedded in a metaphor for dramatic and humorous effect, possibly. Pulling teeth immediately implies a negativity but also carries a sense of empathy and sympathy with the student teacher who has obviously found something (eliciting any response from the learners in this case) particularly unsuccessful in their teaching performance. Finally, supportive and positive interpersonal relationships between the teacher educator and student teacher are the backbone of a good feedback session (Maynard & Furlong, 1995; Randall & Thornton, 2001), and seem to be what teachers want in this context (Bols & Wicklow, 2013). Without this it is likely that any value to be had from other types of talk would be severely diminished. These relationships are built and maintained to a large extent through the type of small talk and phatic communication that occurs at the beginning and end of a TP feedback session, but also through emotionally supportive discourse. In Table 8.2 we see the teacher educator mitigating the face-threat cause by the admission of emotional vulnerability on the part of the student teacher. The TE offers a logical rationale to explain why Nina felt bad after the lesson, signalling an empathy with her, presumably intended to provide emotional support. This role can be demanding (Boote, 2003), and is not one which all educators feel well-equipped to engage in. However, it is crucial in the feedback context if the discussion is not to become what Randal & Thornton (2001) call a degenerative intervention when the communication becomes argumentative or breaks down completely. This is not something that we have yet seen happen in any of the many feedback sessions we have gathered as data for our research, probably because all parties, especially the educators, are acutely aware of the potential for this to happen and therefore mitigate in appropriate ways throughout the feedback.

Pause for Reflection

1. What is your experience of feedback with a teacher educator?
2. Do you think feedback with a teacher educator is a necessary part of the reflective process or could you manage quite well without it? Why/Why not?

SUMMARY

The primary focus in this chapter was on the post-observation feedback session between a student teacher and a teacher educator. The main aim of such encounters is to collaboratively reflect on the practice teaching, review and narrate it, identify puzzles and problems, and explore possible solutions to these which might potentially improve future practice. We organized the chapter around case studies of two contrasting feedback sessions with teachers Maria (who had some pre-program experience) and Nina (who had no pre-program experience). The sections in this chapter take the reader through the ways in which these interactive feedback sessions might begin by establishing co-constructive dialogic relationships. We then detail how they move through more focused reflection on specific issues through one episode for each teacher as an exemplar of a number of repeated such episodes that may take place. Both cases develop quite differently, with Maria engaging in a relatively mature way but all the while being directed fairly explicitly by the teacher educator. By contrast, Nina embarks on a rather frantic and emotional flow of talk almost akin to a monolog, which allows little opportunity for the TE to elicit, focus, or direct in any meaningful way. The ways in which both feedback sessions come to a conclusion provide further evidence of a contrast in approach, engagement, and potential impact. The final section of the chapter categorizes, with examples from the two cases, typical types of talk that we might expect to find in this kind of post-observation spoken feedback interaction.

Chapter 9
Conclusions and Looking Forward

INTRODUCTION

In this book, we have explored the role of RP in the professional preparation of novice teachers of EFL in the context of an MA in TESOL program at a HE institution in Ireland, highlighting the benefits of using a data-led approach to RP and the ways in which it can be integrated and targeted to the needs of novices over the course of TP to support their professional development. Drawing on reflective data from the TEC corpus, including the spoken and written reflections generated as part of the PENSER reflective process, it has been possible to present an evidence-based account of the range of challenges that novice teachers of EFL typically experience on the TP journey in key areas of EFL pedagogy, and how these were addressed through systematic and targeted RP across a range of individual and collaborative modes of communication. This has also demonstrated the enhanced critical understanding that was gained in relation to key aspects of EFL pedagogy and related issues and concerns, as a crucial starting point to developing appropriate responses. In so doing, this book has expanded data-led research within the RP research paradigm and has brought a more bottom-up perspective to the existing academic literature in this field which, as many have observed, is long overdue (Farr et al., 2019; Walsh & Mann, 2015). In this final chapter, we will summarize the key findings from the RP-related research drawn on in this book and explore their implications for future directions in RP and ELTE. From this, we will offer suggestions as to the ways in which reflective practice can also be used for ongoing CPD and how in-service teachers of EFL can be offered opportunities to reflect on their ever more challenging professional practices, within the supportive environment of a CoP, in the pursuit of best educational practice.

KEY EMPIRICAL FINDINGS AND IMPLICATIONS FOR ELTE

The corpus-based RP research drawn on in this book has revealed that novice teachers of EFL experience a wide range of challenges and concerns over the course of their TP experience in key areas of EFL pedagogy and that this can pose a threat to their developing sense of teacher identity and self-efficacy. Through up-close analyses of the reflective data, it was possible to trace how they responded to these difficulties, and the role played by RP in the process. For instance, the analysis has shed light on the challenging issue of how novices with little experience or knowledge of EFL learners and the EFL learning environment can effectively plan language lessons for different learner groups, as is a goal and a requirement of TP. In the case of the novices in our study, this dilemma was seen to be exacerbated by an initial lack of language awareness and formal linguistic knowledge which made it difficult for them to identify the needs and abilities of EFL learners at different proficiency levels. These limitations left many of the group feeling stressed and unable to cope in the early weeks of TP, with one of the novices describing this as a 'feeling of drowning.' These findings are consistent with existing accounts which have shown that in the early days of TP, novices often feel a strong sense of inadequacy as they become more aware both of the professional challenges that lie ahead, and their own lack of knowledge, which they may have underestimated previously. After all 'teaching is a complex activity, and second language teaching has been considered as yet especially complex' (Harvey & Vásquez, 2015: 91). This can explain why emotions can often run high at this initial stage when they come face-to-face with these realities, as their reflections have confirmed.

This book has also demonstrated how, through targeted and guided RP accompanied by classroom observations, team teaching and discussions with experienced teachers acting as mentors, and collaborative tasks with peers, novices gradually become more familiar with the systems, routines, and requirements of the EFL teaching environment, and from this, the nature of the knowledge and skills they would need to develop as future EFL practitioners. For instance, over the course of the first PENSER reflective cycle, they developed a growing awareness of the central role of course books in the EFL curriculum, and of their advantages and limitations. They also became more knowledgeable concerning the wide range of materials, tasks, and resources that are available to supplement course books, and of the criteria that EFL practitioners need to apply to determine their suitability for different learner groups. This enabled them to move away from an initial preoccupation with workload and their own failings, towards actively seeking out ways to enhance the quality of their planning and preparation, keeping the needs of their learners in mind, with evidence of a growing self-confidence in their ability to do so.

Similarly, this approach provided a systematic and holistic framework to support novice teachers' professional development as they grappled with their new classroom management role, at the heart of which lay their relationship with learners, allowing them a safe space in which to voice their initial anxieties and concerns and to explore the affective dynamics of teaching and learning in the L2 classroom environment. Here, the reflective data revealed that they were able to progress from experiencing an initial a sense of intimidation with some learner groups to actively seeking out ways to develop a stronger sense of teacher identity and authority, which in turn led to a growing sense of teacher purpose and self-efficacy and a more pleasant and engaged classroom environment for all.

The novices were particularly challenged in their language teacher role, typically lacking confidence in their ability to teach the target models of grammar, lexis, and pronunciation that form the core components of the EFL curriculum. As expected, this was most acute in the early days of TP when they were still becoming familiar with this subject knowledge. In many cases, this also stemmed from their shared perception that learners often held a superior formal knowledge of the language. These findings confirmed the disadvantages that novices from a native English background can experience due to an initial lack of language awareness and formal language knowledge, which have been well-documented in the ELTE research literature (A. Farrell, 2019; Walsh, 2006). However, as the group gained in knowledge in this area, and through their active engagement in RP and action-based research, the reflective data revealed evidence of growing teacher self-agency and learning.

As they moved through the final reflective cycle, and gained more experience of classroom teaching, their reflections turned to challenges of a more mature and critically-oriented nature, such as the quality of the input and interactions they were providing for learners as they performed key pedagogical functions, and the broader question of the suitability of the use of different varieties of English, which again, seems indicative of professional growth. Their reflections offered a clear sense that over time, and through the complementary use of corpus-based awareness-raising initiatives, they became more insightful as to the relationship between language use and language learning, and the nature and role of both teacher talk and student talk in the EFL classroom context and the types of interactional strategies that teachers can use in order to support the learning process. In their later reflections, there was also evidence of a growing awareness and questioning of the normative dimensions underlying EFL, with opportunities provided for them to gain vital understandings of sociolinguistic trends around English at the international level and to explore what this might mean for their own future professional practices, by means of targeted and guided critically-oriented RP.

In providing empirical evidence of the types of challenges that novice teachers of EFL can be expected to face at different stages of their TP journey, and the various ways in which RP can be used to enable them to develop appropriate responses, this book can provide the basis for fruitful classroom discussions with novice teachers of EFL more widely to explore common problems and issues that they are likely to share, and which they must learn to cope with and address strategically, and the considerations involved. In this way, this book can help to inform our theoretical understanding of the complexities involved in becoming an EFL teacher today in terms of the knowledge base, skills, and critical insights this now requires.

IMPLICATIONS FOR REFLECTIVE PRACTICE AND FUTURE RESEARCH

The RP-based research presented in this book offers important implications for RP. It has brought to light the benefits that can be gained for novice teachers at the beginning and early career stages from engaging in RP across a range of modes. It has also highlighted the ways in which the diverse modes can work in a complementary way to create a space for them to express their thoughts and wishes, to explain their beliefs and values, to reflect retrospectively and on future events, in order to understand them more fully, to offer opinions, reactions, and thoughts while at the same making evaluations, with the aim of revising thinking and actions, and to rationalize thoughts and actions, and ultimately, to aid their professional growth. For instance, it has uncovered the kind of guided and targeted RP that teacher educators can provide to foster awareness-raising and collaborative learning, and there is some evidence that it also helped move the student teachers on to more critically-oriented reflections. It has also shown that collaborative dialog with more experienced educators can serve as a bridge to the professional teaching community and help student teachers to feel a part of it. Collaborative RP with peers was also seen to bring benefits in the cognitive and affective realms as it created opportunities for student teachers to co-construct new understandings on the basis of their shared experience, and to articulate and share their concerns, as well as to offer each other emotional support. Meanwhile, novice teacher individual reflections in TP diaries were found to lead to greater depth in their analytical thinking, which suggests that this mode allowed them more time to think and process their ideas. The TP portfolios also allowed for more open and honest reflections on their own teaching practice and performance. These varied RP modes thereby served in a complementary way to encourage the novices to reflect deeply on their practices.

This book has also confirmed the wide range of cognitive, social, and affective benefits that can accrue when student teachers engage in RP with peers and more expert others across varied modes of communication. It has also highlighted the ways in which CL can be used with RP to raise student teacher awareness of the language teacher role across its multiple complexities, to help prepare them for the difficult decisions and choices that EFL practitioners must make today. These findings are important as they provide further empirical support for the incorporation of integrated and holistic approaches to RP on teacher education programs, such as that provided by the PENSER framework and process (Farr & Riordan, 2015; Farrell, 2016a; Mann & Walsh, 2017; Riordan, 2018). This book has demonstrated the ways in which this can successfully be achieved and as such offers obvious practical applications that can help to support student teachers on their TP journey, and advance language teacher education going forward.

It is intended that the research presented in this book can serve as a springboard for further RP-based research in the ELTE field, to help bring a more bottom-up empirical perspective to the academic literature in this field. As such, it has started to address the historic gap for RP research that can offer practical guidelines as to how best to prepare novice EFL teachers for their future more complex role. In this regard, it also illustrates the huge potential for comparative RP-based studies undertaken in different ELTE contexts and settings, which can help build a more complete picture of the educational needs of new recruits to the global EFL profession, and how they are being addressed through RP and complementary educational approaches. This book could also provide a basis for further RP-based research that traces the development of novice teachers as they move on to become teaching professionals in different contexts and settings, since it has identified areas where ongoing issues and challenges may arise, as well as offered a framework which can be adapted for teachers at the in-service stage of their careers, to allow them to explore these and other challenges they might be experiencing in their everyday professional practices, in a supportive and holistic way. This brings us to the final section of this chapter which discusses RP in the context of CPD.

REFLECTIVE PRACTICE FOR CONTINUOUS PROFESSIONAL DEVELOPMENT

The focus in this volume was clearly on the reflections of teachers during the course of their teacher education program. Most of them had little, if any, pre-program teaching experience. However, as well as the immediate aim of reflecting in order to improve teaching on the practicum during the course of formal education programs, we would argue that the more important dimension of structured reflection during this period was to hone reflective skills so that teachers could embed these into their future practices, post-program. It is now accepted that only a very small amount of teacher development actually takes place during initial teacher education programs, underscoring the importance of developing good habits to implement over the duration of one's professional career. Indeed, Johnson & Golombek (2011: xi) highlight that teacher professional development is 'a complicated, prolonged, highly situated, and deeply personal process that has no start or end point.' Even in contexts where there may be no formal imperative to engage in professional development, it behoves us as professionals to find the motivation and relevant pathways to not only maintain our practices to appropriate standards but to develop further. This is especially important in a changing educational landscape and with the continuous rapid developments in educational technologies, as we have become all too aware during the recent Covid-enforced moves to online and blended modes of learning.

We would like to end this chapter, and indeed this volume, by outlining a range of ways in which teachers can continue to improve and develop their practices, particularly in contexts when they may begin to feel complacent as their professional careers progress and mature. There is no ubiquitous pathway or activity for all teachers so each must choose their own. The following are just some suggestions:

- Attending webinars, seminars, conferences, and other formal education events, many of which are now conveniently available online
- Engaging in peer observations, critical reflections, and supportive discussions
- Eliciting feedback from students and senior teachers or line managers
- Joining online communities of practice such as teacher Twitter groups
- Reading professional or academic publications
- Conducting simple classroom action research projects (see Sjölund et al., 2022 for a review of research-practice partnerships)
- Sharing insights and research with the professional community through publications, or more informal modes such as blogs

- Taking leadership roles such as becoming a Director of Studies, Head of School, etc.
- Partaking in professional networking groups (for example, Beauchamp et al., 2022)
- Enrolling for more advanced programs of study such as an MA program, or even something shorter such as an MOOC or a Digital Badge.

Pause for Reflection

1. Do any of these activities appeal to you more than others and why?
2. Do you think this might change in your future career?

Whichever activities are selected, the real road to improvement comes through systematic reflection before, during, and after these engagements so that action for change is ultimately achieved. T. S. C. Farrell (2019: 58) articulates six interconnected principles of reflective practice, which we remind the reader of by way of conclusion:

- Principle 1: Reflective Practice is Holistic
- Principle 2: Reflective Practice is Evidence-Based
- Principle 3: Reflective Practice Involves Dialog
- Principle 4: Reflective Practice Bridges Principles and Practices
- Principle 5: Reflective Practice Requires an Inquiring Disposition
- Principle 6: Reflective Practice is a Way of Life

Regardless of any institutional or governing body dictating standards of professional development and reflective practice, it will only really have the desired effect when the teacher decides on their own journey. So we wish you Bon Voyage!

References

Abdel-Latif, M. (2020). Corpus literacy instruction in language teacher education: Investigating Arab EFL student teachers' immediate beliefs and long-term practices. *ReCALL*, 33(1): 1–15. https://doi.org/10.1017/S0958344020000129

Acheson, K. A., & Gall, M. D. (1987). *Techniques in the Clinical Supervision of Teachers*. New York: Longman.

Ahmed, M. K. (1994). Speaking as cognitive regulation: A Vygotskian perspective on dialogic communication. In J. P. Lantolf & G. Appel (eds.), *Vygotskian Approaches to Second Language Research* (pp. 157–171). New Jersey: Ablex.

Akbari, R. (2007). Reflections on reflection: A critical appraisal of reflective practices in L2 teacher education. *System*, 35(2): 192–207. https://doi.org/10.1016/j.system.2006.12.008

Aldrich, R. (2006). *Lessons from History of Education: The Selected Works of Richard Aldrich*. London and New York: Routledge.

Allwright, D., & Bailey, K. M. (1991). *Focus on the Language Classroom: An Introduction to Classroom Research for Language Teachers*. Cambridge: Cambridge University Press.

Ambrosetti, A., & Dekkers, J. (2010). The interconnectedness of the roles of mentors and mentees in pre-service teacher education mentoring relationships. *Australian Journal of Teacher Education*, 35(6): 42–55. https://doi.org/10.14221/ajte.2010v35n6.3

Andrews, S. (2007). *Teacher Language Awareness*. Cambridge: Cambridge University Press.

Argyris, C., & Schön, D. A. (1974). *Theory in Practice: Increasing Professional Effectiveness*. San Francisco: Jossey-Boss.

Baguley, N. (2019). 'Mind the gap': Supporting newly qualified teachers in their journey from pre-service training to full-time employment. In S. Walsh & S. Mann (eds.), *The Routledge Handbook of English Language Teacher Education* (pp. 125–136). New York and London: Routledge.

Baker, A., & Murphy, J. (2011). Knowledge base of pronunciation teaching: Staking out the territory. *TESL Canada Journal*, 28(2): 29. https://doi.org/10.18806/tesl.v28i2.1071

Barkhuizen, G. (2017). Language teacher identity research: an introduction. In G. Barkhuizen (ed.), *Reflections on Language Teacher Identity Research* (pp. 1–11). London and New York: Routledge.

Barkhuizen, G. (2021). *Language Teacher Educator Identity*. Cambridge: Cambridge University Press.

Barnes, J., Belsky, K., Broomfield, A., & Edward, M. (2006). Neighbourhood deprivation, school disorder and academic achievement in primary schools in deprived communities in England. *International Journal of Behavioral Development*, 30(2): 127–136. https://doi.org/10.1177/0165025406063585

Beauchamp, G., Chapman, S., Risquez, A., Becaas, S., Ellis, C., Empsen, M., Farr, F., Hoskins, L., Hustinx, W., Murray, L., Palmaers, S., Spain, S., Timus, N., White, M., Whyte, S., & Young, N. (2022). Moving beyond the formal: Developing significant networks and conversations in higher education: Reflections from an interdisciplinary European project team. *Teaching in Higher Education*. https://doi.org/10.1080/13562517.2022.2056833

Beck, C., & Kosnik, C. (2002). Components of a good practicum placement: Student teacher perceptions. *Teacher Education Quarterly*, 29: 81–98.

Berliner, D. C. (1986). In pursuit of the expert pedagogue. *Educational Researcher*, 15(7): 5–13. https://doi.org/10.3102/0013189X015007007

Biber, D., Johansson, S., Leech, G., Conrad, S., & Finegan, E. (1999). *Longman Grammar of Spoken and Written English*. London and New York: Longman.

Bogdan, R., & Biklen, S. K. (1982). *Qualitative Research for Education: An Introduction to Theory and Methods*. Boston: Allyn and Bacon.

Bols, A., & Wicklow, K. (2013). Feedback – What students want. In S. Merry, M. Price, D. Carless, & M. Taras (eds.), *Reconceptualising Feedback in Higher Education: Developing Dialogue with Students* (pp. 19–29). New York and London: Routledge.

Bolton, G. (2014). *Reflective Practice: Writing and Professional Development*. London and California: Sage.

Boote, D. N. (2003). Teacher educators as belief and attitude therapists: Exploring psychodynamic implications of an emerging role. *Teachers and Teaching: Theory and Practice*, 9(3): 257–277. https://doi.org/10.1080/13540600309377

Borg, S. (2003). Teacher cognition in language teaching: A review of research on what language taechers think, know, believe, and do. *Language Teaching*, 36(2): 81–109. https://doi.org/10.1017/S0261444803001903

Borg, S. (2006). *Teacher Cognition and Language Education: Research and Practice*. London and New York: Continuum.

Boulton, A. (2017). Corpora in language teaching and learning. *Language Teaching*, 50(4): 483–506. https://doi.org/10.1017/S0261444817000167

Boulton, A., & Tyne, H. (2014). Corpus-based study of language and teacher education. In M. Bigelow & J. Ennser-Kananen (eds.), *The Routledge Handbook of Educational Linguistics* (pp. 301–312). New York: Routledge.

Boz, Y. (2008). Turkish student teachers' concerns about teaching. *European Journal of Teacher Education*, 31(4): 367–377. https://doi.org/10.1080/02619760802420693

Braun, S. (2005). From pedagogically relevant corpora to authentic language learning contents. *ReCALL*, 17(1): 47–64. https://doi.org/10.1017/S0958344005000510

Breyer, Y. (2009). Learning and teaching with corpora: Reflections by student teachers. *Computer Assisted Language Learning*, 22(2): 153–172. https://doi.org/10.1080/09588220902778328

Brezina, V., & Flowerdew, L. (2017). *Learner Corpus Research: New Perspectives and Approaches*. Oxford: Bloomsbury.

Brickhouse, T. C., & Smith, N. D. (2000). *The Philosophy of Socrates*. Boulder, CO: Westview Press.

Brookfield, S. (1995). *Becoming a Critically Reflective Teacher*. San Francisco: Jossey-Bass.

Brophy, J. (1986). Classroom management techniques. *Education and Urban Society*, 18(2): 182–194. https://doi.org/10.1177/0013124586018002005

Browers, A., & Tomic, W. (2000). A longitudinal study of teacher burnout and perceived self-efficacy in classroom management. *Teaching and Teacher Education*, 16(2): 239–253. https://doi.org/10.1016/S0742-051X(99)00057-8

Brown, P., & Levinson, S. (1987). *Politeness: Some Universals in Language Usage*. Cambridge: Cambridge University Press.

Burns, A. (2010). *Doing Action Research in English Language Teaching: A Guide for Practitioners*. New York: Routledge.

Buzzelli, C. A., & Johnston, B. (2002). *The Moral Dimensions of Teaching: Language, Power and Culture in Classroom Interaction*. New York: Routledge Falmer.

Cabrera, M. P., & Martínez, P. B. (2001). The effects of repetition, comprehension checks, and gestures, on primary school children in an EFL situation. *ELT Journal*, 55(3): 281–288. https://doi.org/10.1093/elt/55.3.281

Canagarajah, S. (2005). Critical pedagogy in L2 learning and teaching. In E. Hinkel (ed.), *Handbook of Research in Second Language Teaching and Learning* (pp. 931–949). Mahwah, NJ: Lawrence Erlbaum Associates.

Carter, R., & McCarthy, M. (1997). *Exploring Spoken English*. Cambridge: Cambridge University Press.

Carter, R., & McCarthy, M. (2006). *Cambridge Grammar of English: A Comprehensive Guide to Spoken and Written Grammar and Usage*. Cambridge: Cambridge University Press.

Carter, R., & Nunan, D. (Eds.). (2001). *The Cambridge Guide to Teaching English to Speakers of Other Languages*. New York: Cambridge University Press.

Chambers, A. (2010). What is data-driven learning? In A. O'Keeffe & M. J. McCarthy (eds.), *The Routledge Handbook of Corpus Linguistics* (pp. 345–358). New York: Routledge.

Chambers, A., Farr, F., & O'Riordan, S. (2011). Language teachers with corpora in mind: From starting steps to walking tall. *Language Learning*, 39(1): 85–104. https://doi.org/10.1080/09571736.2010.520728

Chinnery, G. M. (2006). Emerging technologies. Going to the MALL: Mobile Assisted Language Learning. *Language Learning and Technology*, 10(1): 9–16.

Conway, P. F., & Clark, C. M. (2003). The journey inward and outward: A re-examination of Fuller's concerns-based model of teacher development. *Teaching and Teacher Education*, 19(5): 465–482. https://doi.org/10.1016/S0742-051X(03)00046-5

Copland, F. (2008). Deconstructing the dicourse: Understanding the feedback event. In S. Garton & K. Richards (eds.), *Professional Encounters in TESOL* (pp. 5–23). London: Palgrave.

Copland, F. (2010). Causes of tension in post-observation feedback in pre-service teacher training: An alternative view. *Teaching and Teacher Education*, 26(3): 466–472. https://doi.org/10.1016/j.tate.2009.06.001

Copland, F. (2011). Negotiating face in feedback conferences: A linguistic ethnographic analysis. *Journal of Pragmatics*, 43(15): 3832–3843. https://doi.org/10.1016/j.pragma.2011.09.014

Copland, F. (2012). Legitimate talk in feedback conferences. *Applied Linguistics*, 33(1): 1–20. https://doi.org/10.1093/applin/amr040

Copland, F., & Mann, S. (2010). Dialogic talk in the post-observation conference: An investment for reflection. In G. Park, H. P. Widodo, & A. Cirocki (eds.), *Observation of Teaching: Bridging Theory and Practice through Research on Teaching* (pp. 175–191). Munich: LINCOM.

Corder, S. P. (1967). The significance of learner's errors. *International Review of Applied Linguistics*, 5: 161–170. https://doi.org/10.1515/iral.1967.5.1-4.161

Council of Europe. (2001). *The Common European Framework of Reference for Languages: Learning, Teaching, Assessment*. Cambridge: Cambridge University Press.

Coy, M. W. (ed.). (1989). *Apprenticeship: From Theory to Practice and Back Again*. New York: State University of New York Press.

Crookes, G. (2003). *A Practicum in TESOL: Professional Development through Practice*. New York: Cambridge University Press.

Cullen, R. (1998). Teacher talk and the classroom context. *ELT Journal*, 52(3): 179–187. https://doi.org/10.1093/elt/52.3.179

Cullen, R. (2002). Supportive teacher talk: The importance of the F-move. *English Language Teaching Journal*, 56(2): 117–127. https://doi.org/10.1093/elt/56.2.117

Cunningsworth, A. (1995). *Choosing Your Coursebook*. Oxford: Heinmann.

DeCarrico, J. S. (2001). Vocabulary learning and teaching. In M. Celce-Murcia (ed.), *Teaching English as a Second or Foreign Language* (pp. 285–299). Boston: Heinle & Heinle.

Derwing, T. M., & Munro, M. J. (2005). Second language accent and pronunciation teaching: A research-based approach. *TESOL Quarterly*, 39(3): 379–397. https://doi.org/10.2307/3588486

Derwing, T. M., & Munro, M. J. (2015). *Pronunciation Fundamentals: Evidence-Based Perspectives for L2 Teaching and Research*. Amsterdam and Philadelphia: John Benjamins. https://doi.org/10.1075/lllt.42

Dewey, J. (1916). *Democracy in Education*. New York: Macmillan.

Dewey, J. (1933). *How We Think: A Restatement of the Relation of Reflective Thinking to the Educative Process* (revised edition). Boston: D. C. Heath.

Donaghue, H. (2020a). Teachers and supervisors negotiating identities of experience and power in feedback talk. *The Modern Language Journal*, 104(2): 401–417. https://doi.org/10.1111/modl.12633

Donaghue, H. (2020b). 'Time to construct positive identities': Display questions in post observation teacher feedback. *Classroom Discourse*, 11(3): 193–208. https://doi.org/10.1080/19463014.2019.1581626

Dunn, W. (1999). *Sensory Profile*. Oxford: Pearson.

Edge, J. (1984). Feedback with face. *ELT Journal*, 38(3): 204–206. https://doi.org/10.1093/elt/38.3.204

Edge, J., & Richards, K. (1998). Why *best practice* is not good enough. *TESOL Quarterly*, 32(3): 569–576. https://doi.org/10.2307/3588127

Ellis, N. C. (2002). Frequency effects in language processing: A review with implications for theories of implicit and explicit language acquisition. *Studies in Second Language Acquisition*, 24: 143–188. https://doi.org/10.1017/S0272263102002024

Emmer, E. T., & Stough, L. M. (2001). Classroom management: A critical part of educational psychology, with implications for teacher education. *Educational Psychologist*, 36(2): 103–112. https://doi.org/10.1207/S15326985EP3602_5

Evertson, C. M., Emmer, E. T., Sandford, J. P., & Clements, B. S. (1983). Improving elementary classroom management: A basic training programme for beginning the year. *The Elementary School Journal*, 184(2): 56–72.

Evertson, C. M., & Weinstein, C. S. (2006). Classroom management as a field of enquiry. In C. M. Evertson & C. S. Weinstein (eds.), *Handbook of Classroom Management: Research, Practice and Contemporary Issues* (pp. 3–17). New Jersey: Lawrence Erlbaum Associates.

Farr, F. (2003). Engaged listenership in spoken academic discourse: The case of student–tutor meetings. *Journal of English for Academic Purposes*, 2(1): 67–85. https://doi.org/10.1016/S1475-1585(02)00035-8

Farr, F. (2005). Relational strategies in the discourse of professional performance review in an Irish academic environment: The case of language teacher education. In K. Schneider & A. Barron (eds.), *The Pragmatics of Irish English* (pp. 203–234). Berlin: Mouton de Gruyter.

Farr, F. (2006). Modality in context: Spoken language, variety and the classroom. In A. Gallagher & M. Ó. Laoire (eds.), *Language Education in Ireland: Current Practice and Future Needs* (pp. 165–184). Dublin: IRAAL.

Farr, F. (2007). Spoken language as an aid to reflective practice in language teacher education: Using a specialised corpus to establish a generic fingerprint In M.-C. Campoy & M.-J. Luzón (eds.), *Spoken Corpora in Applied Linguistics* (pp. 235–258). Bern: Peter Lang.

Farr, F. (2008). Evaluating the use of corpus-based instruction in a language teacher education context: Perspectives from the users. *Language Awareness*, 17(1): 25–43. https://doi.org/10.2167/la414.0

Farr, F. (2010). How can corpora be used in teacher education? In A. O'Keeffe & M. McCarthy (eds.), *Routledge Handbook of Corpus Linguistics* (pp. 620–632). London and New York: Routledge.

Farr, F. (2011). *The Discourse of Teaching Practice Feedback. An Investigation of Spoken and Written Modes*. New York: Routledge.

Farr, F. (2015). *Practice in TESOL*. Edinburgh: Edinburgh University Press.

Farr, F. (2022). How can corpora be used in teacher education? In A. O'Keeffe & M. J. McCarthy (eds.), *The Routledge Handbook of Corpus Linguistics* (2nd edition) (pp. 456–468). Abingdon: Routledge.

Farr, F., & Farrell, A. (2017). PENSER: A data-informed reflective practice framework for novice teachers. *The European Journal of Applied Linguistics and TEFL*, 6(2): 85–103.

Farr, F., Farrell, A., & Riordan, E. (2019). *Social Interaction in Language Teacher Education*. Edinburgh: Edinburgh University Press.

Farr, F., & Karlsen, P. H. (2022). Corpus linguistics and Data Driven Learning (DDL): Pedagogy, participants, perspectives. In E. Csomay & R. Jablonkai (eds.), *The Routledge Handbook of Corpora in English Language Teaching and Learning* (pp. 329–343). London: Routledge.

Farr, F., & Murray, L. (eds.). (2016). *The Routledge Handbook of Language Learning and Technology*. London and New York: Routledge.

Farr, F., & O'Keeffe, A. (2019). Using corpus approaches in English Language Teacher Education. In S. Walsh & S. Mann (eds.), *The Routledge Handbook of English Language Teacher Education* (pp. 268–282). New York: Routledge.

Farr, F., & Riordan, E. (2012). Students' engagement in reflective tasks: An investigation of interactive and non-interactive discourse corpora. *Classroom Discourse*, 3(2): 126–143. https://doi.org/10.1080/19463014.2012.716622

Farr, F., & Riordan, E. (2015). Tracing the reflective practices of student teachers in online modes. *ReCALL*, 27(1): 104–123. https://doi.org/10.1017/S0958344014000299

Farrell, A. (2019). *Corpus Perspectives on the Spoken Models Used by EFL Teachers*. New York and London: Routledge.

Farrell, A., & Baumgart, J. (2019). Building partnerships between post-primary schools and ESOL teacher education programmes in the Irish context. In F. Mishan (ed.), *ESOL Provision in the UK and Ireland: Challenges and Opportunities* (pp. 211–231). Amsterdam: Peter Lang.

Farrell, T. S. C. (1998). Reflective teaching: The principles and practices. *English Teaching Forum*, 36(4): 10–17.

Farrell, T. S. C. (2004). *Reflective Practice in Action. 80 Reflection Breaks for Busy Teachers*. California: Corwin Press.

Farrell, T. S. C. (2012). Reflecting on reflective practice: (Re)Visiting Dewey and Schön. *TESOL Journal*, 3(1): 7–16. https://doi.org/10.1002/tesj.10

Farrell, T. S. C. (2015). *Promoting Teacher Reflection in Second Language Education: A Framework for TESOL Professionals*. New York: Routledge.

Farrell, T. S. C. (2016a). Anniversary Article. The practices of encouraging TESOL teachers to engage in reflective practice: An appraisal of recent research contributions. *Language Teaching Research*, 20(2): 223–247. https://doi.org/10.1177/1362168815617335

Farrell, T. S. C. (2016b). *From Trainee to Teacher: Reflective Practice for Novice Teachers*. Sheffield: Equinox.

Farrell, T. S. C. (2016c). Teacher-Researchers in action: Teachers research! *ELT Journal*, 70(3): 352–355. https://doi.org/10.1093/elt/ccw034

Farrell, T. S. C. (2017). 'Who I am is how I teach': Reflecting on language teacher professional role identity. In G. Barkhuizen (ed.), *Reflections in Language Teacher Identity Research* (pp. 183–188). London and New York: Routledge.

Farrell, T. S. C. (2018). *Research on Reflective Practice in TESOL*. New York and London: Routledge.

Farrell, T. S. C. (2019). *Reflective Practice in ELT*. Sheffield: Equinox.

Farrell, T. S. C. (2021). *TESOL Teacher Education: A Reflective Approach*. Edinburgh: Edinburgh University Press.

Farrell, T. S. C. (2022). *Reflective Practice in Language Teaching (Elements in Language Teaching)*. Cambridge: Cambridge University Press.

Farrell, T. S. C., & Lim, P. C. P. (2005). Conceptions of grammar teaching: A case study of teachers' beliefs and classroom practices. *TESL-EJ*, 9(2): 1–13.

Feiman-Nemser, S. (2006). A teacher educator looks at *Democracy and Education*. In D. T. Hansen (ed.), *John Dewey and Our Educational Prospect: A Critical Engagement with Dewey's Democracy and Education* (pp. 129–146). New York: State University of New York Press.

Flowerdew, L. (2015). Data-driven learning and language learning theories. In A. Leńko-Szymańska & A. Boulton (eds.), *Multiple Affordances of Language Corpora for Data-Driven Learning* (pp. 15–36). Amsterdam: Benjamins.

Freeman, D. (1991). 'To make the tacit explicit': Teacher education, emerging discourse, and conceptions of teaching. *Teaching and Teacher Education*, 7(5/6): 439–454. https://doi.org/10.1016/0742-051X(91)90040-V

Freeman, D. (2016). *Educating Second Language Teachers*. Oxford: Oxford University Press.

Freeman, D., Webre, A.-C., & Epperson, M. (2019). What counts as knowledge in English language teaching? In S. Walsh & S. Mann (eds.), *The Routledge Handbook of English Language Teacher Education* (pp. 13–24). New York and London: Routledge.

Friginal, E. (2018). *Corpus Linguistics for English Teachers: New Tools, Online Resources, and Classroom Activities*. New York: Routledge.

Fuller, F. F. (1969). Concerns of teachers: A developmental conceptualization. *American Educational Research Journal*, 6(2): 207–226. https://doi.org/10.3102/00028312006002207

Fuller, F. F., & Brown, O. H. (1975). Becoming a teacher. In K. Ryan (ed.), *Teacher Education (74th Yearbook of the National Society for the Study of Education)* (pp. 25–52). Chicago: University of Chicago Press.

Gardner, R. C., & Lambert, W. E. (1972). *Attitudes and Motivation in Second-Language Learning*. Rowley, Mass: Newbury House Publishers.

Garrett, P., & Shortall, T. (2002). Learners' evaluations of teacher-fronted and student-centered activities. *Language Teaching Research*, 6(1): 25–57. https://doi.org/10.1191/1362168802lr096oa

Gibbs, G. (1988). *Learning by Doing. A Guide to Teaching and Learning Methods*. London: Further Education Unit at Oxford Polytechnic.

Glasser, W. (1986). *Control Theory in the Classroom*. New York: Harper and Row Publishers.

Golombek, P. R. (1998). A study of language teachers' personal practical knowledge. *TESOL Quarterly*, 32(3): 447–464. https://doi.org/10.2307/3588117

Golombek, P. R., & Johnson, K. E. (2019). Materialising a Vygotskyian-inspired language teacher education pedagogy. In S. Walsh & S. Mann (eds.), *The Routledge Handbook of English Language Teacher Education* (pp. 25–37). New York and London: Routledge.

Grabe, W. (2010). Revisiting the MLA Report on reconfiguring foreign language programs: The role of reading. *Reading in a Foreign Language*, 22(1): 11–14.

Graddol, D. (2006). *English Next*. London: British Council.

Grossman, P. (2011). Framework for teaching practice: A brief history of an idea. *Teachers College Record*, 113(12): 2836–2843. https://doi.org/10.1177/016146811111301205

Grossman, P., Compton, C., Igra, D., Ronfeldt, M., Shahan, E., & Williamson, P. (2009). Teaching practice: A cross-professional perspective. *Teachers College Record*, 111: 2055–2100. https://doi.org/10.1177/016146810911100905

Grossman, P., Hammerness, K., & McDonald, M. (2009). Redefining teaching, re-imagining teacher education. *Teachers and Teaching: Theory and Practice*, 15(2): 273–289. https://doi.org/10.1080/13540600902875340

Hall, G. (2019). Locating methods in ELT education. In S. Walsh & S. Mann (eds.), *The Routledge Handbook of English Language Teacher Education* (pp. 285–298). New York and London: Routledge.

Hanson-Smith, E. (2006). Communities of practice for pre- and in-service teacher education In P. Hubbard & M. Levy (eds.), *Teacher Education in CALL* (pp. 301–315). Amsterdam: John Benjamins.

Harvey, J. K., & Vásquez, C. (2015). Preparing for the complexities of teaching: Modeling conceptual thinking in post-observation conferences. *Ilha do Desterro*, 68: 91–103. https://doi.org/10.5007/2175-8026.2015v68n1p91

Hawkins, M. R. (2004). Social apprenticeships through mediated learning in language teacher education. In M. R. Hawkins (ed.), *Language Learning and Teacher Education: A Sociocultural Approach* (pp. 89–110). New York: Multilingual Matters.

Heirdsfield, A. M., Walker, S., Walsh, K., & Wilss, L. (2008). Peer mentoring for first-year teacher education students: The mentors' experience. *Mentoring & Tutoring: Partnership in Learning*, 16(2): 109–124. https://doi.org/10.1080/13611260801916135

Holliday, A. (2005). *The Struggle to Teach English as an International Language*. Oxford: Oxford University Press.

Howatt, A. P. R., & Widdowson, H. G. (2004). *A History of ELT*. Oxford: Oxford University Press.

Ingersoll, R. M., & Smith, T. M. (2003). The wrong solution to the teacher shortage. *Educational Leadership*, 60(8): 30–33.

Izadinia, M. (2017a). From swan to ugly duckling? Mentoring dynamics and preservice teachers' readiness to teach. *Australian Journal of Teacher Education*, 42(7): 66–83. https://doi.org/10.14221/ajte.2017v42n7.5

Izadinia, M. (2017b). Pre-service teachers' use of metaphors for mentoring relationships. *Journal of Education for Teaching*, 43(5): 506–519. https://doi.org/10.1080/02607476.2017.1355085

Jay, J., & Johnson, K. (2002). Capturing complexity: A typology of reflective practice for teacher education. *Teaching and Teacher Education*, 18: 73–85. https://doi.org/10.1016/S0742-051X(01)00051-8

Jenkins, J. (2004). Research in teaching pronunciation and intonation. *Annual Review of Applied Linguistics*, 24: 109–125. https://doi.org/10.1017/S0267190504000054

Jenkins, J. (2007). *English as a Lingua Franca: Attitudes and Identity*. Oxford: Oxford University Press.

Jenkins, J. (2009). English as a lingua franca: Interpretations and attitudes. *World Englishes*, 28(2): 200–209. https://doi.org/10.1111/j.1467-971X.2009.01582.x

Jenset, I. S., Klette, K., & Hammerness, K. (2018). Grounding teacher education in practice around the world: An examination of teacher education coursework in teacher education programs in Finland, Norway, and the United States. *Journal of Teacher Education*, 69(2): 184–197. https://doi.org/10.1177/0022487117728248

Johnson, D. W., & Johnson, R. T. (1999). Making cooperative learning work. *Theory into Practice*, 38(2): 67–73. https://doi.org/10.1080/00405849909543834

Johnson, K. E. (2009). *Second Language Teacher Education: A Sociocultural Perspective*. New York and London: Routledge.

Johnson, K. E. (2015). Reclaiming the relevance of L2 teacher education. *Modern Language Journal*, 99(3): 514–528. https://doi.org/10.1111/modl.12242

Johnson, K. E., & Golombek, P. R. (2002). *Teachers' Narrative Inquiry as Professional Development*. New York: Cambridge University Press.

Johnson, K. E., & Golombek, P. R. (2011). *Research on Second Language Teacher Education: A Sociocultural Perspective on Professional Development*. New York: Routledge.

Johnson, K. E., & Golombek, P. R. (2016). *Mindful L2 Teacher Education: A Sociocultural Perspective on Cultivating Teachers' Professional Development*. New York and London: Routledge.

Kachru, B. (1992). World Englishes: Approaches, issues and resources. *Language Teaching*, 25(1): 1–14. https://doi.org/10.1017/S0261444800006583

Kagan, D. (1990). Ways of evaluating teacher cognition: Inferences concerning the Goldilocks Principle. *Review of Educational Research*, 60(3): 419–469. https://doi.org/10.3102/00346543060003419

Katz, L. G. (1972). Developmental stages of preschool teachers. *The Elementary School Journal*, 73(1): 50–54. https://doi.org/10.1086/460731

Kinginger, C. (2002). Defining the Zone of Proximal Development in US foreign language education. *Applied Linguistics*, 23(2): 240–261. https://doi.org/10.1093/applin/23.2.240

Kolb, D. (1984). *Experiential Learning: Experience as the Sources of Learning and Development*. Englewood Cliffs, NJ: Prentice Hall.

Kozulin, A. (1998). *Psychological Tools: A Sociocultural Approach to Education*. Cambridge, MA: Harvard University Press.

Kramsch, C. (1998). *Language and Culture*. Oxford: Oxford University Press.

Kumaravadivelu, B. (1999). Critical classroom discourse analysis. *TESOL Quarterly*, 33(3): 453–484. https://doi.org/10.2307/3587674

Labaree, D. F. (2004). *The Trouble with Education Schools*. New Haven, CT: Yale University Press.

Lantolf, J. P., & Appel, G. (1994). Theoretical framework: An introduction to Vygotskian approaches to second language research. In J. P. Lantolf & G. Appel (eds.), *Vygotskian Approaches to Second Language Research* (pp. 1–32). New Jersey: Ablex.

Lasagabaster, D., & Sierra, J. M. (2005). Error correction: Students' versus teachers' perceptions. *Language Awareness*, 14(2/3): 112–127. https://doi.org/10.1080/09658410508668828

Lave, J., & Wenger, E. (1991). *Situated Learning: Legitimate Peripheral Participation*. Cambridge: Cambridge University Press.

Leńko-Szymańska, A. (2017). Training teachers in data driven learning: Tackling the challenge. *Language Learning and Technology*, 21(3): 217–241.

Levy, M. (2009). Technologies in use for second language learning. *The Modern Language Journal*, 93(1): 769–782. https://doi.org/10.1111/j.1540-4781.2009.00972.x

Li, L. (2019). Teacher cognition and teacher expertise. In S. Walsh & S. Mann (eds.), *The Routledge Handbook of English Language Teacher Education* (pp. 335–349). New York and London: Routledge.

Littlewood, W. (2007). Communicative and task-based language teaching in East Asian classrooms. *Language Teaching*, 40(3): 243–249. https://doi.org/10.1017/S0261444807004363

Ma, Q., Tang, J., & Lin, S. (2021). The development of corpus-based language pedagogy for TESOL teachers: A two-step training approach facilitated by online collaboration. *Computer Assisted Language Learning*: 1–30.

Macaro, E. (2005). Codeswitching in the L2 classroom: A communication and learning strategy. In E. Llurda (ed.), *Non-Native Language Teachers: Perceptions, Challenges, and Contributions to the Profession* (pp. 63–84). Boston, MA: Springer.

Macaro, E., Curle, S., Pun, J., An, J., & Dearden, J. (2018). A systematic review of English medium instruction in higher education. *Language Teaching*, 51(1): 36–76. https://doi.org/10.1017/S0261444817000350

Mann, S., & Walsh, S. (2017). *Reflective Practice in English Language Teaching: Research-Based Principles and Practices*. New York and London: Routledge.

Martin, N. K., Yin, Z., and Baldwin, B. (1998) Construct validation of the attitudes & beliefs on classroom control inventory. *The Journal of Classroom Interaction*, 33(2): 6–15.

Martin, N. K., & Shoho, A. R. (2000). Teacher experience, training, & age: The influence of teacher characteristics on classroom management style. Annual Meeting of the Southwest Educational Research Association, January 27–29, Dallas, Texas.

Matsuda, A. (2012). *Principles and Practices of Teaching English as an International Language: Rethinking Goals and Approaches*. Oxford: Oxford University Press.

Maynard, T., & Furlong, J. (1995). Learning to teach and models of mentoring. In T. Kerry & A. Shelton-Mayes (eds.), *Issues in Mentoring* (pp. 10–24). London and New York: Routledge in association with The Open University.

McCarten, J. (2007). *Teaching Vocabulary: Lessons from the Corpus, Lessons for the Classroom*. Cambridge: Cambridge University Press.

McCarthy, A., & Farr, F. (2022). Role models and motivators in English language learning in the Japanese high school context. *TESL-EJ*, 26(2): (pp. 1–20). https://doi.org/10.55593/ej.26102a2

McCarthy, M. (2020). Fifty-five years and counting: A half-century of getting it half-right? *Language Teaching*: 1–12.

McNeely, S. R., & Mertz, N. T. (1990). Cognitive constructs of pre-service teachers: Research on how student teachers think about teaching. Annual Meeting of the American Educational Research Association, Boston, 1990.

Medgyes, P. (1992). Native or non-native: Who's worth more? *ELT Journal*, 46(4): 340–349. https://doi.org/10.1093/elt/46.4.340

Medgyes, P. (1994). *The Non-Native Teacher*. Houndsmills: Macmillan.

Mercer, N. (1995). *The Guided Construction of Knowledge. Talk amongst Teachers and Learners*. Philadelphia: Multilingual Matters.

Mishan, F. (2004). Authenticating corpora for language learning: A problem and its resolution. *ELT Journal*, 58(3): 219–227. https://doi.org/10.1093/elt/58.3.219

Mishan, F. (2005). *Designing Authenticity into Language Learning Materials*. Bristol: Intellect.

Mishan, F. (2013). Modes of delivery. In B. Tomlinson (ed.), *Applied Linguistics and Materials Development* (pp. 287–302). London: Bloomsbury.

Mishan, F., & Timmis, I. (2015). *Materials Development for TESOL*. Edinburgh: Edinburgh University Press.

Mishra, P., & Koehler, M. J. (2006). Technological pedagogical content knowledge: A framework for teacher knowledge. *Teachers College Record*, 108(6): 1017–1054. https://doi.org/10.1177/016146810610800610

Mompean, J. A., & Fouz-González, J. (2016). Twitter-based EFL pronunciation instruction. *Language Learning and Technology*, 20(1): 166–190.

Morton, T., & Gray, J. (2018). *Social Interaction and English Language Teacher Identity*. Edinburgh: Edinburgh University Press.

Mukherjee, J. (2006). Corpus linguistics and language pedagogy: The state of the art – and beyond. *English Corpus Linguistics*, 3: 5–24.

Munby, H. (1989). Reflection-in-action and reflection-on-action. *Current Issues in Education*, 9(1): 31–42.

Murphy, B., & Riordan, E. (2016). Corpus types and uses. In F. Farr & L. Murray (eds.), *The Routledge Handbook of Language Learning and Technology* (pp. 388–403). London and New York: Routledge.

Murphy, D. (2011). An investigation of English pronunciation teaching in Ireland: ELT in Ireland presents a number of interesting issues when it comes to the question of pronunciation. *English Today*, 27(4): 10–18. https://doi.org/10.1017/S0266078411000484

Murray, D. E., & Christison, M. (2011). *What English Language Teachers Need to Know Volume II*. New York and Oxon: Routledge.

Murray, N. (2010). Pragmatics, awareness-raising, and the cooperative principle. *English Language Teaching Journal*, 64(3): 293–301. https://doi.org/10.1093/elt/ccp056

Murray-Harvey, R., Slee, P. T., Lawson, M. J., Silins, H., Banfield, G., & Russell, A. (2000). Under stress: The concerns and coping strategies of teacher education students. *European Journal of Teacher Education*, 23(1): 19–35. https://doi.org/10.1080/713667267

Nation, I. S. (2001). *Learning Vocabulary in Another Language*. London: Klett Sprachen.

Nguyen, H. T. M. (2017). *Models of Mentoring in Language Teacher Education*. New York: Springer.

Nguyen, H. T. M., & Ngo, N. T. H. (2017). Learning to reflect through peer mentoring in a TESOL practicum. *ELT Journal*, 72(2): 187–198. https://doi.org/10.1093/elt/ccx053

Nicaise, E. (2021). *Native and Non-Native Teacher Talk in the EFL Classroom: A Corpus-Informed Study*. London and New York: Routledge.

Nunan, D. (2017). Language teacher identity in teacher education. In G. Barkhuizen (ed.), *Reflections on Language Teacher Identity Research* (pp. 164–169). London and New York: Routledge.

O'Brien, T., & Beaumont, M. (2000). *Collaborative Research in Second Language Education*. Stoke-on-Trent: Trentham.

O'Keeffe, A., & Farr, F. (2003). Using language corpora in language teacher education: Pedagogic, linguistic and cultural insights. *TESOL Quarterly*, 37(3): 389–418. https://doi.org/10.2307/3588397

O'Keeffe, A., McCarthy, M. J., & Carter, R. (2007). *From Corpus to Classroom*. Cambridge: Cambridge University Press.

O'Leary, M. (2013). *Classroom Observation: A Guide to the Effective Observation of Teaching and Learning*. New York and London: Routledge.

O'Leary, M. (2012). Exploring the role of lesson observation in the English education system: A review of methods, models and meanings. *Professional Development in Education*, 38(5): 791–810. https://doi.org/10.1080/19415257.2012.693119

O'Neill, S., & Stephenson, J. (2012). Does classroom management coursework influence pre-service teachers' perceived preparedness or confidence? *Teaching and Teacher Education*, 28(8): 1131–1143. https://doi.org/10.1016/j.tate.2012.06.008

Oliver, R. M., & Reschly, D. J. (2007). *Effective Classroom Management: Teacher Preparation and Professional Development. TQ Connection Issue Paper*. National Comprehensive Center for Teacher Quality. Retrieved from: http://files.eric.ed.gov/fulltext/ED543769.pdf

Oliver, R. M., Wehby, J. H., & Reschly, D. J. (2011). Teacher classroom management practices: Effects on disruptive or aggressive student behavior. *Campbell Systematic Reviews*, 7(1): 1–55. https://doi.org/10.4073/csr.2011.4

Oxford, R. (1997). Cooperative learning, collaborative learning, and interaction: Three communicative strands in the language classroom. *Modern Language Journal*, 81(4): 443–65. https://doi.org/10.1093/elt/ccy050

Papageorgiou, I., Copland, F., Viana, V., Bowker, D., & Moran, E. (2019). Teaching practice in UK ELT Master's programs. *ELT Journal*, 73(2): 154–165. https://doi.org/10.1093/elt/ccy050

Parkay, F. W., Greenwood, G., Olejnik, S., & Proller, N. (1988). A study of the relationships among teacher efficacy, locus of control, and stress. *Journal of Research & Development in Education*, 21(4): 13–22.

Patterson, G. R., Debaryshe, B. D., & Ramsey, E. (1989). A developmental perspective on antisocial behavior. *The American Psychologist*, 44(2): 329–335. https://doi.org/10.1037/0003-066X.44.2.329

Pennington, M. C. (1990). A professional development focus for the language teaching practicum In J. Richards & D. Nunan (eds.), *Second Language Teacher Education* (pp. 132–152). Cambridge: Cambridge University Press.

Pennington, M. C., & Richards, J. C. (2016). Teacher identity in language teaching: Integrating personal, contextual, and professional factors. *RELC Journal*, 47(1): 5–23. https://doi.org/10.1177/0033688216631219

Pennycook, A. (2000). English, politics, ideology: From colonial celebration to postcolonial performativity. In T. Ricento (ed.), *Ideology, Politics and Language Policies: Focus on English* (pp. 107–119). Amsterdam: John Benjamins.

Prodromou, L. (2008). *English as a Lingua Franca: A Corpus-based Analysis*. London: Continuum.

Prodromou, L., & Mishan, F. (2008). Materials used in Western Europe. In B. Tomlimson (ed.), *English Language Teaching Materials: A Critical Review* (pp. 193–212). London: Continuum.

Randall, M., & Thornton, B. (2001). *Advising and Supporting Teachers*. Cambridge: Cambridge University Press.

Reppen, R. (2010). *Using Corpora in the Language Classroom*. Cambridge: Cambridge University Press.

Richards, J. C. (2001). *Curriculum Development in Language Teaching*. Cambridge: Cambridge University Press.

Richards, J. C. (2008). Second language teacher education today. *RELC Journal*, 39(2): 158–177. https://doi.org/10.1177/0033688208092182

Richards, J. C. (2017). Teacher identity in second language teacher education. In G. Barkhuizen (ed.), *Reflections in Language Teacher Identity Research* (pp. 139–144). New York: Routledge.

Richards, J. C., & Lockhart, C. (1994). *Reflective Teaching*. New York: Cambridge University Press.

Richards, J. C., & Rodgers, T. S. (2001). *Approaches and Methods in Language Teaching*. Cambridge: Cambridge University Press.

Richards, K. (2006). Being the teacher: Identity and classroom conversation. *Applied Linguistics*, 27(1): 51–77. https://doi.org/10.1093/applin/ami041

Riordan, E. (2012). Online reflections: The implementation of blogs in language teacher education. In F. Farr & M. Moriarty (eds.), *Learning and Teaching. Irish Research Perspectives* (pp. 195–224). Berlin: Peter Lang.

Riordan, E. (2018). *TESOL Student Teacher Discourse: A Corpus-Based Analysis of Online and Face-to-Face Interactions*. London: Routledge.

Riordan, E., & Farr, F. (2015). Facilitating identity construction through narratives: A corpus-based discourse analysis of student teacher discourse. In Y. L. Cheung, S. B. Said, & K. Park (eds.), *Advances and Current Trends in Language Teacher Identity Research* (pp. 161–174). New York and London: Routledge.

Riordan, E., & Murray, L. (2010). A corpus-based analysis of online synchronous and asynchronous modes of communication within language teacher education. *Classroom Discourse*, 1(2): 181–198. https://doi.org/10.1080/19463014.2010.514728

Rodgers, C. R., & Raider-Roth, M. B. (2006). Presence in teaching. *Teachers and Teaching: Theory and Practice*, 12(3): 265–287. https://doi.org/10.1080/13450600500467548

Rogerson-Ravell, P. (2011). *English Phonology and Pronunciation Teaching*. London: Bloomsbury.

Sachs, J. (2005). *Teacher Education and the Development of Professional Identity: Learning to be a Teacher*. London: Routledge.

Schmitt, N. (2000). *Vocabulary in Language Teaching*. Cambridge: Cambridge University Press.

Schmitt, N., & McCarthy, M. (1997). *Vocabulary: Description, Acquisition and Pedagogy*. Cambridge: Cambridge University Press.

Schön, D. (1983). *The Reflective Practitioner: How Professionals Think in Action*. New York: Basic Books.

Schön, D. (1987). *Educating the Reflective Practitioner: Toward a Design for Teaching and Learning in the Professions*. San Francisco: Jossey-Bass.

Schwab, J. J. (1959). The 'impossible' role of the teacher in progressive education. *The School Review*, 67(2): 139–159. https://doi.org/10.1086/442488

Scrivener, J. (1994). *Learning Teaching*. Oxford: Macmillan.

Seidlhofer, B. (2001). Closing a conceptual gap: The case for a description of English as a lingua franca. *International Journal of Applied Linguistics*, 11(2): 133–158. https://doi.org/10.1111/1473-4192.00011

Shavelson, R. J., & Stern, P. (1981). Research on teachers' pedagogical thoughts, judgements, decisions, and behavior. *Review of Educational Research*, 51(4): 455–498. https://doi.org/10.3102/00346543051004455

Shulman, L. S. (1986). Those who understand: Knowledge growth in teaching. *Educational Researcher*, 15(2): 4–14. https://doi.org/10.3102/0013189X015002004

Shulman, L. S. (1987). Knowledge and teaching: Foundations of the new reform. *Harvard Educational Review*, 57: 1–22. https://doi.org/10.17763/haer.57.1.j463w79r56455411

Shulman, L. S. (1998). Theory, practice, and the education of professionals. *The Elementary School Journal*, 98(5): 511–526. https://doi.org/10.1086/461912

Shulman, L. S. (2004). *The Wisdom of Practice: Essays on Teaching, Learning, and Learning to Teach*. San Francisco: Jossey-Bass.

Sjölund, S., Lindvall, J., Larsson, M., & Ryve, A. (2022). Mapping roles in research-practice partnerships – A systematic literature review. *Educational Review*, 1–29. https://www.

tandfonline.com/doi/10.1080/00131911.2021.2023103 https://doi.org/10.1080/00131911.2021.2023103

Skinner, B. F. (1953). *Science and Human Behavior*. New York: Simon and Schuster.

Spalding, E., Wilson, A., & Mewborn, D. (2002). Demystifying reflection: A study of pedagogical strategies that encourage reflective journal writing. *Teachers College Record*, 104(7): 1393–1421. https://doi.org/10.1177/016146810210400704

Spiro, J. (2013). *Changing Methodologies in TESOL*. Edinburgh: Edinburgh University Press.

Stiffler, J. (2010). *Classroom Management Plan*. Retrieved from: https://templaterepublic.com/wp-content/uploads/Classroom-Seating-Chart-01.pdf.

Swain, M. (1985). Communicative competence: Some roles of comprehensible input and comprehensible output in its development. In S. Gass & E. Varonis (eds.), *Input in Second Language Acquisition* (pp. 235–253). Rowley: Newbury House.

Talbert, J. E., & Mclaughlin, M. W. (2002). Professional communities and the Artisan Model of teaching. *Teachers and Teaching: Theory and Practice*, 8(3/4): 325–343. https://doi.org/10.1080/135406002100000477

Tao, Q. (2010). The evolution and implications of small class reform policies in Asian countries and regions. *Modern Education Management*, 3: 102–105.

Thornbury, S. (1996). Teachers research teacher talk. *ELT Journal*, 50(4): 279–289. https://doi.org/10.1093/elt/50.4.279

Thornbury, S. (2019). Methodology texts and the construction of teachers' practical knowledge. In S. Walsh & S. Mann (eds.), *The Routledge Handbook of English Language Teacher Education* (pp. 509–521). London and New York: Routledge.

Timmis, I. (2002). Native-speaker norms and International English: A classroom view. *ELT Journal*, 56(3): 240–249. https://doi.org/10.1093/elt/56.3.240

Tomlinson, B. (1998). Introduction. In B. Tomlinson (ed.), *Materials Development in Language Teaching* (pp. 1–24). Cambridge: Cambridge University Press.

Tomlinson, B. (2001). Materials development. In R. Carter & D. Nunan (eds.), *The Cambridge Guide to Teaching English to Speakers of Other Languages* (pp. 66–71). Cambridge: Cambridge University Press.

Tomlinson, B. (2003). Humanizing the coursebook. In B. Tomlinson (ed.), *Developing Materials for Language Teaching* (pp. 162–173). London: Continuum.

Tomlinson, B. (2012). Materials development for language learning and teaching. *Language Teaching*, 45(2): 143–179. https://doi.org/10.1017/S0261444811000528

Tsui, A. B. M. (1996). Reticence and anxiety in second language learning. In K. M. Bailey & D. Nunan (eds.), *Voices from the Language Classroom* (pp. 145–167). Cambridge: Cambridge University Press.

Tsui, A. B. M. (2003). *Understanding Expertise in Teaching*. Cambridge: Cambridge University Press.

Van der Veer, R., & Yasnitsky, A. (2015). Vygotsky the published: Who wrote Vygotsky and what Vygotsky actually wrote. In A. Yasnitsky & R. Van der Veer (eds.), *Revisionist Revolution in Vygotsky Studies* (pp. 73–93). London and New York: Routledge.

Vásquez, C. (2004). 'Very carefully managed': Advice and suggestions in post-observation meetings. *Linguistics and Education*, 15(1–2): 33–58. https://doi.org/10.1016/j.linged.2004.10.004

Vásquez, C., & Reppen, R. (2007). Transforming practice: Changing patterns of participation in post-observation meetings. *Language Awareness*, 16(3): 153–172. https://doi.org/10.2167/la454.0

Vygotsky, L. S. (1978). *Mind in Society: The Development of Higher Psychological Processes*. Cambridge, MA: Harvard University Press.

Vygotsky, L. S. (1986). *Thought and Language*. Cambridge, MA: MIT Press.

Waks, L. J. (2001). Donald Schon's philosophy of design and design education. *International Journal of Technology and Design Education*, 11(1): 37–51. https://doi.org/10.1023/A:1011251801044

Wallen, M., & Kelly-Holmes, H. (2006). 'I think they just think it's going to go away at some stage': Policy and practice in teaching English as an additional language in Irish primary schools. *Language and Education*, 20(2): 141–161. https://doi.org/10.1080/09500780608668718

Walsh, S. (2001). *Characterising Teacher Talk in the Second Language Classroom: A Process Model of Reflective Practice*. PhD, Queen's University, Belfast.

Walsh, S. (2006). *Investigating Classroom Discourse*. London and New York: Routledge.

Walsh, S. (2010). What features of spoken and written corpora can be exploited in creating language teaching materials and syllabuses? In A. O'Keeffe & M. McCarthy (eds.), *The Routledge Handbook of Corpus Linguistics* (pp. 333–344). London and New York: Routledge.

Walsh, S. (2011). *Exploring Classroom Discourse: Language in Action*. London and New York: Routledge.

Walsh, S. (2013). *Classroom Discourse and Teacher Development*. Edinburgh: Edinburgh University Press.

Walsh, S., & Mann, S. (2015). Doing reflective practice: A data-led way forward. *English Language Teaching Journal*, 69(4): 351–362. https://doi.org/10.1093/elt/ccv018

Wang, S., & Vásquez, C. (2012). Web 2.0 and second language learning: What does the research tell us? *CALICO*, 29(3): 412–430. https://doi.org/10.11139/cj.29.3.412-430

Warford, M. K., & Reeves, J. (2003). Falling into it: Novice TESOL teacher thinking. *Teachers and Teaching: Theory and Practice*, 9(1): 47–65. https://doi.org/10.1080/1354060032000049904

Waring, H. Z., & Creider, S. C. (2021). *Micro-Reflection on Classroom Communication: A FAB Framework*. Sheffield: Equinox.

Warschauer, M., & Liaw, M.-L. (2011). Emerging technologies for autonomous language learning. *Studies in Self Access*, 2(3): 107–118. https://doi.org/10.37237/020302

Wertsch, J. V. (1985). *Vygotsky and the Social Formation of Mind*. Cambridge, MA and London: Harvard University Press.

Wertsch, J. V. (1998). *Mind as Action*. Oxford: Oxford University Press.

White, P. (2000). Dialogue and inter-subjectivity: Reinterpreting the semantics of modality and hedging. In M. Coulthard, J. Cotterill, & F. Rock (eds.), *Working with Dialogue* (pp. 67–80). Tübingen: Max Niemeyer.

Widdowson, H. G. (1984). The incentive value of theory in teacher education. *ELT Journal*, 38(2): 86–90. https://doi.org/10.1093/elt/38.2.86

Willis, D. (1990). *The Lexical Syllabus: A New Approach to Language Teaching*. London: Collins ELT.

Woods, D. (1996). *Teacher Cognition in Language Teaching: Beliefs, Decision-Making and Classroom Practice*. Cambridge: Cambridge University Press.

Wragg, E. C. (2012). *An Introduction to Classroom Observation* (Classic Edition). Oxon: Routledge.

Yazdanmehr, E., & Akbari, R. (2015). An expert EFL teacher's class management. *Iranian Journal of Language Teaching Research*, 3(2): 1–13.

Young, T. J., & Walsh, S. (2010). Which English? Whose English? An investigation of 'non-native' teachers' beliefs about target varieties. *Language, Culture and Curriculum*, 23(2): 123–137. https://doi.org/10.1080/07908311003797627

Zavershneva, E. I. (2010). 'The Way to Freedom' (On the publication of documents from the family archive of Lev Vygotsky), *Journal of Russian and East European Psychology*, 48(1): 61–90. https://doi.org/10.2753/RPO1061-0405480103

Zeichner, K., & Liston, D. P. (2014). *Reflective Teaching: An Introduction* (2nd edition). New York and London: Routledge.

Zimmerman, D. H. (1998). Identity, context and interaction. In C. Antaki & S. Widdicombe (eds.), *Identities in Talk* (pp. 87–106). Thousand Oaks, CA: Sage.

Zwozdiak-Myers, P. (2012). *The Teacher's Reflective Practice Handbook*. Abingdon and New York: Routledge.

Index

www.ingramcontent.com/pod-product-compliance
Lightning Source LLC
LaVergne TN
LVHW010444080826
844660LV00026B/1213

9781781798492